K9 COPS

POLICE DOGS OF THE WORLD

K9 COPS

POLICE DOGS OF THE WORLD

NIGEL ALLSOPP

BIG SKY PUBLISHING
www.bigskypublishing.com.au

Big Sky Publishing Pty Ltd
PO Box 303, Newport, NSW 2106, Australia
Phone: (61 2) 9918 2168
Fax: (61 2) 9918 2396
Email: info@bigskypublishing.com.au
Web: www.bigskypublishing.com.au

Cover design and typesetting: Think Productions

National Library of Australia Cataloguing-in-Publication entry : (pbk)
Author: Allsopp, Nigel.
Title: K9 cops: police dogs of the world / Nigel Allsopp.
ISBN: 9781921941764 (pbk.)
Notes: Includes bibliographical references.
Subjects: Police dogs.
Dewey Number: 636.7376

National Library of Australia Cataloguing-in-Publication entry : (ebook)
Author: Allsopp, Nigel.
Title: K9 cops [electronic resource] : police dogs of the world / Nigel Allsopp.
ISBN: 9781921941818 (ebook)
Notes: Includes bibliographical references.
Subjects: Police dogs.
Dewey Number: 636.7376
Printed in China through Bookbuilders

CONTENTS

Acknowledgements xii

    Consultants xii

    Contributors xii

Introduction xiv

Part 1: Canine Law Enforcement 1

Policing and Police Dogs: A History 2

    Policing in ancient times 2

    Early dog days in Europe and London 4

        The 19th century 5

        The 20th century 7

    North American dogs at work 10

Dog Breeds Used for Law Enforcement 14

    Airedale terriers 14

    Belgian shepherd (Malinois) 15

    Bloodhounds 15

    Border collies 15

    Boxers 15

    Doberman pinschers 16

    German shepherd 16

    Labradors 16

    Rottweilers 17

    Spaniels 17

Selecting Dog Handlers and Dogs 18

    Handler selection 18

    Police dog selection 20

        Temperament 21

        Physical characteristics 21

Specialist dog selection 22

Basic Training 23

    The learning process 25

    Assessments 27

Specialist Roles for Dogs in Law Enforcement 29

    Police dogs 32

    Tracker dogs 32

    Riot control dogs 34

    Specialist explosives detection dogs 35

    Specialist narcotic detection dogs 41

    Search and rescue dogs 41

    Human remains detection dogs 43

Advanced Training 49

    Tactical operations 49

    Canine First Aid 51

    Transportation 56

    The maritime environment 57

    Special Weapons and Tactics (SWAT) 59

Protecting the Borders 62

Border protection 65

    US Border Protection 65

    German Border Police 69

    Finland's Border Guards 70

    Federal Border Guard Service of Russia 70

    Ukraine Border Guards 72

    Belarus Border Guard 72

    The Canada Border Services 72

The Future of Police Dogs 76

Part 2: An A–Z of Police Canine Units around the World 79

Australia 80

    The Australian Federal Police 80

Tasmania 82

Northern Territory 83

Queensland 84

NSW Police 86

WA Police Dog Squad 90

Victoria 90

South Australia 92

Belgium 94

Canada 98

Toronto Police Dog Services 98

Royal Canadian Mounted Police (RCMP) 104

The Edmonton Police 108

Chile 111

China 112

Columbia 114

Czech Republic 115

Denmark 118

Estonia 120

Finland 121

France 124

Germany 125

Greece 128

Hong Kong 128

Hungary 131

India 133

Indonesia 135

Iraq 137

Israel 139

Italy 142

Japan 147

Jersey 147

Jordan 148

Kenya 149

Lithuania 152

Nepal 153

Netherlands 154

New Zealand 156

Norway 160

Poland 162

Republic of Ireland 165

Republic of Serbia 167

Russia 168

Singapore 169

Slovenia 171

South Africa 177

Spain 179

Sweden 182

Switzerland 184

Taiwan 186

Turkey 186

United Kingdom 189

   England 190

      Metropolitan Police Dogs 191

      Devon and Cornwall Police 194

      North Yorkshire Police Dog Section 196

      Surrey Police 198

Scotland 203

   Strathclyde Police 203

   Fife Constabulary Dog Section 205

   Tayside Police Dog Section 206

Wales 207

British Specialist Police K9 Units 212

Ministry of Defence Police 212

The Civil Nuclear Constabulary 214

British Transport Police 214

United States of America.. 217

Bakersfield Police Department K9 Unit........................... 217

Anchorage Police Department's K9 Unit 219

LAPD 220

NYPD... 221

St Paul Minnesota 222

Orange County 224

Anaheim Police Department Canine Detail.................. 224

Fullerton K9 Program.. 226

Orange County Sheriff's Department 226

Honolulu Police Canine Unit 228

New England State Police K9 unit 229

Sacramento Sheriff's Department 230

United States Specialist Canine Units................................... 235

United States Park Police Canine Unit.............................. 235

The Bureau of Alcohol, Tobacco, Firearms and Explosives (ATF) 235

CIA K9 Corps... 237

The Pentagon 238

Transit Police.. 239

Airport Police... 241

San Diego Harbour Police... 245

Los Angeles School Police Department (LASPD) 245

US Forest Service 246

Zimbabwean Republic Police 249

Police K9 acronyms... 253

Bibliography.. 259

Books.. 259

Journals... 259

Websites... 259

*I dedicate this book to my dad, Barry Allsopp, who inspired me
to follow my dreams and still looks over my shoulder.*

Don't Grieve for Me

Author unknown

Don't grieve for me, I served you well
I loved you more than you could ever tell
I am now an angel in blue
I laid my life on the line for you
I wore my badge with honour every day
to keep citizens safe and out of harm's way
So when you see a badge worn with pride
Remember their comrades and friends who have died.

ACKNOWLEDGEMENTS

Consultants

Deputy Steve Brown, Orange County Sheriff's Department

Mick Cicolini, Queensland Police Service, Specialist Dog Instructor

Paul Henry, Government and Defence Veterinary Surgeon

Mick Martin, RNZAF Police — ex-Royal Army Veterinary Corps

Stephen Palmer, Queensland Police Service — Police Dog Instructor

Commanding Officer Lt John Pappas, NYPD Transit Bureau Canine Unit

Brad Smith, West Covina Police Department, Subject matter expert — Canine Tactical Ops

Contributors

Australia: Lauren McMahon, Tasmanian Police Dog Unit

Canada: Nancy Sample, Royal Canadian Mounted Police

Canada: Sgt Tom Pallas, Canine Unit Edmonton Police Service

Canada: Sgt David Bessason, Supervisor/Trainer K9 Unit Winnipeg Police Service

Czech Republic: Lenka Chlebcova, Czech Police Canine

Estonian: Lieutenant Jüri Pajusoo, Border Guard Service Dogs Training Centre Chief

Finland: Walczuk Ewa, Embassy of Finland

Guam: Mark Torre, Guam Police Dept

Hungary: Major Iblya Gati- Hungarian Police

Ireland: Superintendent John Gilligan Garda, Dublin

Jersey: Sgt Canham Charles, State of Jersey Police

Republic of Lithuania: Aster Galdikaite

Republic of Serbia: Dusan Vukasinovic, First Counsellor

Scotland: David McKelvie, Fife Constabulary

Scotland: Rory Duncan, Tayside Dog Section

Singapore: Pak Ooi Tart, Police K-9 Unit Singapore

Spain: Gabinete Mando Unico, Spanish Police Dogs

UK: Ian Kelly, Isle of Man Constabulary

UK: Ron Harney, Ministry of Defence Police

UK: Russ Jackson, Metropolitan Police

UK: Dyfed-Powys Police Service

UK: Insp Mark Hobrough, South Wales Dog Unit

USA: David Ferrel, USDA Forest Service

USA: Capt Alexnder Ahlo, Honolulu PD

USA: Sgt Mitzi Grasso, LAPD

USA: Senior Police Officer John Taylor, Los Angeles School Police Department

USA: Paul Dunnom, St Paul Canine Unit

USA: Officer Brian Griffeth, Ohio

USA: Brook Sims, City of Orlando

USA: Sarah Lagasse, Pentagon Police

INTRODUCTION

Dogs and humans have cooperated to perform many tasks over the years in war and peace, from hunting, tracking, guarding, haulage and rescue work. Dogs have continually shown that they can provide both valuable assistance and warm companionship. A police dog is a dog that is trained specifically to assist police and other law enforcement personnel in their work. Police dogs are also referred to as 'K9s' in many countries.

The main purpose for a police K9 is locating something or someone; tracking or searching for people, or detecting a substance. Police dogs can basically be divided into two main types: general purpose police dogs (PD) and detection dogs. PDs are typically German shepherds or similar breeds used for tracking and criminal work. They are also called patrol dogs or general duties dogs in some countries. These dogs are often seen in the back of a police vehicle and are generally the most numerous in a department. Detection dogs can be explosive detection dogs (EDD), narcotic detection dogs (NDD), or be trained in cadaver detection or search and rescue (SAR).

Recent events in the 21st century have highlighted the important role law enforcement dogs play in the daily war against terrorism and major criminal activities. Dog teams serve as a potent force multiplier, as seen with great effect in the military. One police dog in a riot control incident is worth twenty men as a physiological deterrent to would-be agitators. Police officers often call on police dog teams to back them up in dangerous situations. There is a saying in police dog circles in the USA: 'If a member of the public is in trouble they call 911; when a cop is in trouble they call K9'.

Few humans can match the versatility and loyalty of a police dog as a partner in everyday police work. Police dogs can chase suspects, track them if they are hidden and guard them when they are caught. They are trained to respond viciously if their handler is attacked, and otherwise not to react at all unless they are commanded to do so by their handler. Police dogs are also used tactically in special response operations throughout the world. These are known by different names, including SWAT (Special Weapons and Tactics) and SRT/SRG (Special Response Team or Group).

This book explores the history and current use of police dogs, their different roles over the years and what future dogs have in modern law enforcement. I have included the most well known police dog squads from several countries and many I have worked with. In countries such as the United States and United Kingdom, to name just two, there are too many agencies to list, so I have selected only a few from each. Some specifics and names have been deliberately withheld for security reasons. This includes a deliberate omitting of detailed training techniques. There are plenty of myths out there about how dogs are trained — dog training after all is an art form based on a science — so I don't want to let the bad guys know how we do it.

The photographs have been supplied by handlers both current and retired, and by various official government sources such as embassies, others are official releases on websites.

Police dogs are an enigma to most people. They are the front line in crime fighting and regarded as elite in any force. Even serving officers view them from a distance. It takes a considerable amount of time and experience in general police duties to even be allowed to apply for a dog handler's position and the competition is fierce.

I wrote this book to give an insight into the role of police dogs and I couldn't have done it without the help of their handlers. I would like to give a special thanks to serving K9 officers who have proofread the chapters pertaining to their country's programs and helped make this book the accurate and authoritative reference I wanted it to be.

PART 1
Canine Law Enforcement

POLICING AND POLICE DOGS: A HISTORY

Policing is seen to be a fairly modern concept but in reality it is a very old profession thanks to the ugly side of humanity. Police have always been the few that protect and serve the many. One thing is certain: as soon as police forces were established it did not take long for members to bring along a canine partner. In many cases these were for companionship and self-protection; later it was realised that police could use their dogs' advanced senses to locate criminals and items of interest.

Police dogs have a long but somewhat disjointed history throughout the world. Records show that prior to 1899 dogs were used by law enforcement personnel; however, there was not a formal training program and most often the dogs were companions at night for patrolling policemen.

Law enforcement canines were initially used by the military or appointed feudal systems to aid people in various activities. These initially included the suppression of the population by the local lord having large dogs as personnel body guards, which he occasionally loosed on his subjects. Appointed persons such as tax collectors would have a large dog to protect the money they had raised whilst proceeding from town to town. Many dogs in early times were regarded as war dogs and there is a slight blur between the two functions until society established its first police forces instead of using the army to deal with matters.

Policing in ancient times

Law enforcement in Ancient China was carried out by 'prefects'. Prefects were government officials appointed by local magistrates just as modern police report to judges. Under each prefect were sub-prefects, who helped collectively with law enforcement of the area.

In Ancient Greece, publicly owned slaves were used by magistrates as police. In Athens, a group of 300 Scythian slaves was used to guard public meetings to keep order and for crowd control, and also assisted with dealing with criminals, handling prisoners, and making arrests.

The Romans had three urban cohorts stationed in Rome, created by Augustus. Tacitus clearly stated their duties 'to control the slaves and those citizens whose natural boldness gives way to disorderly conduct, unless they are overawed by force'. The cohorts were regarded part of the Imperial Army and had considerable power; in effect they were the first military police force in history. The urban cohorts were responsible for law and order and acted as a dedicated police force. Before its decline, the Roman Empire had a relatively effective law enforcement system. Under the reign of Augustus, when the capital had grown to almost 1 million inhabitants, 14 wards were created; the wards were protected by seven squads of 1000 men called Vigiles, who guarded against fires and served as night watchmen. Large mastiff-type breeds of dogs were used to attack crowds and protect the watch men.

In merry old England the local lords and nobles were responsible for maintaining order in their lands, and often appointed a constable, sometimes unpaid, to enforce the law. Later on in England a system of sheriffs and investigative juries developed under the Anglo-Saxons to provide basic security and law enforcement. After the Norman Conquest, these institutions remained although their roles changed. Sheriffs in particular were responsible for keeping law and order, although they were responsible to the king and represented his interests. Fewters, the first professional dog handlers in Norman service, used tracker dogs such as bloodhounds to track down offenders.

Europe had the *Hermandades*, or 'brotherhoods'; peacekeeping associations of armed individuals. As medieval Spanish kings often could not offer adequate protection, protective municipal leagues began to emerge in the 12th century against bandits and other rural criminals. As one of their first acts after the war of succession, Ferdinand and Isabella established the centrally organised and efficient Holy Brotherhood as a national police force. They adapted an existing brotherhood to the purpose of a general police force, appointing officials who were endowed with large powers of summary jurisdiction even in capital cases. The original brotherhoods continued to serve as modest local police units until their final suppression in 1835. Dogs, often strays, were used as early warning systems at night.

The first police force in the modern sense was created by the government of King Louis XIV in 1667 to police the city of Paris, then the largest city in Europe. The royal edict, registered by the Parliament of Paris on 15 March 1667 created the office of lieutenant general of police, who was to be the head of the new Paris police force, and defined the task of the police as 'ensuring the peace and quiet of the public and of private individuals, purging the city of what may cause disturbances, procuring abundance, and having each and every one live according to their station and their duties'.

Early dog days in Europe and London

Imagine a 19th century constable walking the beat in the bustling cities of Paris, London, Berlin or New York. At this time the only weapon the constable had at his disposal was a night stick. On-duty injuries and deaths became a topic of great concern. Criminals armed with knives or pistols were quick to take advantage of the meagrely armed constable. In 1896, Dr Ham Gross had a cutting-edge notion for decreasing the injuries and deaths of constables patrolling the night beats by teaming them up with canine partners. In his book, *Yearbook of the Austrian Constabulary*, Gross referred to canines as 'ideal, ever-watchful companions of the constable in his arduous official rounds, gifted with senses far more acute than those of his master'. Law enforcement officials throughout Europe loved Gross' idea and many employed canines in their agencies.

The first recorded instance of the use of dogs in police work was to guard naval docks in St Malo, France in the early part of the 14th century. However, from as early as the Middle Ages, money was set aside in towns and villages in England to pay for the upkeep of bloodhounds to be used by parish constables to track down outlaws and criminals.

In fact, during the reign of King Henry I, documents showing the staffing levels of the royal palaces refer to the appointment of a constable who, with the aid of a marshal, 'shall maintain the stables, kennels and mews, and be responsible for protecting and policing the whole court'.

During the 12th and 13th centuries, the forces of law and order were employed by the barons and landowners to protect their privileges. Restrictions were placed upon the right to own a dog, which were divided into three classes: small dogs, which were unlikely to be a threat to hunting, were unrestricted; dogs that had natural hunting instincts, such as greyhounds and spaniels, were barred altogether; and larger breeds were only allowed if used for security purposes and if their claws were removed. Constables used these larger breeds such as the bloodhounds more for their own protection than the ability to apprehend villains. A point worthy of note is that the bloodhounds of those times were described as 'unreliable, bad-tempered and savage', but even then displayed an uncanny ability to track through the marshes and bogs which bordered the highways of that time.

In Scotland bloodhounds became known as 'slough dogs' and it is from this name that the word 'sleuth', usually applied to a detective, is derived. By the beginning of the 19th century, people were leaving rural areas to move into larger cities and towns. Large country estates were breaking down into smaller units and with this change came the decline in the popularity of the dog as a hunter and enforcer of the law. At about this point in history, people of all classes began to treat their dogs as domestic pets rather than working animals, and size and appearance became as important as temperament and working ability.

The 19th century

The period of the Napoleonic Wars saw extreme outbreaks of violence and lawlessness in England and the existing forces of law and order — the parish constables and the Bow Street Runners (the first police force in London) — were overwhelmed. As a result private associations were formed to help combat crime. Night watchmen were employed to guard premises with many of these individuals provided with firearms and dogs to protect themselves from the criminal elements. In 1829 Sir Robert Peel established London's Metropolitan Police, the first professional body to police the whole metropolitan area. From 1835 onwards, police forces were set up in the larger boroughs and cities, as well as in the counties, so that by the end of the century, professional policemen were policing the whole country.

One of the first real attempts to use dogs to aid police in the detection of crime and the apprehension of a criminal was in 1888 occurred when two privately owned bloodhounds, Barnaby and Burgh, were used in a simple tracking test set by the then Commissioner of the Metropolitan Police, Sir Charles Warren, with a view to using them in the hunt for the Victorian murderer, Jack the Ripper. The results were far from satisfactory, with one of the hounds biting the Commissioner and both dogs later running off, requiring a police search to find them.

Police dogs were officially recognised as being of value on the European continent as early as 1859, with the Belgium Police in Ghent using dogs to patrol with the night shift.

Ghent, Belgium is the first city in the world known to have established a school where dogs were trained for law enforcement work. In March 1899 Ghent purchased three dogs and soon after, seven more. These dogs were trained for police work. The Ghent program attracted wide attention and prompted other cities on the continent to use dogs in law enforcement. German officers who studied in the Ghent system made favourable reports and by 1910 there were 600 towns in Germany using police dogs. Several police forces in France, Hungary, Austria and Italy as well as other Belgium police forces did so too. The first force in England to use handler/dog teams was the Hull and Barnsley Railway Police. In about 1908 these police used Airedale terriers imported from Belgium and trained in England for basic obedience and man work to help deal with rowdy seamen returning to the Hull docks after shore leave. The dogs were also used to protect premises and goods at dockside.

The first engraving of a police dog in Belgium, 1899.

Germany, France, Austria and Hungary soon followed with dogs becoming an accepted part of the official police establishment. The dogs employed at this time were aggressive animals that could inspire fear, protect their handler against attackers and be prepared to tackle courageously anyone found lurking in the ill-lit streets or open spaces. The breeds most commonly used by the end of the 19th century in these countries were Belgian and German shepherds, boxers, Dobermans and Airedales (imported from England).

In 1895, dogs were used by the French police to combat street gangs in Paris. The success of these dogs led to the first major step forward in the development of the modern police dog in Germany. It was here, in the late 1890s, that the first scientific and planned development took place with experiments in breeding, training and utilisation. By 1899, rapid progress had been made in the field of dog training with the development of the German shepherd dog as a breed and the formation on 22 April 1899 of the *Vereins für Deutsche Schäferhunde* or SV (The German Shepherd Dog Society). In 1903 the SV staged civilian police dog trials that encompassed control, criminal work and nose work exercises. The police authorities were impressed but were not convinced that the intensive efforts expended on training and the costs involved were justified by the results. The primary object of the police dog at this time was still seen to be that of only a deterrent.

The 20th century

In 1908, the North Eastern Railway Police who used Airedales to put a stop to theft from the docks in Hull formed the first recognised UK Police Dog Section. By 1910 the British Transport Commission Police had taken over, experimenting with other breeds such as labradors, Dobermans and finally, the German shepherd or Alsatian as it was then known.

After World War I despite the success of the transport police dogs, the police authorities in the United Kingdom continued to show a lack of interest in the use of dogs as an aid to police work. Dogs were considered beneficial as long as they did not cost money or require special training (some of my modern day colleges would argue that nothing has changed). In keeping with this attitude, in 1914 official authority was granted for 172 constables in the Metropolitan Police in London to take their own pet dogs on patrol with them; a motley crew of sheepdogs, retrievers, collies, terriers, spaniels, mongrels and even one Pomeranian.

By this time in Europe dogs were being used for a variety of purposes, and in 1920 a government school was established in Greenheide, Germany for the training of dogs for use in the field of law enforcement. Dogs were trained in basic obedience, tracking and searching with organised dog training centres being set up in various locations. The impressive results achieved on the continent could not be ignored forever, and in 1934 a committee was set up to investigate the whole question surrounding the use of police dogs in the United Kingdom. An interesting excerpt from *The Times* dated 15 January 1938 gives an interesting insight into the thinking of senior police officers of the time in regard to the use of dogs. Colonel Hoel Llewellyn, Chief Constable of Wiltshire was quoted as follows: 'A good dog with a night duty man is as sound a proposition as you can get. The dog hears what the constable does not, gives him notice of anyone in the vicinity, guards his master's bicycle to the death, and remains mute unless roused. He is easily trained and will go home when told to do so with a message in his collar.'

Bearing in mind that this was a statement from a pro-dog man of the times, it's no wonder that the authorities failed to understand the true worth of the dog in the role of law enforcement for a number of years to come.

Britain has a long tradition of using police dogs, which are used for tracking down offenders, crowd control and bite-work. They play an important part in all around Britain; from two-man police units in the small counties to over a hundred in large metropolitan divisions.

It was not until the 1930s that the police forces of the United Kingdom finally realised the potential of the police dog. In order to establish the best breed to be employed as a police service dog, a Home Office committee was set up in 1934 to establish an experimental dog training school in Washwater, near Newbury. The committee concluded that a multi-purpose dog, trained to carry out all disciplines, was not possible, and that tracking and other work would have to be divided. The committee reported in 1937 that the experiments at the dog training school showed that the best breed of dog for following a scent was the bloodhound, and the best breed of dog for general patrol purposes was the labrador.

Experiments had been done in crossing fell hounds with labradors and otter hounds to bloodhounds, but both sets of crosses left something to be desired. As a result of the committee's conclusions, recommendations were made that chief constables consider the use of dogs in police work, and it was once again left to the individual chief police officer to decide the worth of employing dogs in his respective police force. In 1938 two specially trained black labradors were introduced into the Metropolitan Police as general patrol or 'utility' dogs. However, they were transferred in 1940 to the Cheshire Constabulary. With the outbreak of World War II, any further efforts to introduce dogs into a policing role in the United Kingdom were abandoned. The British Army, though, increased its use of working dogs throughout the war period.

The interest of the UK police forces was revived in 1946, when the Metropolitan Police established a small dog section and purchased six labradors, deploying them in South London. The labradors proved their worth on their first night on patrol when they were used in the arrest of two American servicemen. In 1948, the first German shepherd police dog had arrived in London. By 1954, the Metropolitan Police Dog Section was growing rapidly and a working party of police officers from the United Kingdom visited Germany. By this stage, the German police had been using working dogs for some years. German shepherd dogs were brought into the UK and designated to various police forces. A standing committee was formed to coordinate the breeding, supply and training of police dogs throughout the United Kingdom and it was from this point on that the working police dog came into its own in the United Kingdom. From these early beginnings the use of police dogs grew across Europe and around the world.

The end of World War II brought a crime wave to the shores of the United Kingdom, generally attributed to the presence of returning servicemen. It also brought the appointment of Chief Constable of the Surrey Constabulary to Sir Joseph Simpson KBE, a man who had a lifelong interest in gundogs and who saw clearer than most the possibilities of adapting the natural abilities and qualities of the dog to the specialist requirements of the police service. By good fortune, the Surrey Constabulary also employed an officer who had taken part in many of the unrewarding experiments to try and prove the value of the trained dog in police work; his name was Sergeant Harry Darbyshire.

This liaison set in motion the first positive effort to convince the Home Office and police forces throughout the United Kingdom of the true worth of a well-trained dog. With Darbyshire's enthusiasm and ideas and Simpson's leadership and influence, the Surrey police headquarters at Mount Brown in Guildford became the epicentre of breeding and training of the modern police dog. Within a short space of time the Surrey police dogs were touring the country giving demonstrations to other police forces, while at the same time, Sir Joseph Simpson was bringing his influence to bear on the kennel club and other senior police officers. Slowly, they began to understand and appreciate the potential value of the police service dog.

After a careful study of the work carried out by Harry Darbyshire, Sir Joseph Simpson reached a number of important conclusions on which further developments and progress were to be based. The most far-reaching of these was to discard the accepted notion that all police dogs should be divided into two classes: tracking dogs and criminal work patrol dogs. The evidence pointed to the fact that some breeds of dogs were capable of being trained to carry out both disciplines. He also concluded that there should be a more rigorous selection process when accepting dogs for police work, which was the first step towards the notion that the police service should breed their own animals in an attempt to produce the ideal police dog.

In 1948 a new breed of police dog was used on the streets of London for the first time, the Alsatian wolf dog, later known as the Alsatian or German shepherd dog. The first of this breed in London was called Smokey and such was the impression that he made, that a further twelve Alsatians together with another seven labradors were purchased. The Metropolitan Police Dog Section was growing so rapidly that a central dog training school was established at Imber Court, and by 1950 the total number of trained dogs in the force numbered 90.

In England a major recommendation of the Home Office Working Parties that visited police dog centres in Germany in 1955 and 1956 was the establishment of a central registry of all dogs used in Great Britain for police purposes. Chief Constable P. Eric St. Johnston of Lancastershire Constabulary was asked to set up a registry at the county police headquarters at Hutton. The registry was put into use in January 1960. The principal objectives in setting up the registry are essentially:

- To record specific information about all dogs used in police work in England and Wales

- To note police dogs considered for breeding so that the quality of police dogs may be improved

- To assist the police forces in acquiring suitable dogs

North American dogs at work

In British North America, policing was initially provided by local elected officials. For example, the New York Sheriff's Office was founded in 1626, and the Albany County Sheriff's Department in the 1660s. In the colonial period, policing was provided by elected sheriffs and local militias as in their mother countries dogs often accompanied these men but were not officially on the pay role as police dogs are today.

British Bobbies have used German shepherds since World War I. The dogs were called Alsatians due to anti-German sentiment at the time.

In Canada, the Royal Newfoundland Constabulary was founded in 1729, making it the first police force. It was followed in 1834 by the Toronto Police, and in 1838 by police forces in Montreal and Quebec City. A national force, the Dominion Police, was founded in 1868. Initially the Dominion Police provided security for parliament, but its responsibilities quickly grew. The famous Royal Northwest Mounted Police was founded in 1873. Spitz-type breeds were used not for traditional attack roles but as transportation; dogs were the first patrol cars.

In 1789 the US Marshals Service was established, followed by other federal services such as the US Parks Police (1791) and US Mint Police (1792). The first city police services were established in Philadelphia in 1751, Richmond, Virginia in 1807, Boston in 1838, and New York in 1845. The US Secret Service was founded in 1865 and was for some time the main investigative body for the federal government. Every one of these agencies now maintains a K9 unit. There are more than 900,000 sworn law enforcement officers now serving in the United States.

The New York City Police program was developed in 1907. Since 1907 more than 1000 US police forces have had K9 units at some time or presently do. There have been two distinct eras in the United States in the police canine programs. The earlier era ran from 1907 to 1952 and included 13 programs and 12 police forces. (There were no canine programs in the United States from 1952 to 1954.) The modern era began in 1954 and continues today.

In the 21st century our canine friends have not only adapted to police work but have also established themselves as integral members of law enforcement teams. Police across the world have not overlooked dogs as important partners in the war on crime and disorder. Not only do our canine friends help us to deter criminals and safeguard the public (would you want to take on a German shepherd?), they also offer us something quite unique: an amazing sense of smell. A dog's nose is many times more sensitive than a human's and so is ideal for tracking or detecting, whether it is drugs, criminals, bombs, stolen property, or people who have lost their way. The canine sense of smell is so finely tuned that they can be trained to detect a number of different substances. Police dogs are a huge asset to the police service.

There is no standard breed that is best for police work. Here a border collie is used to search for illegal substances at a checkpoint for entry into the Pentagon in the USA.

DOG BREEDS USED FOR LAW ENFORCEMENT

We have a special bond with dogs, a bond more special than with any other animal. Of all the animals on earth, we are the closest to the dog. In police work the reason we use dogs is because they are trainable: we can take a dog with high hunt drive, condition its behaviour, and train it to detect and respond to the presence of humans or other odours.

Many breeds of dogs have been used in law enforcement throughout history. (Throughout this book I use the term 'law enforcement' to include all dogs that work for agencies which fight crime whether it be to track down a suspect thief or apprehend a person smuggling an illegal item into the country.)

In Ancient Rome, for example, the urban cohorts employed large, fierce attack dogs to control the masses, and hounds to track down runaway slaves. In Britain Celtic hounds were dogs well respected by royalty and warriors. Hounds were the traditional guardian animals of roads and crossways and are believed to protect and guide lost souls in the Otherworld. The Irish wolfhound was used to hunt wolves and deer, but they were also used to track down poachers, slaves or villagers accused of crimes by the local sheriff.

Airedale terriers

Lieutenant Colonel Edwin Richardson was responsible for the development of messenger and guard dogs in the British Army. Two Airedales (Wolf and Prince) were used as message carriers. However, prior to this, in 1906, Richardson tried to interest the British Police in using dogs to accompany officers, for protection on patrol at night. Airedale terriers were selected for duty as police dogs because of their intelligence, good scenting abilities and their hard, wiry coats, which were easy to maintain and clean.

At the beginning of the Russo-Japanese war in 1904, the Russian embassy in London contacted Lieutenant Colonel Richardson for help acquiring dogs for the Russian Army, trained to take the wounded away from the battlefields. He sent Airedale terriers, for communication and sanitary services. Although these original imports perished, Airedale terriers were reintroduced to Russia in the early 1920s for use by the Red Army and Civilian Police as guard and tracker dogs. Before the adoption of the German shepherd as the dog of choice for law enforcement and search and rescue work, the Airedale terrier often filled this role throughout the world.

Belgian shepherd (Malinois)

The Belgian shepherd (Malinois) is a breed of dog sometimes classified as a variety of the Belgian shepherd dog rather than as a separate breed. In Belgium, Germany, the Netherlands and other European countries, as well as in the United States, Canada and Australia, the Malinois is bred primarily as a working dog for detection and police work. The United States Secret Service uses the breed exclusively.

Bloodhounds

A bloodhound (also known as the St Hubert hound, first bred in 1000 AD by monks at the St Hubert Monastery in Belgium) is a large breed of dog famed for its ability to follow scents hours or even days old over great distances. The combination of keen nose and powerful drive to track give it its place as top scent hound and have led it to be used to track escaped prisoners, missing persons and for police work. Bloodhounds are famous for their scenting abilities and are still used today by some US police departments for tracking fugitives and for cadaver recovery.

Border collies

The border collie is a breed of herding dog that originated along the borders of England, Wales and Scotland. Is it widely considered to be the most intelligent breed of dog in the world. Because of their skills, border collies make excellent search and rescue dogs in lowland, mountain and urban areas. They have been trained in air-scenting, ground-scenting and as cadaver dogs in many police forces.

Boxers

Developed in Germany in the late 1800s, the boxer is part of the Molosser dog group; a stocky, medium-sized, short-haired dog. The coat is smooth and fawn or brindled, with or without white markings. Boxers are brachycephalic (they have broad, short skulls), and have a square muzzle, mandibular prognathism (an underbite), very strong jaws and a powerful bite ideal for hanging on to large prey, including man. These strong and intelligent animals have been used by many European police K9 units.

Doberman pinschers

Doberman pinschers were first bred in the town of Apolda by Karl Friedrich Louis Dobermann, in the German state of Thüringia around 1890, following the Franco-Prussian War. Its qualities soon became apparent to both the German police and military; by World War II it is estimated that more than 200,000 war dogs were trained. The US established seven Doberman War Dog Platoons that were sent to the European theatre and the Pacific. Dobermans were credited for saving many American lives and are the official Marine Corps War Dog. Several police forces use Dobermans as their main breed of police dog.

German shepherd

The German shepherd dog (GSD, also known as an Alsatian), is a breed of large-sized dog that originated in Germany. German shepherds are a relatively new breed of dog, whose origins date back to 1899 according to its breeding club, the *Verein für Deutsche Schäferhunde* (VS). As part of the herding group, the German shepherd is a working dog developed originally for herding sheep. Because of its strength, intelligence and abilities in obedience training the German government began to use the dog for military purposes and make them ideal companions for police officers today. They are especially well known for their police work, and are used for tracking criminals, patrolling troubled areas, and detection and holding of suspects. The German shepherd is one of the most widely used breeds in scent-work roles. These include search and rescue, cadaver searching, narcotics detection, explosives detection and accelerant detection, amongst others. They are suited for these lines of work because of their ability to work regardless of distractions.

Labradors

The modern labrador's ancestors originated on the island of Newfoundland, now part of the province of Newfoundland and Labrador, Canada. The breed emerged over time from the St John's water dog, also an ancestor of the Newfoundland dog (to which the labrador is closely related). Labradors are intelligent digs with a good work ethic and generally good temperaments. Common working roles for labradors include hunting, tracking and detection (they have a great sense of smell), and as guide dogs, police and military working dogs. They are perhaps the most popular and commonly used specialist search dog in law enforcement.

Rottweilers

The Rottweiler, or *Metzgerhund* ('Butchers Dog'), is a medium to large size breed originating in Germany as a herding dog. Rottweilers worked as draught dogs, pulling carts to carry meat and other products to market. The breed is an ancient one, whose history stretches back again to the Roman Empire. One route the army traveled was through Württemberg and on to the small market town of Rottweil. The principal ancestors of the first Rottweiler's during this time was supposed to be the Roman droving dog, local dogs the army met on its travels. The Rottweiler was officially recognised in 1910 as a police dog in Germany.

Spaniels

The spaniel is an old breed, appearing in paintings as early as the 1600s. It is possibly the ancestor of modern spaniels, springer spaniels and cocker spaniels, which were not recognised as separate breeds until the 1800s. The purpose of the breed was as a hunting dog. As such they are ideally suited to explosive and firearms searching, utilising their natural scenting abilities.

There are of course many other dogs that have been used by various police forces throughout the world. I have just highlighted the most common types used today. Not all police dog are pure breeds. Many a mongrel (a dog or bitch whose sire and dam who owe their make-up to any number of different breeds) has served the police services with heroic distinction. Many have given the ultimate sacrifice.

SELECTING DOG HANDLERS AND DOGS

Handler selection

The careful selection of persons suitable for training as dog handlers is vital to the successful employment of dogs for police purposes. At all stages of training and operation, the handler and the dog work as a team, often with the minimum of supervision. The selection of suitable personnel for training is therefore no less important than the careful selection of dogs. People to be considered for training as dog handlers must be sound, experienced police officers whose mental alertness, equable temperament and willingness to persevere are above average. The nature of the training and subsequent operational work calls for a high standard of physical fitness. It is no good having all the academic talents in the world if you cannot lift a dog over a two-metre fence or carry a weight of 40 kilograms (your average police dog) for half a kilometre. If your police dog is injured you must be able to get it to a vet; you may be far from your patrol vehicle conducting a track of an offender when an injury occurs.

Austrian police dog handler. Being a dog handler is not exclusively for males; many police forces embrace female handlers in their ranks.

Previous experience with animals may well be an advantage but the lack of it is not necessarily a disqualification in the case of an otherwise suitable officer. It is important, however, that a handler should have a forceful character with a determination to succeed and a cheerful disposition which will be reflected subsequently in the behaviour of his dog. A handler with a brusque or nagging disposition will confuse and may easily ruin a dog. Voice modulation is vital to be able to give the dog quick, sharp, clear commands.

In cases where a police dog is to be kennelled at the home of the handler, serious consideration should be given to checking the home background, to determine whether all members of the family are supportive of the job requirements. Adequate kennelling facilities must be available to ensure that interference with and disturbance of the dog is minimised. Many police departments have a rule that dog handlers be married as this provides a stable life for the dog and aids its sociability.

Being a dog handler is a seven-day-a-week job. Many departments pay allowances to handlers because unlike general police officers who can hang up their gun and relax on their days off, a dog handler has to groom, feed and clean up after the department's property on his days off. Some agencies, predominately the Military and Customs, believe dogs are a tool and when you're off duty your K9 is in the agency's kennel complex. I believe this is very limited thinking; it's usually based on fiscal considerations, so that the department doesn't have to pay for kennel housing or patrol cars as transport. You simply cannot have the same rapport with an animal, which your life may depend on, if you treat it like a part-time piece of kit, then lock it away after use. In my humble opinion you should live and work with your pack. I based part of my selection process as Dogmaster of the Defence Force on this commitment; if a potential handler didn't want to take his K9 home he was not accepted into my unit.

The devotion of the handler to the dog and to duty must be without question: the former will ensure a mutual confidence and respect which will be shown in the dog's attitude to work, and the latter is an operational necessity, particularly in squads where the number of police dogs is small. The technical ability of handlers can only be really judged after they have been allocated a dog to undertake a 'familiarisation course', or when they commence full training.

Many familiarisation courses thus test the physical fitness of handlers to check if they are able to look after the dog's welfare as stated and to be able to keep up with it while tracking. Physical dexterity and agility is also tested as dog training often requires quick and sudden changes of pace and direction. Being able to listen to commands and repeat them may sound simple but is very important because it is the handler who effectively trains the dog.

A good handler is not only an alpha personality; he or she must be able to work in both a small team environment and on their own. This is why dog handlers the world over are recruited from the force not the street. Dog handlers must have excellent general police skills including weapons and investigative abilities prior to being considered, which in most forces means several years of service first. Although it's true to say that all dogs can be trained, not all people can give that training. Getting a dog to want to use its abilities to order is a skill in itself.

Police dog selection

The selection of police dogs is perhaps even more demanding than the selection of handlers. Only half a dozen dogs out of a hundred viewed and tested will even make it to the beginning of a course and then not all of them will finish it. Producing a dog suitable in all respects for police work requires knowledge and care in the initial selection of animals for a training course. There are no hard and fast rules regarding particular breeds as individual dogs of any breed vary considerably in their mental approach to the training, and in their ability to assimilate such training. So the selection of dogs considered suitable for training as police dogs must be based on experience and must be done with extreme care. A department should not send the duty handler out to select dogs; rather it should send a very experienced operator/trainer. In many police or military forces the remount section, as it is often called, is staffed by senior non-commissioned officers (SNCOs) whose sole function is to select dogs. It must be appreciated that shortcomings in any individual dog may not become apparent until the training is well advanced. No useful purpose will ever be served by persevering with dogs which are in any way lacking the essential qualifications.

The requirements of the police service may be met in two ways:

- Breeding at authorised breeding establishments

- Acquiring young dogs at an age suitable to commence or be prepared for training

There is some difference of opinion about the best age at which training should begin, but experience has shown that the best results are obtained if training is undertaken when the dogs are between 12 and 18 months old. So when breeding dogs for police purposes, the long unproductive upbringing of puppies must be taken into account.

Police forces throughout the world are finding it difficult to acquire suitable dogs for policing. Breeders often aim for features opposite to the qualities police are looking for. Unfortunately the German shepherd is a breed which suffers from this; breeding for exaggeration in the show ring, exaggeration in size and breeding purely for profit has resulted in the production of a lot of animals of marginal physical, mental and genetic soundness. This is a long way from the original features envisaged by Captain Max von Stephanitz, the founder of the German shepherd dog in 1899, when he first bred this ideal working dog. Therefore many agencies are trying to breed their own dogs to counter these modern physical weaknesses.

An alternative to direct breeding for police purposes is the acquisition of suitable dogs at or near the age when they are ready to begin training. In Australia, for example, a great deal of money was recently spent by several government agencies to travel to Eastern Europe to source good old-fashioned quality stock and frozen semen, which will be used for improving breeding stock.

Temperament

Gone are the days of recruiting land sharks; years ago police dogs were often unapproachable by anyone except the handler. Today police dogs have to be more socialised. This does not mean soft or that any person can come up too close to them. The public just do not expect the dog wagon to rock from one side to the other with a large, hairy German shepherd bearing its teeth out the window as Grandma walks past on her Zimmer frame. So people who select police dogs look for certain traits. The characteristic expression of the dog gives the impression of perpetual vigilance, fidelity, liveliness and watchfulness; alert to every sight and sound, with nothing escaping attention. Fearless, but with a suspicion of strangers as opposed to the immediate friendliness of some breeds. A police dog should possess highly developed senses. It should be strongly individualistic and possess a high standard of intelligence. Three of the most outstanding traits are incorruptibility, discernment and ability to reason.

Physical characteristics

Police dogs don't necessarily need to be pure breed (a pure breed dog is one whose sire and dam are of the same breed, likewise their parents are descendants of the same breed). But for many reasons most forces use pedigree stock. The general appearance of a police dog no matter what breed is a well-proportioned dog showing great suppleness of limb, neither massive nor heavy, but at the same time free from any suggestion of weediness. It must not approach the greyhound type. The body is rather long, strongly boned, with plenty of muscle, obviously capable of endurance and speed and of quick and sudden movement. The gait should be supple, smooth and long-reaching, carrying the body along with the minimum of up-and-down movement, entirely free from stiltedness.

The head and skull of a potential police dog is perhaps the most important area and should be looked at in depth. After all we rely on and use a police dog for its enhanced abilities such as sight, scent, hearing and in the case of criminal work the ability to bite an offender. All of these systems are in the skull.

The head is proportionate to the size of the body: long, lean and clean cut, broad at the base of the skull, but without coarseness, tapering to the nose with only a slight stop between the eyes. The skull is slightly domed and the top of the nose should be parallel to the forehead. The cheek must not be full or in any way prominent and the whole head when viewed from the top should be much in the form of a V, well filled in under the eyes. There should be plenty of substance in foreface, with a good depth from top to bottom. The muzzle is strong and long and, while tapering to the nose, it must not be carried to such an extreme as to give the appearance of being overshot. It must not show any weakness. The lips must be tight fitting and clean. The nose must he black. Teeth are clean, sound and strong, gripping with scissor like action.

SPECIALIST DOG SELECTION

All of the desired recruiting traits for general police dogs are the same for specialist search dogs; however, the breeds are usually different. Many police agencies use labradors or similar hounds known for their scenting abilities. It is true that these breeds of dogs tend to be perceived by the public as less aggressive and therefore more acceptable working around a crowded airport terminal or railway station.

Explosive detection dogs (EDD) are passive response, retrieve reward detection dogs. In other words the dog is trained to work the 'scent cone' from the target odour to the source. Once the source is pinpointed, the dog offers conditioned passive response consisting of a sit or down position combined with an intensely focused stare at the source of the target odour. In practice this method provides a very safe and accurate way of indicating the exact location of the source of the target odour, not just a generalised indication that the target odour exists in the area. The EDD is not taught to play with the source or target odour, or to expect a reward from the handler, rather the EDD is taught that the reward, generally a verbal phrase or a play item, will always come from the exact point of the source, not from the handler.

Many other detection dogs are trained at least initially with an active response; they will physically try to retrieve the scent object. This could be a narcotic scent or human remains odour in a container of some sort (so the dog doesn't mouth and contaminate the substance and for safety in the case of drugs). This active response has some advantages as the dog literally finds the source, the item itself; however, this is not the way for explosives detection because of booby traps. All specialist detection dogs can work on or off lead. Obedience training in specialist detection dogs is measured and minimal. It is important for these types of dogs to possess an amount of independence because handlers rely on them to locate an odour, not be directed to it. This way a search dog can at least initially search large areas independently until the handler decides a more detailed search is required.

BASIC TRAINING

Most police dog courses for general patrol dogs are approximately 13 weeks duration. Over that time they receive instruction in tracking, man-work, obedience, search and agility. Many police schools train not only their own service but those of neighbouring police states or counties. Some also train the military and other government agencies such as Customs, aviation security and search and rescue organisations.

Not every police force has its own dog training school. Many countries cooperate with either the defence department or federal police assets, or send handlers to a larger police department for training. Some countries even send their perspective handlers overseas to train. For example, the British Army's Royal Army Veterinary Corps has trained dozens of Commonwealth Military and police force canines. In the United States federal agencies have combined to train specialist canines. This ensures fiscal savings as well as uniformity and standards, enabling multi-agency cooperation for homeland defence.

As another example, the National Police of Haiti, in 2011, acquired six specialised dogs, trained in the detection of narcotics, explosives and currencies. The Canine Unit is now at work, at the international airport in Port-au-Prince, the regional airport and the port. The dogs, purchased and trained through United States government funding, were offered to the Haitian Government through the Narcotics Affairs Section of the US Embassy in Port-au-Prince, Haiti, as part of the continued support of the United States to strengthen the capacity of the National Police of Haiti. One of the six dogs will be used for the detection of explosives and one for the detection of money. Canine operations are conducted in cooperation with the US DEA (Drug Enforcement Administration).

A recently certified Iraqi Police officer with his new dog. Iraq has embraced the use of dogs, especially explosive detection dogs, in order to help their country in the war against terrorism. Most police dogs are trained by US or Croatian instructors.

The learning process

Although the figures vary depending on who you speak to, a dog inherits approximately 75 per cent of its knowledge, learnt behaviour accounts for 15 per cent (observing parents) and taught knowledge (training) accounts for less than 10 per cent. A canine therefore acts or reacts if all else fails on its basic instincts and the four basic responses (the four Fs) of fight, flight, feed and reproduction! We harness natural instincts to train a police dog. For example, we harness the protection instinct to defend the handler; we use the hunting instinct in tracking and search. We can use a dog's natural instincts for tasks such as tracking, detection of explosives or narcotics and search and rescue. In the right environment a dog can detect intruders up to 1000 metres away using its natural senses of smell, hearing and sight.

The formula used in most military and police organisations for training dogs is RAR: recognition, association and repetition. Added to this is voice modulation; praise and timing are vital. For example, in food detection dogs we want a passive alert (not picking up the object or moving it with their nose). So once the dog initially responses to the stimulus or odour we immediately reward it; the dog associates what we want via command and the reward for correctly alerting on that odour. All done as a big, positive game. With repetition the dog associates the smell with command and reward. It isn't as simple as this, of course; there are many other factors (but this is not a training manual).

For patrol dogs the most important of all training skills is obedience; it is the fundamental base to all other training. It is pointless training your dog to retrieve an object if it will not obey the command to return it to you. To train a police dog in gun steadiness on the range it is essential to command him to stay, not jump up and try to mouth the gun or bite you because it has already associated gun fire with crime work.

Therefore obedience control is the groundwork on which all successful training is based. The successful teaching of obedience is brought about by a series of repetitive habit-forming exercises, taught on command and put into practice under guidance. When teaching a dog a new exercise it can't be expected to be immediately aware of what is to be done or how to associate a command with the required action. Before it does so the same command, tone of voice and guided action is carried out on numerous occasions (repetition and association).

Care must be taken to avoid boredom for both dog and handler. The various exercises which constitute general obedience are introduced in a certain sequence; all pieces that fit together like a jigsaw puzzle. The dog must thoroughly grasp each exercise before progressing to another. It must be borne in mind that dogs, just like human beings, are diverse in character. Some are quicker to respond to training, others are more sensitive, and all have their off moments. The handler needs to trust the trainer to get them and their dog to the end goal — sometimes a new handler is unclear about what the finished puzzle looks like. A little bit of knowledge is dangerous and the last thing a trainer wants is the student to get ahead too fast and miss out on vital groundwork (or parts of the puzzle).

Words of command should be clear and concise, and therefore preferably confined to single syllables. It is the sound and tone of the voice, not the volume, which controls the dog. The quieter the commands are given the better, as this will not only compel the dog to pay attention but help to build up its concentration. Commands must not be repeated too much (nagging) or exercises continued for too long and overtiring the dog.

The dog, from the first day of training, must never be allowed to ignore a command or fail to complete one given. The dog must never be allowed to suspect that there is ever a possibility of being able to avoid a command. To allow one to be ignored for any reason whatsoever can give a dog a false impression which, if allowed to develop, will make many problems in the ensuing training and may even result in a dominance challenge (the dog thinking he's the boss not the handler).

Infinite patience is needed when showing the dog what it is required to do. Faults must be corrected at the time. Timing is also one of the most important skills a dog handler has to possess. Giving the right phrase at the right time will help the dog associate with the right thing to do. Late timing can either do nothing or at worst confuse the dog.

Disobedience must be met with firmness once it is certain that the dog has clearly understood the meaning of the command and has learnt the exercise correctly. The dog does not understand our standards of right and wrong and it is important, from a training point of view, that we do not wrongly credit it with these powers when considering the right application of correction. The use of physical punishment should under no circumstances ever be considered a training measure. Proper use of the check chain, the verbal command or admonition and the withholding of praise are usually sufficient correctives. As stated, dogs are diverse in character and it is important that correction fits the temperament of the dog as well as the misdeed.

Working happiness should prevail throughout the training by giving plenty of praise. This praise must be given even if the dog has had difficulty in doing its exercise but has completed it successfully. The manner and amount of such praise needed will vary with each dog but, having been praised suitably, the dog will know that it has done the right thing and the subsequent repetitive commands will be made much easier to enforce. A training session should always finish on both a happy and successful note. Control in training does not only mean control over the dog. It is essential that the handler has control over himself. Any loss of temper, with the consequent aftermath of faulty training, will completely confuse the dog and make difficult the mutual understanding which is so essential between handler and dog.

General police dogs are also taught agility to ensure they can jump any obstacle they encounter during operational tasking. They need the ability to scale a wall, jump a fence or ditch, or jump through a vehicle or residential window.

Criminal work, also known by several names including bite-work or man-work, is a police dog's reason for being. Criminal work comes in many forms such as attack on a violent criminal, defending the handler from attack, riot control training, or building search for a hidden offender.

Criminal work is the end result, in many cases, of the offender's confrontation with police. Up to this point a police dog has tracked the offender from the commission of his offence; the dog may have located stolen items on the way or similar evidence. Finally the police dog has confronted the offender, warned him or her by physical presence or a vocal growl. If this is not enough for the person in question or he tries to harm the handler, then the next thing the offender sees is the inside of a hospital ward.

Assessments

Assessments are conducted all the way through a dog's training course. Many dogs might find themselves withheld from training if they are deemed suitable but just don't have what it takes at present. Others may be assessed as weak in one of the areas and deemed unsuitable to continue police training. This could mean a complete re-team for a handler whose 13-week course has just turned into a 26-week course because he or she has to start all over again with a new dog. There are also handlers who do not pass these physically demanding courses and they are returned to their old jobs within the force. It is sad to say that in the old days when police dogs trained in criminal work were deemed too vicious, they were often given what was called the lead aspirin (a bullet). Thankfully today all dogs can be re-teamed with a suitable family.

A formal assessment is given prior to the dog's graduation. The dog is trained usually once a week after graduation in a formal squad environment with all other K9 members of the unit. Individually a handler will train his dog on a daily basis. Dogs are not a tool you can store on the shelf until needed and expect them to function, they are a living animal with a capacity to learn and forget. They must be used and trained daily. The next step in training is tactical and operational exposure.

Xanto's Tenacity

What makes a good police dog? As well as the required physical attributes it's also about character. Police dogs have a dangerous job and some sadly die on duty protecting their handlers and making the streets safe for you. One such dog was Xanto from the Garland Police Department in the USA. Xanto and his human partner, Brian Griffeth, were called to track a suspect who had committed a carjacking and aggravated robbery. Xanto tracked the offender to his hiding place in thick bushland; after several verbal warnings by the handler to come out the dog was sent in to apprehend the offender. During this time the handler heard a yelp. An ice pick was found at the scene, but there were no visible signs of injury to Xanto. In fact, he had been stabbed in the side on his body that night but the wound had closed up. Over the next few weeks Xantos health deteriorated and finally he succumbed to the wound. It was not until an autopsy was done that the internal injury was found. Xanto only had a short career of two years' service but in that time he apprehended 49 suspects, 7 of them after the ice pick injury in the last weeks of his life. Even on the same night of his death he tracked an offender several kilometres. A true K9 hero.

SPECIALIST ROLES FOR DOGS IN LAW ENFORCEMENT

Over the centuries police dogs have had several roles mainly as night watchdogs and protectors for the constable and to track down wanted persons. In modern times specific duties have been defined for police dogs where they can give the best service. These include the detection of illegal substances such as narcotics, the detection of explosives, the detection of food items or animal products at border control points and, of course, the detection of undesirable persons.

Many sheriff departments use part-time dog teams to broaden their operational capabilities as and when needed such as cadaver detection dogs or search and rescue dogs. These types of specialist teams usually do not have enough work to be part of the full-time strength of most departments but are used by police volunteers with great success. Likewise for budget constraint reasons some police departments use their limited dog resources by multi-skilling them. For example, training their general purpose police dogs in firearms detection or locating cannabis.

The military is often the prime user of this type of dog, using military police patrol K9s that can also carry out a search for explosives at a vehicle checkpoint (VCP) at a base's main gate. The only problem with these multi-skilled working dogs is that their primary role and focus is and has been criminal work; that is, apprehending offenders. They have completed the usual 13-week course in policing and patrol on the streets. After a year or so on the job biting bad guys the K9 then might do a week long course in cannabis detection as its secondary role. Many dogs may go on for weeks doing their primary role before a chance to search for drugs occurs. That's the problem; we train them to bite bad guys days on end then want the K9 to switch on and leave people alone in a crowded environment and look for a scent without biting anyone. For the basic mind of a K9 it's quite an ask and no wonder some dogs bite people while conducting a drug search in a residence. The local head of the department then has to go on TV and justify what's happened. Some people — usually the criminal's family — call for the euthanasia of the dog or try to get money from the department.

In this chapter I outline some basic roles that police dogs have been used for over the centuries. These roles have supported police personnel using their senses and physical abilities.

The working dog group such as German shepherds have been used as police and protection dogs while hounds have been used as tracker dogs. This is a very broad statement as dogs and mongrel crosses of all breeds have been used in the police service. The roles in which police dogs can be used is also evolving: apart from the traditional general purpose K9 and explosives and drug specialists dogs are also used for currency detection, illegal produce (food and animal products), icon detection (much used in the former Soviet Union in the 1980s to prevent a flood of national religious treasures being bought on the black market and smuggled across the borders). Arson or accelerant detection dogs are used in the investigation of suspicious fires and recently there has been an increase in search and rescue dogs due to natural and man-made disasters.

Police dogs are great force multipliers their role is defence of a handler or to prevent other greater uses of force such as an offender having to be shot. Many commanders forget that the use of a police dog biting an offender may have saved a more deadly option from occurring.

Superior Senses

Why have we used dogs in law enforcement? Well, in addition to all the fine qualities that dogs have as team members they have visual and olfactory sensory abilities that are literally many times superior to ours; they can catch an offender and subdue or intimidate them more quickly with non-lethal force than a human if required.

Among a dog's abilities that far exceed a man is its sense of smell. Dogs are reported to have many times the number of receptors in their nose, compared to a human, and the olfactory part of their brain (devoted to smell) is much larger. This gives them the ability to detect very faint odours and to discriminate between very slight differences in chemical composition. Dogs rely on their sense of smell much the same way humans rely on their eyesight.

This story demonstrates their abilities. After a routine traffic stop Officer Whyte of the Manchester Police Service became suspicious of the occupants of the vehicle, so he used his dog to conduct an air scent around the outside. Ace, his K9 partner, a cross-trained narcotic detection dog, alerted his partner to an area of the vehicle where several capsules of heroin were located under the driver's seat. As the occupants were removed from the vehicle Ace again indicated, this time on one of the passengers — a small bag of marijuana was located inside his anal cavity.

Police dogs

General purpose police patrol dogs are the most commonly used in the service. Originally police dogs were only trained to defend their handler, who was usually operating at night by himself. They indicated the presence of prowlers and were released to either bite and hold or bail up a suspect until the handler arrived.

Today the patrol dog is trained to detect personnel, pursue, attack and hold any intruder who attempts to avoid apprehension or escape from custody or uses deadly force against any person. Releasing the dog constitutes the conscious application of physical force. As well as being highly obedient and trained in obstacle agility they are true multipurpose dogs as they can track, search for offenders or missing persons and attack on command.

Tracker dogs

Some sheriff and police departments, especially in the USA, employ dogs solely for the purpose of tracking. Tracking is the bread and butter of police K9 work; without an ability to track and find a criminal that has fled from an incident their use is limited to biting bad guys. Tracker dogs not only pursue felons but can find missing persons. They have been used by humans for centuries all over the world to track down poachers, offenders and runaway slaves.

The military has made extensive use of tracker dogs in South East Asia. This group was called a combat tracker team. The purpose of a combat tracker team was to re-establish contact with the 'elusive enemy', reconnaissance of an area for possible enemy activities, and to locate lost or missing friendly personnel. Most departments today, however, cannot afford to operate dogs that perform a single duty so general purpose police dogs are trained in tracking as one of their primary functions, the others being criminal bite work and defence of their handler.

The effectiveness of tracking dogs is highly dependent upon the terrain, the age of the track, the weather and the number of contaminating paths that cross the subject's path. The dog in its wild state depended to a large extent on its nose for survival and it is a scientific fact that a dog has a sense of smell immeasurably keener than that of a human being. Use of this characteristic is the means by which a dog is able, under certain conditions, to track an offender.

The theory of scent is a wide and complex subject but for practical police purposes may be divided into broad categories: ground scent and wind scent.

Ground scent, which is followed by the dog when tracking is caused by human contact with the ground resulting in disturbance. The slightest movement of the soil or the crushing of grass, other vegetation and insect life, leaves, particles and drops of moisture lying on the ground, all give a scent and thus denote a trail. Some of this scent will obviously adhere to the crushing instrument; for example, the footwear, and may be carried in this way for some distance from one type of ground to another. Experience has shown that the dog depends to a large extent on this effect from crushing when following a track.

Windborne scent attracts the dog when searching. It is airborne scent from the individual or object and may be the personal odour from the body of the person, be a characteristic of the object or may be the result of some previous human contact. The scent of the article itself may be alien to the particular ground on which it lies, such as a piece of sawn or broken wood lying on grassland. The amount of personal odour varies according to constitution, health, clothing, nourishment, activity, mental condition and state of cleanliness. It is greatly intensified when there is physical exertion.

Wind scent may also include occupational odours carried in the clothing of the wearer. In some circumstances they may be very characteristic and distinctive.

Using its acute sense of smell the dog becomes conscious of the scent through the air it breathes. The degree of discernment therefore varies with the concentration of the scent which in turn varies with the rate of evaporation, air movement and type of country over which the scent is set up. Quite obviously the most important feature affecting scent from an operational point of view is time. The more quickly a dog can be brought to follow a scent the more successful the result is likely to be.

A factor affecting scent is whether it has been subject to evaporation, so it is greatly affected by climatic conditions. Generally speaking scenting conditions are most favourable:

- In mild, dull weather
- When the temperature of the ground is higher than the air i.e. normally at night
- In areas where the ground is sheltered

Factors which adversely affect scent are:

- Hot sunshine
- Strong winds
- Heavy rainfall after the scent has been set up

Tracking is an essential part of a general police dog's function. The ability to track down an offender after an incident ensures continuity of evidence and puts the suspect at the scene when caught.

Frost and snow may have either the effect of preserving or destroying a scent depending on whether this occurs before or after the scent has been set up. Pedestrian or vehicular traffic will quickly disperse a scent.

Tracking is a complex art and is one which must be interpreted with great care when working a dog under practical conditions. There will be innumerable occasions when the accepted theories are contradicted by the dog's ability and willingness to follow a scent that under accepted conditions should be non-existent. The only true test is for the dog to be given the opportunity to establish whether or not working conditions prevail. Good handlers learn to read their dogs quickly and trust them.

Riot control dogs

Riot control, crowd control, public safety response — these are just a few names given to police squads that control a large group of demonstrators. Police dog handlers will encounter this task at some point. High ranking commissioned officers are usually required to authorise the use of dogs at a riot. In riot control and public disorder operations the police dog can be employed to attack armed aggressors that try to hide in the crowd. In such cases the employment of a police dog provides the on-site commander with an additional step in the escalation of force that ranges from the use of batons to the use of firearms.

One thing all riot control operations have in common is their high media profile and the often negative attention they receive. Journalists seem often in a position to take a photograph of a police dog in an aggressive stance but never seem to capture the spitting, verbal abuse, rock throwing, fire bomb wheeling mass of agitators outnumbering police hundreds to one. This is obviously a better photo opportunity for them rather than reporting the dogs preventing the escalation of violence and some crowd members being crushed.

Specialist explosives detection dogs

One of the specialised canine units which perform military and police functions is the police or other civilian agency explosive detection dog teams. Due to their specialist nature and relative small numbers many units conduct inter-agency training and tasks. In Queensland each week I train alongside members of the Army, Air Force and Federal Police. Within the United States the Airforce train explosive detection dog teams (EDD) teams for civilian departments, and in Australia and New Zealand many military EDD teams are trained by the State Police.

During events such as the World Summit, Olympic Games or Heads of State meetings, police dogs can be spotted searching for explosives at vital entry points or routinely searching public gathering points and vehicles.

Many police dog operations tend to go unnoticed by the public as searches tend to be conducted after hours prior to a VIP's arrival at a facility. A dignitary's residence will be patrolled by guard dogs at night, often going unnoticed. In fact, wherever there is a major venue involving VIPs you will always find in the organisational chart dog teams tasked with explosive search or perimeter security functions. The United States Secret Service employs explosive detection dogs in relative large numbers for the protection of a single entity.

Police dogs are perhaps at their most valuable when they are trained to detect explosives. Just as with narcotics, trained police K9s can detect minuscule amounts of a wide range of explosives, making them invaluable for protecting entry points and patrolling within secure installations. These dogs are capable of achieving over a 90 per cent success rate in bomb detection.

Few other criminal acts create such concern and fear in the hearts of a nation's citizens as a series of bombings. It is no coincidence that organised crime and terrorist groups routinely use explosive materials as a means of achieving their violent goals. Whether the objective is murder, intimidation, extortion or governmental disruption, the bomb is a favourite and effective weapon of the criminal element. One of the most effective countermeasures to the use of explosives is the deterrent value and the detection capabilities of the EDD team.

Explosive detector dogs are used every day, in a variety of ways, to search and secure buildings, schools, vehicles, luggage, and planes. Unlike other equipment in the bomb squad the explosive detection dog is motivated by a reward, whether it is a toy or food. The main reason for using specialist detection dogs is their speed and accuracy. A dog can search a room or vehicle faster than a team of humans. Dogs can also search more safely than we can. Rather than open the luggage to search it, we run the dog along the seams. If the dog responds, you can suspect the presence of explosive odour then call for an explosives technician. The same procedure can be used to search vehicles, lockers and other areas. With the dog, we don't have to open the locker or vehicle to search it, thus making the search much safer. Without the dog, we must open the item to be searched causing an unsafe practice as well as taking too much time. With all searching principals involving explosive devices safety equals time over target. The less time you expose yourself to the potential danger the safer you are.

The hardest job the explosive detector dog handler has is to educate his department and other bomb squad members about the use of the dog, the dog's limitations and proper deployment. The dog is trained to detect explosives, and that is what it does. When problems arise, they are usually not the fault of the dog, but rather the fault of the handler or trainer. Like any piece of equipment used by the bomb squad, the dog has limitations. Heat and humidity are two factors that will limit the dog's search time.

For years, modern science has been trying to duplicate the dog's nose. To this day, we cannot develop or manufacture a machine that is as sensitive or accurate as a dog's nose. Thousands of olfactory glands in the dog's nose can't be wrong. The best way to describe how the dog's nose works is this analogy referred to in the United States Police Canine Association magazine. You are cooking a meal in the kitchen. What we smell in the living room is a combination of all those ingredients simmering on the stove. The dog smells each individual ingredient in the soup. The dog's nose is able to break down the odour and separate the ingredients. So when terrorists try to mask the explosive odour with other odours, it does not work. The dog can still smell the explosives through the masking odours.

One of the sad and dangerous ironies of EDDs is they tend to be forgotten between headlines. Using the United States as an example, after the first World Trade Center bombing in 1993 every police department was rushing to equipment itself with EDDs, but after eight years of nothing happening many departments lost interest in this role, usually due to budget constraints. Well, a short time after this timeframe September 11 happened and again there was a rush to employ EDDs. The problem was that most of the top handlers and trainers had moved on. Another eight or so years is coming up since that tragedy and with few major attacks by terrorists in the US many departments are considering downsizing again. This is one area where police should not let their guard down.

Some departments have combined the detection of explosives with firearms. Firearms and explosive detection dogs (FEDD) are vital to today's police operations. The majority of warrants executed could do with the presence of an FEDD. Most self-respecting drug dealers wouldn't be seen anywhere without a gun for protection. Motorcycle gangs are also prime candidates for weapons searches in there club houses or vehicles. I have been involved in warrants with both these groups over the years and due and there are usually always numerous weapons located.

An important role for police dogs is crowd/riot control; one police dog is worth 50 protesters. The media often focuses on dogs when used as crowd control, showing them as aggressive and dangerous.

The Secret Service Uniformed Division, USA

The Secret Service Uniformed Division was established in 1922 as the White House Police Force, and fully integrated into the Secret Service in 1930. With more than 1300 officers today, the Uniformed Division is responsible for security at the White House Complex, the vice president's residence, the Department of the Treasury (as part of the White House Complex), and foreign diplomatic missions in the Washington, DC area.

Uniformed division officers carry out their protective responsibilities through a network of fixed security posts, foot, bicycle, vehicular and motorcycle patrols. Part of this unit is the Canine Explosives Detection Unit (K9): In the 1970s, the Secret Service Uniformed Division created the K9 division, which paired specially trained dogs with handlers, or K9 Technicians. These special dogs have been trained to detect drugs, explosives and firearms.

Although German shepherds were first used, the Secret Service now uses many Belgian Malinois dogs from Holland. Known for their adaptability to new climates and environments and their work drive, these dogs are exceptional members of the Secret Service. They generally work between seven and eleven years in the Secret Service. At night, after a busy day's work, they go home with their handlers, where they are part of the family.

Secret Service K9 units patrol the grounds of the White House as well as inside. The dogs do periodic searches of the White House before and after guests and tours arrive. They also search every incoming delivery and vehicle. The dogs are cross-trained in patrol and explosives. There are dog teams on duty 24–7. The K9 Unit travels all over the United States in support of the President. This might mean searching Air Force One many hours before the President arrives to enplane. They will deploy prior to any major event and function to search the area for explosive devices.

Depending on the overseas destination that the President is attending members of the K9 Unit may be required to travel internationally. Such was the case during a trip to India when the media got hold of a story about how well the K9s are looked after. While US President George W Bush was checking into the presidential suite at one of Delhi's top hotels, a group of canines belonging to his security detail were enjoying similar comfort nearby. Some 17 dogs belonging to the K9 Unit of the US Secret Service were also put up at top Delhi five-star hotels. The German shepherds and labradors were staying in rooms which cost more than $200 a night. Delhi police have their own dog squads which were used to comb all the locations the President of the United States was to visit. But while the Indian dogs retreated to their kennels, the Secret Service K9 squad were taken back to the comfort of their air-conditioned hotel rooms.

BORSTAR Canines, USA

In the United States the Customs and Border Protection (CBP) Canine Program remains a major component in the ability of protecting US homeland security—over 1200 CBP canine teams expedite inspections along US borders. They work tirelessly to combat terrorist threats, stop the flow of illegal narcotics, detect unreported currency, firearms, concealed humans, smuggled agriculture products and explosives. Within this organisation BORSTAR Canines or Border Patrol Search, Trauma, and Rescue Teams are highly specialised units that are capable of responding to emergency search and rescue situations in the United States. They were first established in San Diego in 2001.

BORSTAR agents and their canine partners play a crucial role in locating fallen agents, civilians, and illegal aliens. The teams are commonly used in dangerous terrain and inclement weather to locate victims. Through the use of land navigational skills and the global positioning systems, canine teams are brought into areas where the missing person is likely to be found. Many times the victims are located in remote, rugged terrain where helicopter deployment of the dogs is not only critical but the only option because of the physical demands placed on the searchers. While at the National Canine Facility, the BORSTAR canine teams are trained in rappelling, helicopter operations and boat operations. In addition, the canines are trained in various environments, such as snow, desert, pine forest, mountains and swampland. The San Diego Sector's BORSTAR Canine Team has had unparalleled success. In one single year the BORSTAR Canine Team tracked over 132 undocumented aliens, rescued 25 undocumented aliens, and rescued one 4-year-old US citizen.

Specialist narcotic detection dogs

Police drug dogs provide an invaluable service in the war on drugs as they're able to detect illegal substances despite efforts of concealment. Dogs trained in drug detection are normally used at airfields, border crossing entry points and other places where there is a need for anti-contraband measures. This includes private homes and workplaces under warrant searches. Dogs are used to prevent the use of illegal substances causing dangerous workplace environments by affected persons.

These dogs often have to be capable of searching in or around populated areas, so many tend to be breeds acceptable to people as unthreatening types. For example, many spaniels and labradors are used. Some departments use German shepherds and some cross-train there general duties patrol dogs to locate narcotics. Sometimes this results in the odd nip from a police dog, but you have to remember that despite the headlines of the local paper stating 'Police dog savages a man during search', the police are there for a reason to search for drugs and the victim is not likely to be Mother Teresa.

Search and rescue dogs

Search and rescue dogs (SAR) are trained to indicate casualties lying in obscure places; casualties that are difficult for collecting parties to locate. In cases of severe shock or haemorrhage, minutes saved in locating casualties often mean the difference between life and death. The Red Cross dogs were by far the most organised and successful canine unit in this field during World War I. The dogs carried medical supplies and canteens to wounded soldiers. They were trained to not recognise dead soldiers. If a soldier was found unconscious the dogs would return to their handlers and lead them to the location of that soldier. The Red Cross dogs often worked at night and relied on their olfactory abilities to find soldiers. This type of dog is more likely to be used today by civilian volunteer organisations.

There are three main types of search and rescue:

- Mountain rescue — search and rescue operations specifically in rugged and mountainous terrain

- Ground search and rescue — search and rescue operations in remote regions

- Urban search and rescue — structural collapse operations conducted in a city usually after a natural disaster

A Queensland Police explosive detection dog searching in rubble for unexploded devices. In many countries the EDD teams are attached to Bomb Squads and work closely with bomb technicians, who make the device safe after the dogs find it.

Search and rescue (SAR) dogs detect human scent. Although the exact processes are still debated it may include skin rafts (scent-carrying skin cells that drop off living humans at a rate of about 40,000 cells per minute), evaporated perspiration, respiratory gases, or decomposition gases released by bacterial action on human skin or tissues. Added to this are smells of the person's occupation, crushed insects walked on, right down to the brand of boot polish — all these kinds of scents make up a scent picture to the dog. That's just the nose. Then there is heartbeat detection or the sound a victim may make. It is thought a dog can hear a heartbeat some 50 metres away. Of course all of this is affected by time and environmental conditions.

From their training and experience, search and rescue dogs can be classified broadly as either air scenting dogs or tracking dogs. They also can be classified according to whether they 'scent discriminate', and under what conditions they can work. Scent discriminating dogs have proven their ability to alert only on the scent of an individual person, after being given a sample of that person's scent. Non-scent discriminating dogs alert on or follow any scent of a given type, such as any human scent or any cadaver scent.

Air scenting dogs primarily use airborne human scent to home in on subjects, whereas trailing dogs rely on scent of the specific subject. Air scenting dogs typically work off-lead, are non-scent discriminating (e.g. locate scent from any human as opposed to a specific person), and cover large areas of terrain. These dogs are trained to follow diffused or windborne scent back to its source, return to the handler and indicate contact with the subject, and then lead the handler back to the subject. Handler technique, terrain, environment and atmospheric conditions determine the area covered by air scenting dogs, although a typical search area may several kilometres and scent sources can be detected from a distance of 500 metres or more.

Specific applications for SAR dogs include wilderness, disaster, cadaver, avalanche, and drowning search and recovery.

In wilderness SAR applications, air scenting dogs can be deployed to high-probability areas whereas tracking/trailing dogs can be deployed from the subject's last known point or the site of a discovered clue.

Human remains detection dogs

Human remains detection or cadaver dogs are used to locate the remains of deceased victims. Depending on the nature of the search, these dogs may work off-lead (e.g. to search a large area for buried remains) or on-lead (to recover clues from a crime scene). Air scenting and tracking/trailing dogs are often cross-trained as cadaver dogs, although the scent the dog detects is clearly of a different nature than that detected for live subjects. Cadaver dogs can locate entire bodies (including those buried or submerged), decomposed bodies, body fragments (including blood, tissues, hair, and bones), or skeletal remains; the capability of the dog is dependent upon its training. These dogs were used post the major bushfires in Australia recently and again in New Zealand after the Christchurch earthquake, sadly with great effect.

Avalanche dogs work similarly to air scenting, disaster or cadaver dogs, and must be able to rapidly transition from a wilderness SAR-air scenting scenario to a disaster scenario focused on pinpointing the subject's location.

Training for Search and Rescue

Training is a time-consuming and comprehensive process for both the dog and the handler. Obedience training is essential for the dog's safety, and to maintain professionalism in law enforcement and the public audience.

The 'games' technique is particularly effective with these dogs bred for search and rescue (such as hunting and sporting breeds) but has also been successful with working and herding dog breeds. A commonly used approach is to base training on herding, prey/pursuit and pack instincts: initial training for puppies usually involves run-away games where the handler runs from the puppy and hides a short distance away. Basic instincts drive the puppy to locate the subject, initially by sight but with the association of human scent. To advance this training, the subject hides further away or longer times pass between departure of the subject and release of the dog. The dog is forced to rely increasingly on scent to locate the subject. Eventually, the dog can be transitioned to search without seeing the subject depart by simply giving the command used when it's released during basic run-away training. During all stages, finding the subject is reinforced by multiple means (praise, play or food treats).

Air scenting dogs are trained to track human scent to its source, be it human or traces of a human, but this basic process has been elaborated and improved upon: dogs now are commonly also trained in recall/refind and indication. The entire process may begin with the command 'Go find!', indicating that the dog is to search until the find is made. After the find, the dog can be trained to return to the handler (recall), perform a trained indication (often a bark coupled with some form of meaningful touching of the handler, such as a paw placed on the handler's leg or a 'sit-stay' at the handler's feet), and return to the subject (refind, sometimes cued with the 'Show me!' command). Once the handler is with the subject, the dog is released (and during training, rewarded). Dogs are trained in the recall/refind shuttle between the handler and the source until the handler and subject are within sight (this builds on the dog's natural pack instinct). This is of greatest use in situations where the dog may be ranging from the handler (wilderness air scenting) or the subject may be concealed or out of sight (e.g. at night, hidden in brush), but is less useful for dogs trained for close-quarters searches (e.g. cadaver and drowning dogs).

An alert by an air scenting dog can be distinct from an indication (although for a dog that uses a natural indication, the two may not be distinguishable). Both involve the handler being able to read the dog's behaviour. Alerts are instances where an air scenting dog detects human scent but has not located the subject or source. Alerts can be recognised by a change in the dog's behaviour—pointing, following a scent upwind, circling, or following scent up terrain or obstructions, training techniques for search dogs are not written in stone. There are many different techniques for training a dog for this type of work.

K9s at the World Trade Center

Disaster dogs are used to locate victims of catastrophic or mass casualty events (e.g. earthquakes, landslides, building collapses, aviation incidents). Disaster dogs rely primarily on air scent, and may be limited in mass-casualty events by their inability to differentiate between survivors and recently-deceased victims.

Hundreds of search and rescue (SAR) dogs from SAR units across the country were used to assist recovery efforts at Ground Zero after the tragic events at the World Trade Center on September 11, but a special group of canines worked tirelessly from the first day of the tragedy.

These smart, tough and loyal animals were from the New York Police Department K9 Unit, a subunit of the NYPD Emergency Service unit. While the K9 unit narrowly escaped injury when the towers came down, the NYPD Emergency Service Unit lost 14 officers at the World Trade Center.

The K9 Unit consists of 30 German shepherd, cross-trained patrol dogs and three bloodhounds and 34 officers. The NYPD K9 Unit used their special abilities to locate victims in the millions of tons of rubble that was once the Twin Towers.

While the unit needed and welcomed the other great K9 units and organisations, the NYPD K9 Unit remained working at the site for four months.

Then headed by Lt. Dan Donadio, the NYPD K9 Unit assisted the NYPD in subway patrol, tracking and criminal apprehension, in addition to search and recovery. Lt. Donadio's job at the WTC site was to supervise and direct the deployment of Police K9 resources at the site and throughout

New York City. The handlers have custody of their dogs 24 hours a day, at home and at work, allowing for a close personal bond between the handler and dog. Formed in 1980, the unit also has responded to other major disasters, including the first World Trade Center bombing in 1993 and the Oklahoma City bombing in 1995.

Specially trained search and rescue dogs like those from NYPD K9 locate victims based on their sharp sense of smell. Overcoming noise, distraction and their own fatigue, these dogs tirelessly climbed over and under debris, through shards of steel and glass, looking for survivors. An advanced search and rescue dog can search more than hundreds of square metres of rubble, and a cadaver dog can locate human remains the size of a nail.

In September 11 the job was both dangerous and challenging, but the dogs worked continuously, ignoring cuts and injuries to complete their task. At the World Trade Center site, the dogs from NYPD K9 worked alongside their human handlers day and night for months, searching through acres of dangerous rubble, and inhaling potentially dangerous dust and smoke, full of tiny particles of asbestos, plastics and concrete.

They also had some help from international SAR dog teams. Trakr was a German shepherd police dog who along with his handler, Canadian police officer James Symington, discovered the last survivor of the September 11 attacks at the World Trade Center in New York City in 2001. For his accomplishments, Trakr was named one of history's most heroic animals by Time magazine. In 2008 Symington won an essay contest sponsored by BioArts International to find the world's most 'clone worthy dog'; as a result Trakr was cloned, producing five puppies.

Queensland Police Service K9 Special Response Team is used during high risk situations, including hostage and armed offender takedowns.

ADVANCED TRAINING

Tactical operations

After completing a basic course you're not expected to know everything the day you finish and a police dog is no different. After an initial training course a police dog still has much to learn. If you're a handler you hope that on the day you finish your course you will not be thrown into a high risk tactical situation. Hopefully you will have time to introduce your dog to the environment it will be operating in. It is tactically sound to expose your police dog to all things it is likely to encounter in operational situations both during day and night time.

Police dogs (PDs) need to be regularly trained in tactical operations to work alongside groups of friendly forces under fire — this is vital prior to operational deployments. A police dog must be comfortable working around a squad of troops so as not to cause a blue-on-blue incident. Remember PDs do not think or reason like humans; they react on instinct or according to the training they have been exposed too. Therefore if a dog has never been exposed to or trained in a particular situation it will react on instinct only. This, however, may not be the reaction or response required.

PDs are trained to clear stairways and the associated kill zone in that area well ahead of personnel, enabling safer entry during urban house clearing operations. When clearing under houses or in tunnel operations similar to those encountered in Vietnam, having an ability to send in a PD first will save human lives. Likewise once inside a building dogs are used to clear hallways or corridors that can be deadly funnels of fire or may be booby trapped. A dog can also be used inside the building to cover possible criminal escape routes.

All PDs should have range training and be familiarised with the battlefield environment. Some dogs may even act aggressively towards their handler while he or she engages a target. Strict obedience training in combination with reward as range firing is introduced is required. Sometimes cotton wool is placed in the dog's ear canal or ear protection is provided. Range training ensures that a squad of men can tactically engage the enemy around you and your dog and it doesn't freak out or act aggressively to your team. If the dog freaks out during an operation and the handler tries to control the dog while having live rounds loaded, it could possibly endanger the entire police squad.

During urban operations the use of a long line during tactical entry to buildings may be an option. The long line prevents a dog entering out of sight or being pulled in by an offender. Similarly, once the dog has a firm hold on an offender the handler can pull the line with dog and offender attached (just like fishing) out into the open. Some disadvantages of this method are entanglement of the line and the limited distance between you and the bad guy.

An operational street search is the most common type of building search. A handler may do operational street searches on a semi-regular basis. This is when a suspect is still on scene; for example, a trespasser in a warehouse at night. Prior to sending a dog in, a repeated clear audible warning is issued. If it's a multi-level building this may have to be repeated on each floor. A police dog is used for several reasons: once the warning announcement has been given any innocent person in the area has the opportunity to leave; secondly it gives a suspect the opportunity to surrender— a safe option for us all; thirdly if the suspect decides to chance his arm his fear factor will increase, and when that happens his scent pool will increase and make it easier for the dog to locate him. Most officers encourage the dog to bark prior to the release to increase the fear factor.

Just like a police horse, police K9s must be able to work under adverse conditions including near gunfire and load explosions. It is vital that the dog does not react when the handler is firing his or her weapon.

Handlers never expose themselves to a doorway, but this is not true for dogs; if someone approaches a doorway the dog will be able to detect them. The air will typically flow out of an open door giving the dog a great scent picture. Some officers might find it difficult to put their dog in the line of fire but that's what they are for.

When a dog handler enters a building during a high risk situation he or she will always have an armed police officer as a backup, therefore they tend to train for this potentially dangerous situation by getting the dogs used to other officers firing guns in close proximity.

Dogs need to be trained to take commands when the handler is wearing a gas mask because this could occur in a tactical operation. Some dogs react uncharacteristically to the handler when the gas mask is worn. The first time I worn one when training my dog without prior exposure to the mask he freaked out. He was at first puzzled, then reacted like a highly trained police dog — he bit me.

Police dogs should be used to being physically picked up. In an urban environment this may be required to get over large objects especially in urban warfare or entry via an open window. Handlers and other team members practise picking up the dog — there may be a tactical situation where a team member may have to pick up the dog up and pass it to the handler. If a dog is ever wounded, it is useful if it can be lifted onto an object such as a riot shield or stretcher by another squad member. We have heard before of the romantic faithful police dog guarding its injured master even when the medic turned up, this might cost the life of the handler.

Police dogs not only have to be trained to work around friendly forces but they may have to also be trained to work alongside fellow police dogs. The last thing needed is a dog fight in the middle of a tactical operation.

Canine First Aid

An important aspect to operational training is having a sound knowledge of canine first aid. Handlers may be required to patch up a dog in-situ who has been shot or stabbed.

Dogs cannot tell us what hurts and there is usually no vet to call for help in the middle of nowhere at 0200 hours in the morning. Prevention of injury is the key; however, accidents do happen. What a handler does between an injury occurring and veterinary care being available will greatly affect a dog's chances of a full recovery.

Dogs must be physically fit. Many injuries and illnesses seen during operations can be a direct result of lack of prior physical conditioning. Being overweight can increase strain on a dog's heart, lungs and joints. K9 fitness training includes at least two sessions of activity, lasting 15 minutes daily, to maintain muscle mass and maintain cardiovascular health. Dogs should undertake a full medical exam every six months.

Handlers are the ones most likely to see or discover an illness, injury or external parasite infection during a daily inspection, and are the best to judge what is normal in his or her dog. In order to determine if there is a problem, handlers should be familiar with a dog's vital signs. A handler also has the most to lose if his or her dog is not in top physical condition.

Tactical dogs have the highest threat to injury, they are used to enter blind spots or stairwells were officers cannot see. Tactical handlers are usually well trained in K9 first aid.

Garth's Recovery

K9 Garth, a commissioned Tennessee State Trooper and a valued member of his criminal interdiction team, faced early retirement when he tore a ligament in his left knee. After all, a drug dog has to be agile. It's his job to jump on moving baggage conveyor belts in airports, on top of commercial shipping containers and to actively investigate buildings and vehicles.

Garth's handler, Trooper James M Grant, didn't want to give up on the black labrador who had been his partner in sniffing out drug smugglers, money couriers and other felons for more than five years. The Tennessee Highway Patrol decided to send Garth to the College of Veterinary Medicine at the University of Tennessee for surgery and for a follow-up physical therapy program for dogs believed to be the most comprehensive in the nation.

'This dog has participated in raids and apprehensions worth about $500,000. We wanted him returned to maximum potential. If we just did the bare minimum to repair the leg, we would have to retire him,' Grant said. 'That would be like junking a luxury automobile because of a flat tire.'

Garth underwent surgery to repair his cruciate ligament. The day after the operation, Garth's leg was iced down to reduce pain and swelling and he began taking slow walks. Mild electrical stimulation was used to contract his leg muscles and minimise loss of muscle mass until he could use it again.

Gentle range-of-motion manipulation and ultrasound massage were also part of his therapy. When Garth's incision was sealed and he started touching his toe to the ground, he began work on a special piece of equipment the Veterinary College had acquired.

Associate professor and surgeon Dr Darryl Millis worked with a company that builds aquatic therapy units for humans to design the college's new underwater treadmill machine for dogs. It is the first one of its type in the country and is part of a comprehensive physical therapy program for dogs that offers an array of board-certified specialists such as surgeons, internists, anaesthesiologists, radiologists and nutritionists, and a licensed physical therapist, to help manage the dog's care.

The underwater treadmill looks like a Plexiglas box roughly 1.5 metres wide, 2 metres long and 1 metre deep with a treadmill in the bottom. Beside it are a water storage tank, heavy-duty water filters, and controls for the water level and the treadmill speed. The treadmill box is made of clear material so dogs get a sense that they can see where they're going.

'They won't walk into a wall — they're smarter than that,' Millis said.

The dog is placed in the box on the treadmill and the box is filled with water to the dog's chest. When the treadmill starts, the water provides both support and resistance.

'It's really interesting to see how the dogs walk in it,' Millis said. 'They don't panic because the water comes in gradually.

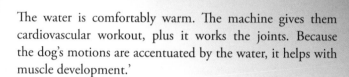

The water is comfortably warm. The machine gives them cardiovascular workout, plus it works the joints. Because the dog's motions are accentuated by the water, it helps with muscle development.'

Labradors are known to like water, and Garth was no exception. He splashed happily on the underwater treadmill and displayed the personality that has made him a favourite with schoolchildren. Trooper Grant and Garth often do talks and obedience demonstrations at elementary schools. Grant illustrates topics such as staying in school and not running across the street by using Garth's obedience to commands. For example, Grant might show children how to refuse to go away with strangers by giving Garth a 'sit and stay' command and enlisting a teacher to try to tempt the dog to move.

Garth returned to work in late November last year.

During his recovery, Garth had a lot of support from his partner. Trooper Grant drove to Knoxville from Nashville to visit him twice a week. They took walks together and played with a ball on the veterinary college lawn.

'It kept up our bond up to see him frequently. And it helped my state of mind,' Grant said. 'On a routine day we work together full time. We're practically inseparable.' Garth lives in a kennel at Grant's home in Nashville.

Transportation

Many operations require deployment via different mediums such as aircraft (fixed wing and helicopter). A police dog should be able to operate in and around this kind of noise with no ill effects. In order to be rapidly deployed to various locations the dog units should be used to being transported by helicopter.

Training includes a theoretical phase in the classroom and a practical part with a stationary rotor and engine used for mounting and dismounting manoeuvres. Before the first flight, a final test on the ground with the motors at full capacity with the rotors in motion is advisable. This is perhaps the most difficult phase. Loud noise prevents the dogs from hearing the reassuring words of his or her handler. The sound frequency produced by the turbines confuses the sensitive hearing of the dogs and the wind produced by the rotor is a new experience for them. This causes a change in focus for the dogs. This is why it is imperative the dogs are trained prior to the need to do it for real.

Police vehicles for K9 units vary — from sedans with specialist back compartments to highly specialised purpose built dog vans. In all cases the dog has good ventilation and space to be comfortable during a shift.

The maritime environment

Water obstacle training and deployment of dogs via maritime transport is not usually a consideration during initial police dog training courses. Most standard agility courses do not have water obstacles and dog training courses seldom expose the dogs to maritime environments. But dogs and handlers need to be able to work in any situation encountered so it's important for handlers to prepare and train dogs for any eventuality, maximising officer safety in any environment. With the war on terrorism spreading into different arenas, interdiction of boats and waterborne craft has taken on even greater importance. Additionally many urban and rural tracks have extensive water crossings and obstacles to consider. Police dogs may also find themselves working around harbour facilities and other maritime locations in the course of their patrols. Police dog teams may have to deploy from a police vessel to another ship underway as part of a waterborne tactical insertion. Likewise specialist narcotic or explosive detection dog teams may be required to board ships, oil rigs and other maritime installations in the course of their duty.

During tracking, police dogs will encounter water obstacles, so both handler and dog must be able to swim confidently across without loss of operational momentum. An example of a training program for canine waterborne preparation:

- Entry and exit from various sized vessels. All vessels seem to share the problem of confined spaces no matter what size they are. Besides being a tactical obstacle and creating fatal funnels at every entry way, confined spaces on board a vessel can also present deadly dangers. Commercial ships present their own hazards such as dangerous gases and vapours, hazardous cargo, heavy cargo which may shift due to insecurity and slippery decks

- Crossing gangways and ladders (special lift harnesses may have to be employed)

- Jumping out of a vessel underway or into shallow water

- Riding as a passenger in a vessel underway to get used to the sights, sound and motion

- Familiarisation with marine environments such as wharf, dock yards and ships

- Bite work in shallow water

As part of water environment training handlers should also consider officer safety when working around potential high risk vessel interceptions. Some examples of the operational skills training a handler must consider are:

- Falling safely either alone or while grappling with a subject from various heights into the water

- Controlling and deploying a firearm while in the water

- Handgun retention while in the water

- Effectively deploying and handling intermediate weapons such as non-lethal (baton and handcuffs) while in the water

- Performing submerged and surface tactics

- Safely assisting or rescuing an injured officer or subject from the water

I have witnessed an operational police dog who could not swim. This was only discovered after the handler had sent his dog into a river to bite an offender!

Training to board vessels underway is physically demanding on the handler and takes considerable practice and fitness. Sometimes a K9 flotation device is placed over a dog's harness.

German human remains detection dogs can even locate a scent from drowned victims under several metres of water.

Special Weapons and Tactics (SWAT)

I use the term SWAT throughout this book, which stands for Special Weapons and Tactic; it is an American acronym and thanks to the movies is well known to most readers. However, tactical teams are known by various names; for example, in Australia the term SRT or Special Response Team is often used. SWAT teams may be confronted with a situation where a suspect is hiding or barricading themselves within a building and a dynamic and quick entry may jeopardise the safety of officers, the suspect and innocent parties.

In situations such as these, a slow and deliberate entry/search would be employed. This requires a team to move slowly and quietly through a building, entering and stealthily clearing each room until the suspect is located, at which point negotiations can start, the suspect can be called out, or a dynamic entry can be employed to surprise and take the suspect into custody. However, slow and deliberate entries are very time consuming and still place human officers at risk as they enter and clear rooms in an attempt to locate a hiding suspect using only their sense of sight. This is where the use of a well-trained canine comes into play.

Police canines use all of their senses to locate their quarry. The most powerful sense they use is their nose, which is thousands of times more sensitive than a human's. The next most powerful sense a dog possesses is its hearing, which far exceeds human capabilities. And lastly, dogs use their eyesight to help them confirm what their eyes and ears have told them; there's a person hiding in the immediate vicinity. Canine searches can be completed much quicker than human searches, regardless of lighting and environmental conditions, and greatly reduce the risk to human officers.

A good SWAT dog is a proven patrol dog that is quiet and very driven, highly interested in searching for people. The canine must be sociable and comfortable working around other SWAT team members and in close quarters and tight spaces. Of tremendous importance is that the dog is very obedient and will obey a handler's commands without hesitation and from a distance. Conversely, SWAT team members must be comfortable around the dog and be confident in its abilities and trust the handler to set limitations as to what the dog can do.

When using the canine in a SWAT search, the dog is used to clear areas of concern for the human officers. The dog is sent before the team on- or off-lead, to clear hallways, rooms or blind corners. The canine sniffs rooms it passes, enters open rooms, and clears open areas by using its superior senses. If the dog does not show an alert, the handler will place the dog in a 'down and stay' using hand signals or very quiet commands, and the SWAT team will move up behind the dog and take a new position of cover. The dog, in essence, becomes the 'point man' to protect the team from any threat that may suddenly appear. The handler then deploys the canine in the same manner until the suspect is located. If a canine locates and alerts on a suspect, the SWAT team can now implement its arrest or negotiations plan and the dog may be moved back until it is needed to assist the arrest team. If the suspect remains concealed and refuses to cooperate, the canine may be used to enter the room and physically apprehend the suspect.

SWAT teams may also choose to use the canine in area searches of large outdoor open areas by providing armed support to the canine handler as they search areas either on or off lead. The use of the canine substantially lowers the risk of a human officer being hurt or killed by walking up on a well hidden suspect and allows for a more thorough search of large areas.

Thankfully, more missions are resolved peacefully and without injury to anyone, than those that are not. It is not uncommon for a suspect to surrender upon hearing the canine alerting to their presence. Most criminals will readily admit they would much rather take their chances in fighting with a human than to be physically apprehended by a canine.

Canines are also used on perimeters in case the suspect tries to flee from an area of concern, and with the primary arrest team in case a suspect tries to fight or run from the arresting officers. In all cases, the use of the canine provides an extra tool for SWAT teams to assist them in conducting their jobs in a safer, more efficient, and reliable manner.

In today's K9 tactical employment it is the norm to be part of a squad or team comprising back-up fire power, signals and a command element. Police dogs must be comfortable working around other squad members and vice-versa.

Fitness is a major consideration for both dog and handler during tactical operations. Not every police K9 handler is suitable to be a special response team dog handler. Many SRT or SWAT teams find it easier to have one of their already qualified members trained as a dog handler rather than finding a dog handler who fits all of SWAT's requirements. Likewise careful selection of a K9 is vital for a SWAT team; not only does it have to be calm under fire but when the word is given it must instantly carry out its task with extreme aggression. You do not use a SWAT dog to get Granny out of a car. SWAT dogs are the right tool for the right job.

I have included this section on border protection dogs because the line between police dogs employed on the streets by police departments and these canines is indistinguishable in the fight against crime. Post 9/11 many countries have enhanced their homeland security assets to fight a wave of illegal immigration and the trafficking of contraband to support terrorist or criminal activities. European countries have a long history of border protection using dogs. This is mainly due to their relatively inexpensive employment costs versus their deterrent values and force multiplier attributes; one dog can effectively patrol and cover an area that 50 men could. In the days before electronic detection devices and night vision equipment the dogs' keen senses were the best all-weather day and night detection systems.

Dogs are used in all types of terrain and weather conditions in European countries and borders such as Mexico/USA. They are also regularly seen at international airports and maritime ports of entry to detect and prevent any substance that might be hostile to a nation's security ranging from agricultural pests to weapons of mass destruction. The United States Air Force in particular trains supply and supplement dog teams at border crossings in Mexico. The United States Coast Guard provides K9 search capabilities in the maritime environment.

In some European countries canines are used in paramilitary teams (separate arms of the military brought in to assist with civilian police duties) including the French Gendarmerie Nationale, the Spanish Civil Guard Service, the Royal Netherlands Marechaussee and Italian Carabinieri.

PROTECTING THE BORDERS

Guardians of the Night

Author unknown

Trust in me my friend for I am your comrade.
I will protect you with my last breath.
When all others have left you
And the loneliness of the night closes in,
I will be at your side.
Together we will conquer all obstacles
And search out those who might wish harm to others.
All I ask of you is compassion,
The caring touch of your hands.
It is for you that I will selflessly give my life

And spend my nights un-rested.

Although our days together

May be marked by the passing of the seasons.

Know that each day at your side is my reward.

My days are measured by

The coming and going of your footsteps.

I anticipate them at the opening of the door.

You are the voice of caring when I am ill.

The voice of authority over me when I've done wrong.

Do not chastise me unduly

For I am your right arm,

The sword at your side.

I attempt to do only what you bid of me.

I seek only to please you and remain in your favour.

Together you and I shall experience

A bond only others like you will understand.

When outsiders see us together

Their envy will be measured by their disdain.

I will quietly listen to you

And pass no judgement.

Nor will your spoken words be repeated.

I will remain ever silent,

Ever vigilant, ever loyal.

And when our time together is done

And you move on in the world,

Remember me with kind thoughts and tales.

For a time we were unbeatable,

Nothing passed among us undetected.

If we should ever meet again on another field

I will gladly take up your fight.

I am a police dog and together

We are GUARDIANS of the NIGHT.

SWAT team dogs are highly trained. They have to be aggressive but controllable when operating near gunfire.

BORDER PROTECTION

US Border Protection

The US Customs and Border Protection detector dogs were introduced on a wide scale in April 1970 as part of a major effort, by the then US Customs Service to interdict narcotics being smuggled through major air/sea and land border ports. Teams consisting of a dog and officer are used to screen arriving aircraft, cargo, baggage, mail, ships, vehicles and passengers. The US Customs and Border Protection is one of the Department of Homeland Security's largest and most complex components, with a priority mission of keeping terrorists and their weapons out of the US. It also has a responsibility for securing and facilitating trade and travel while enforcing hundreds of US regulations, including immigration and drug laws. The mission of the Canine Enforcement Program is to develop, execute and oversee the allocation, training and support of canine resources. These valuable resources combat terrorism, interdict narcotics and other contraband and help to facilitate and process legitimate trade and travel within the core processes of US Customs and Border Protection (CBP).

The CBP Canine Enforcement Program, located within the Office of Field Operations (OFO), Cargo and Conveyance Security, is an integral part of the agency's counter-terrorism and narcotics interdiction strategy. The Canine Training Center Front Royal develops course content and provides training for CBP Officers (K9). Currently there are over 1200 OFO canine teams fulfilling the CBP mission throughout the United States. The vast majority of resources is located along the south-west border, from Brownsville, Texas to San Diego, California. Canine teams are also strategically assigned to other ports of entry around the country, and located at pre-clearance stations abroad.

As their core mission, CBP Officers use specially trained detector dogs to interdict large quantities of illegal narcotic substances, concealed humans, smuggled agriculture products and unreported currency at the nation's ports of entry. The Canine Enforcement Program is also involved in specialised detection programs aimed at combating terrorist threats at borders and international airports.

Although the Canine Training Center is primarily focused on the training and development of OFO Canine Enforcement teams, there are also detector dog training opportunities, on a reimbursable basis, for other federal, state, local, and foreign law enforcement agencies. The program also provides limited assistance to state and local law enforcement entities on a case-by-case basis. The Canine Enforcement Program evaluates each of its teams for detection proficiency once a year. Narcotic detector dogs are tested in their actual work environments on their ability to detect the odours of marijuana, hashish, heroin, cocaine, methamphetamine and ecstasy. Dogs trained to detect other odours, such as currency or non-narcotic hazardous substances, are also evaluated on their detection capabilities regularly. The officers are also evaluated, ensuring that they possess the critical handling skills necessary to successfully deploy an OFO detector dog.

The program continues to train and equip canine teams to maintain the agency's efforts at anti-terrorism, border security, selective targeting, interception of large loads of narcotics, detection of smuggled agriculture products and currency, advanced training of officers, and prevention measures through outreach activities to this country's youth. Through the use of risk management and strategic problem solving techniques, all aspects of the Canine Enforcement Program will continue to be improved and updated to meet the changing needs of CBP and the United States of America.

In 1998, the Canine Enforcement Program established a detector dog breeding program to maximise the number of dogs suitable for detection training. The program, modelled after the Australian Customs Service program, has bred 19 litters to date. The CBP breeding program strives to develop labrador retrievers that are ideally suited for detection work. CBP dogs are bred and cared for in state of the art facilities until they are approximately 12 weeks old. The puppies are then socialised and raised by foster families until they are about a year old. This program relies on the local community around the Canine Enforcement Training Center to raise the puppies in foster homes. In 2003, the Canine Enforcement Program expanded this effort by utilising the Puppies Behind Bars program at selected prisons to enhance the foster program. Once they are ready, they return to the CETC to begin their new career.

The CBP uses a wide variety of dogs including labrador retrievers, golden retrievers, German shepherds, Belgian shepherd (Malinois), and many mixed breeds. The Agriculture side of the canine program uses beagles as well. The most important factor in selecting detector dogs for training is not its breed, but the extent of enthusiasm the dog displays toward retrieving a given object. All potential CBP dogs are tested to see if they possess the inherited traits that make them a likely candidate for detection training. Many dogs are tested, but relatively few are procured. Dogs used by the Canine Enforcement Program can be of either sex, but must be between one and three years of age.

Part 1: Canine Law Enforcement

Border protection has been a vital role for working dogs in the past and continues to grow in importance today. Dogs are used to prevent illegal immigration and smuggling of contraband, and to protect the overall sovereignty of a state. Here two petty officers from the USCG part of Maritime Safety and Security Team (MSST) San Francisco prepare to search for explosives.

The US Coast Guard operates many K9 teams that comprise one guardian and one dog. There are teams at every Deployable Operations Group (DOG) unit. The DOG units include Maritime Safety and Security Team (MSST) Seattle, MSST San Francisco, MSST LA, MSST Galveston, MSST Kings Bay, MSST New York and MSRT Chesapeake.

The US Coast Guard launched the Canine Substance Detection Program approximately one year after the terrorist attacks on September 11, 2001. The program's goal was to enhance detection and deterrence capabilities in the maritime environment, adjacent lands and waterside installations. This initiative is in line with the President's national strategy for Homeland Security, and allows the Coast Guard to support the Department of Homeland Security initiatives such as the Canine Rapid Deployment Force. The Coast Guard canine teams are used in maritime ports, waterways and shoreline facilities, including during boardings of commercial vessels before the vessels reach the United States to help ensure safety of those on the vessel and to prevent illegal or dangerous substances from exiting those vessels coming into the United States.

This mission is not new to the Coast Guard; in fact canine handler was a position or rating from 1943 to 1952. The US Coast Guard had over 3,600 dog teams and three different training sites for the canine teams located in different states. At first however the basic training for the canines and their handlers was held at Front Royal Virginia and it was administered by the Army. Upon completion of the course the canine teams would be stationed everywhere in the United States and they would patrol (walk) the entire boarder. The canines were trained in Sentry and Patrol work, and the best time for them to patrol was at night. Many canine teams confronted and stopped German U-Boats and their crew from completing their mission of infiltration and destruction. Many canine teams stationed in the Pacific North West had to hike to their locations with the canines and all of their support gear and build their bases in the worst of conditions and locations. They would take turns building the camps and patrolling. In some locations the canine handler would have to carry the canine on his back so that they would be able to continue their patrols. In 1952 the Coast Guard disbanded the canine teams and the rating, for what was thought to be forever.

The times have changed since then. The US Coast Guard as a whole changed on September 11, 2001 as did the rest of the United States. The Coast Guard created new units called Maritime Safety and Security Teams or MSSTs and part of the many capabilities the teams would have would be explosive detecting canines. The Coast Guard re-established the canine program after 50 years of not having them. The first of the new canine handlers attended school at Auburn University in Aniston, Alabama, and they pick up the Coast Guard's new and dangerous mission as canine explosive detector teams. The Coast Guard made another change in schools after seeing the progress that was being made by the canine teams. The new school was located in Front Royal Virginia and was run by Customs and Border Protection. Customs had been running its Canine Enforcement Training Center since the 1960s and started instructing the Coast Guard in canine explosive detection in 2004.

The Customs and Boarder Protection course is four months long and the handlers are exposed to many different environments that they will expected to operate in. Upon completion of the four-month canine school the handlers return to their perspective commands, and commence their environmental training as well as trying to locate training aids. Since the canines are trained on live explosives and the Coast Guard does not have any, the canine handlers have to go to their federal, state, and local law enforcement agencies to gain vital training. Because of the need to network with the agencies that has made the relationship, training and experiences with the agencies strong. Every day the canine teams have to train on odour, patterns and exposure to different elements as well as conduct exercise, health checks, health care and more.

German Border Police

In 1946, the Soviet Union formed the *Grenzschutz Polizei*, the Border Police, and the main border between East and West Germany was sealed. In 1961, thousands of East German workers, guarded by troops, began to construct concrete-block and wood barriers and barbed wire fences blocking boulevards, parks, streets, and alleys in the heart of the city of Berlin, as well as the perimeter adjoining the surrounding Communist state of East Germany. Snaking for almost a hundred miles around West Berlin, the Berlin Wall became the Cold War's most potent symbol. Next came an alarmed fence, then dog-runs patrolled by specially trained German Democratic Republics (DDR) German shepherd dogs. In 1974, the original *Grenzschultz Polizei* became the *Grenztruppen*, or border troops. Approximately 100–160 DDR German shepherd dogs were assigned to each *Grenztruppen* battalion. The *Diensthundefuehrer* (Dog Team Leader) was in charge of the overall care and training for the border patrol dogs and their handlers. The *Diensthundefuehrer* had to have basic veterinary skills be proficient in dog training.

The *Grenztruppen* would police minefields, border fences, checkpoints, and watch towers. Hundreds of large dog pens were set up throughout the East German border, including the Berlin Wall. More than 5000 dogs were used just to patrol the Berlin Wall. Dogs were sometimes leashed to a suspended line, within these dog runs, to patrol a strategic area. It was a common part of their training regimen to feed them only once every ten days to keep them lean, aggressive and ferocious. Their keen intelligence made them far more versatile than a mere security dog. They were also worked as trackers and attack dogs. The *Grenztruppen* even created a specialised unit of DDR German shepherds dogs to track deserters in all types of terrain.

In 1990 dismantling of the wall began and the *Grenztruppen* were officially disbanded. Many of the DDR dogs were sold, abandoned or euthanised. Thankfully, a small handful of breeders realised that years of strict East German breeding had produced a magnificent animal and preserved the lineage of this incredible dog.

Finland's Border Guards

During the Cold War, Finland's eastern border was on the northern fringes of the Iron Curtain across Europe, and the closeness of the border aroused both fear and awe. The border was heavily fortified and guarded and there were no contacts between people living on the two sides. Towards the north, the terrain becomes hilly, and in Lapland it's an uninhabited wilderness. Finland and Russia are separated by a 1340 kilometre-long border. This border has been pushed back and forth several times mainly as a consequence of armed conflicts.

Today on the Finnish side, the border is guarded by the Border Guard, and in fact most of its 3100 members of staff are deployed on Finland's eastern border. The most important task of the border guards is to ensure that cross-border passenger traffic goes through the official border crossings and that all formalities are adhered to. There are 13 official border crossings between Finland and Russia. Some 7.2 million people crossed the border between Finland and Russia every year. Finnish Border Guard also makes a contribution to pan-European security. A dog is an invaluable asset. The Finnish Border Guard has about 250 dogs, which have been trained to sniff out drugs, explosives and human tracks.

Federal Border Guard Service of Russia

Many dogs are used by paramilitary border guard units. Once they may have been used to keep people in but they now protect their nation's boarders by conducting drug and illegal alien patrol missions. Today there are many units within Russia that operate dogs in the paramilitary role including border guard units and special police units. The USSR KGB Border Guards use tracker dogs on the mountainous terrain bordering the Soviet Union and Afghanistan. Entry into the KGB Border Guards K9 is highly selective; a recruit has to have an unimpeachable political background.

The Federal Border Guard Service of Russia was created in 1993 tasked with the defence of the longest national border in the world. Russian Border Guards are also stationed outside of Russia most notably in southern Tajikistan, in order to guard the border with Afghanistan. Its modus operandi is to combat any threats to national security in the border area; including terrorism and foreign infiltration. The Federal Border Guard Service operates a large numbers of dogs. These operate under all types of terrain and environmental conditions.

Dogs get a good deal at Russia's border posts: plenty of respect and attention, their own place to sleep and a special diet comprising twice as much meat as the men get. If there's no meat, the dogs get fed canned dog food. That costs more, but the commanding officers know that the expense pays off because the dogs are the most loyal, effective and essential support they can have. Every border post in the ten regional departments of the Federal Border Service (FPS) includes dogs among its personnel. The dogs have their own master – an instructor or dog handler and, like small children, are lavished with constant attention.

'The government can't do without dogs. In the army and navy, they guard arms stockpiles, nuclear installations, closed garrisons; and in the border guards service, they guard the border,' says head of the FPS canine division Lt. Col. Vladimir Yakovlev. 'The dogs usually specialise in different areas. Some track mines, others hunt for drugs or alcohol, and then every post has three or four dogs that can pick up a trail. Dogs are considered strategic weapons, and so figures relating to them are secret.

'Much of the border terrain has gorges, mountains with streams, rivers and dense mountain bush mean that technology is of little use in these conditions, and that is why the dogs are so valuable.'

'The dogs are hugely important on the Tadjik-Afghan border. One dog, Beri, and Senior Warrant Officer Shishin, the dog's master, have detained numerous people illegally crossing the border and detected many weapons, ammunition and 274 kilograms of drugs. In another case, a search dog, Dina, and her instructor Sergei Valiyev, came under fire with their border patrol along the Tadjik-Afghan border. When the fighting was over, Dina helped search the area and discovered five corpses, a sack of heroin weighing nearly 10 kilograms, two Kalashnikovs, ammunition and radio equipment.'

The Dog Training Centre is in the midst of a thick forest and swampland and is surrounded by a concrete fence. With its numerous kennels, enclosures and dogs, it doesn't look much like the average military base. Every year, the centre trains several hundred dogs for the FPS, as well as training dog handlers and instructors. The centre works mostly with Caucasian and German shepherds, but also with spaniels, Rottweilers and Dobermans. Between 10 and 15 different breeds are represented at the centre, serving not only in the FPS, but also as rescue dogs and in the Emergencies Ministry.

Ukraine Border Guards

Ukrainian border guards patrol along the Ukraine-Romania border near the west Ukrainian village of Yablunitsa. Thousands of would-be immigrants from India, Afghanistan, China, Iraq, Somalia, Chechnya and Georgia have begun to choose the 'easy' route to Europe — through Ukraine's Carpathian Mountains. Either duped by smugglers into thinking Ukraine is Romania or Hungary or dumped in a Ukrainian forest, many migrants end their thousands of dollars-worth trips to Europe in Ukraine. Dogs train at the Ukrainian border guard dog training centre near Velyki Mosty village, about 50 kilometres north-west of Lviv. Every year, the biggest dog training centre in the former Soviet Union prepares hundreds of trained dogs for Ukrainian border guards as well as for presidential guards and other special forces.

Belarus Border Guard

The Belarus Government states that no other service needs the assistance of working dogs more than the Border Guard does. Detection of drug trafficking, smuggling weapons and explosives, detainment of illegal immigrants — in all these operations a working dog is the border guard's right hand. Of all the neighbouring states Belarus' border with the European Union is the longest (around 1250 km). According to international organisations the Belarusian section is one of the most reliable sections of the European Union border. More than 90 per cent of border trespassers detained by the Belarusian border guards are the citizens of the frontier regions. Most often perpetrators try to cross the border on foot; this is where the dogs have their most success. Canines go through an intensive training session at the border guard's army department in the village of Smargon. About 300 dogs are under training in the centre, to be used in Belarus customs service, emergency ministry services and border guarding. Belarussian border guards patrol the state border with Poland near the city of Brest, some 360 kilometres south-west of Minsk.

The Canada Border Services

The Canada Border Services Agency (CBSA) currently has 72 detector dog teams strategically located across Canada, serving both travellers and commercial operations. The detector dog teams work in all modes of travel such as air, highway, marine, and rail and in postal and courier centres.

The CBSA has specialised dogs trained in the detection of:

- Narcotics (e.g. cocaine, heroin, ecstasy)

- Firearms

- Currency

- Agriculture products (e.g. pork, beef and chicken) that could contain harmful pests and diseases

The CBSA's Detector Dog Service (DDS) program has been in operation since 1978. At that time, Canada Customs responded to the identified need of providing front-line officers with a more effective method of detecting and interdicting narcotics and firearms. Detector dogs were seen as a possible tool and a pilot project was initiated in Windsor.

The program's reach has extended in recent years, with dogs being used to detect items other than drugs and firearms. In 2003, a currency detector dog pilot project was launched to help CBSA officers with their authorities under the *Proceeds of Crime (Money Laundering) and Terrorist Financing Act*. The currency detector dog teams have now become part of the DDS program.

Since January 2005, the DDS program has included food, plant and animal detector dog teams from the Canadian Food Inspection Agency.

The DDS plays an important role in the detection of prohibited or regulated goods entering the country and in assisting the CBSA to fulfil its border protection mandate by:

- Significantly increasing opportunities to interdict narcotics, firearms, currency and food, plant and animal products

- Deterring smugglers while increasing the public's awareness of the CBSA's innovative enforcement approaches

- Assisting CBSA officers in conducting examinations and eliminating labour-intensive searches

- Improving service to the travelling public by reducing the time needed to screen or examine passengers, luggage and commercial shipments in the least intrusive manner

In addition, detector dog teams assist other law-enforcement agencies in their execution of search warrants for drugs/firearms and currency.

CBSA officers and their detector dogs also conduct demonstrations at schools and for community service groups. During these demonstrations, handlers provide general information on drugs and firearms, currency and food, plant and animal products and demonstrate their dog's trained abilities. This service is aimed at educating young people and the general public while providing information about the CBSA's role as a law-enforcement agency.

Detector dog teams receive intensive training at the CBSA's Learning Centre in Rigaud, Quebec. At the Learning Centre, they are trained to recognise the specific scents that they will be employed to detect, whether the scents are from narcotics, firearms, or agriculture products. They also become familiar with the circumstances and situations under which they will work.

The CBSA offers detector dog services to other enforcement agencies in Canada and abroad, such as police forces in Blainville, Châteauguay, Montréal, Toronto, federal and provincial correctional authorities, US police forces in New York and Florida, and the Bermuda Customs Service.

What the CBSA looks for in a potential detector dog:

- Natural ability and the desire to retrieve
- Good physical condition
- Size (15–40 kilos)
- Alertness
- Boldness
- Temperament
- Sociability

The dog handlers must be border services officers and be dedicated to their job. They may be required to be on call 24 hours a day and must be willing to travel to other locations on short notice. They must also be dedicated to their dogs, while both on- and off- duty.

Post Sept 11 all countries have increased security at airports. Search dogs working around passengers at terminals, like the one above taken at a Canadian airport, are a common sight.

THE FUTURE OF POLICE DOGS

The future looks bright for police dogs. There is no sign of any modern technology being developed anytime soon that will be able to cost-effectively detect an offender, or particular odour, day or night in various environments and do something about it via indication or physical action. What machine can could jump a two-metre ditch, climb or jump over a three-metre wall, swim across a water obstacle and hold a suspect until you arrive?

For decades scientists have been trying to replace the searching capabilities of a police detection dog with machines. So far they have failed. To get anywhere near the capability of a dog the machine has to be the size of a small car. Many such military devices using the same principle and designed for the detection of chemicals in biological warfare are truck-mounted appliances.

At many international airports you see security guards waving a magic wand over baggage to detect narcotic substances. The results of a recent US survey measuring detection success rates showed the following results: machines 14 per cent; humans searching 34 per cent and dogs around 90 per cent.

However, back to basics, the police dog is still one of the world's fastest land animals with 42 sharp teeth heading for the bad guy like a guided missile. Who really needs to improve that?

Dogs in many cultures still strike fear into the hearts of men and comfort their fellow police officers by raising moral. The sheer presence of the dogs at an incident is a huge deterrent for would-be troublemakers, both because of their intimidating size and because the average human is generally scared of being bitten by a police dog. Unfortunately the deterrent value of the work a police dog does is not easily comparible to an accountant or a commanding officer who only reviews his or her budget to arrest ratios. A police dog is expensive to train and maintain, there's no denying that, but one dog unit can achieve the value for money of 25 other officers.

If I were ever going to start up a local sheriff's department I would have a K9 team. For a start you only need one man in the patrol car not two. Single officer patrols are usually dangerous; having to respond to domestic violence calls and felony crimes in progress alone is risky. You can arm your single officer to the teeth — guns, capsicum spray, batons, tasers and other non-lethal equipment —but all of these can either malfunction or be taken off you by a highly aggressive skilled offender. A K9 doesn't malfunction; it is a true force multiplier for a single officer patrol, is highly motivated and will quite literally give its life for you.

As an operational police dog handler I have seen many violent situations de-escalate when a police dog arrives on scene. Just a simple bark from the rear of the dog wagon has made many a want-to-be tough guy readjust his attitude.

The threat of a police dog jumping through the window and ripping into flesh usually works better than the sympathetic voice of a negotiator trying to coax a criminal out.

Dogs provide a vital extra level of search capability, whether they are looking for people, drugs, explosives or arms. They are a cost efficient means to controlling many times their number because of their deterrent value and physical presence.

Police dogs will continue to give future police commanders both a search capacity and force protection capacity.

PART 2

An A–Z of Police Canine Units around the World

AUSTRALIA

One of the earliest known uses of police dogs in Australia was in Queensland in 1912, when they were first introduced for an experimental trial. Results from this trial were disappointing and the dogs were subsequently removed from the service in 1917. Similarly, the Victorian Police Service introduced a privately cross-bred black dog in 1922. Its main purpose appears to have been to break the monotony of the night shift. It too was removed from the service in 1925. By 1932, New South Wales had also established a police dog unit, which was later disbanded in 1954. In 1956, the New Zealand dog unit was established. The New Zealand Police Dog Unit would become instrumental in providing training, information and dogs to their Australian counterparts.

The Australian Federal Police

The Australian Federal Police (AFP) was formed in 1979 following the merger of the former Commonwealth Police and the Australian Capital Territory Police. Historically, the use of dogs within the organisation dates back to the uniformed branch of the former Commonwealth Police and Peace Officer Guard. At the time of the merger, Commonwealth Police explosive detection and general purpose dog handlers based at Brisbane, Sydney and Melbourne airports became members of the newly formed organisation.

Following inception in 1979, the most recent history of the AFP canine program dates back to 1983, when an explosive detection dog and handler were trained with the assistance of the Australian Army. General purpose capability was further developed in 1985, with two handlers trained by the Royal Australian Air Force (RAAF). The following year, the capability was expanded with an additional general purpose dog and handler team trained by NSW Police.

AFP bomb and general purpose dogs were deployed to major airports in Australia until 1990 when the function was assumed by the Australian Protective Service, the government agency created by the separation of the Protective Service component of the AFP in 1984.

During the 1980s, the AFP dogs were kennelled nationally in purpose built facilities; however, throughout the early stages in Canberra, the team was based out of a makeshift kennel located in Barton, ACT, before relocating in 1985 to the ACT Water Police building adjacent to Lake Burley Griffin. This changed when, in 1988, a small purpose built complex was erected at

Majura, ACT, adjacent to the Police Driver Training Facility. The year also saw Queensland Police train a general purpose handler which included a cannabis detection capability for the first time, The AFP then began to train its own general purpose dogs, and included the drug detection capability in selected dogs until 1999.

In 2000, the AFP launched its inaugural dedicated drug detection capability. Trained by Australian Customs Service, this was an integral step in the canine program's ultimate aim of providing a resource to the entire organisation.

The re-integration of the Australian Protective Service into the AFP in 2004 (as part of Australian Government efforts to improve the coordinated response to terrorism), saw the AFP assume responsibility for the deployment of explosive detection canines at Brisbane, Sydney, Canberra, Melbourne and Perth airports.

In 2005, the Wheeler Review into airport security and policing made key recommendations on the structure and operation of Australian airport policing and security. The AFP developed a unified policing model to enhance existing airport security and provide a policing presence at the 11 major Australian airports through community policing, investigations, intelligence gathering, and terrorism deterrence and response.

The year also saw the organisation secure funding to assist in the Federal Government commitment to Asia-Pacific Economic Cooperation (APEC) 2007. National AFP Canine expanded to include an additional 24 police explosive detection dog and handler teams to assist in APEC related operations, and ultimately deployed permanently to the major Australian airports.

Funding was subsequently provided for the construction of a purpose built complex on the original dog squad site at Majura, ACT. Opened for operations in December 2007, and with a state-of-the-art facility built at a cost of $10.8 million, the scope of National AFP Canine was to provide a canine resource to the entire organisation.

The AFP continues to develop canine detection capability, including completing a successful pilot currency detection course in 2008. The training centre is currently running a currency and drug detection course to provide the capability to eight regions around Australia. The portfolio will grow this capability with plans to deploy currency and drug detection dogs to all major regions nationally in the near future. Further, National AFP Canine is training a tactical canine capability to assist the International Deployment Group in tactical and stability response resolutions both nationally and internationally.

National AFP Canine is now established as a specialist multi-disciplinary team that delivers explosive detection, currency and drug detection, general purpose and tactical canine capabilities to the AFP on a national and international scale. The dog handlers in the AFP are a great bunch of individuals. I work regularly with them and we cooperate on many missions in Queensland.

Tasmania

With the prospect of starting a police dog squad in Tasmania, an expression of interest was sought from members to attend an information session, which outlined the requirements and responsibilities to be a handler. Partners and spouses were also encouraged to attend, as the role of the handler required a commitment from both the handler and other people involved in the handler's life. Fifty members and their partners/spouses attended the information session, with only 15 continuing on to the shortlisting process for the three-day selection trial. The Tasmanian Police selected two handlers and they were introduced as part of the State Security Unit in November 2003.

The two handlers that were chosen were paired with two labradors, which were trained as explosive detection dogs. The two dogs were supplied by the Australian Customs Service Labrador Breeding Program and were brother and sister, named Wally and Winnie. Wally and Winnie were assessed as suitable for the passive alert system and were selected for training at the Victoria Police Dog Training Centre.

The two handlers also underwent training to learn about the animals they were paired with. The training involved learning about their hunting and detecting instincts and what drives and motivates the dogs. They also completed a purpose designed veterinarian course; learning the make-up of the dog, the different names of their bones and body parts, and how different injuries and strains impact on the working dog.

The two labradors were trained using a 'feeding/training' regime, meaning that every day, for at least one hour, the dogs were required to detect odours, for which their reward for detection was food — this in turn becomes their feeding regime. As there are no central kennelling facilities, the dogs are with their handlers all the time.

The squad's success was marked with its expansion, and in June 2008 the Tasmanian Dog Squad received a further two recruits, the drug detecting labradors Flicka and Yuli. They arrived from Australian Customs in January

2008 and endured a rigorous training course at the Tasmanian Police Academy before becoming operational.

In April 2009, the two original squad dogs were awarded with Canine Service Medals. The medals honoured five years' service with the Tasmania Police Service. Initially the dogs' role was to deter activity associated with the import and export of explosive substances on the *Spirit of Tasmania*. However, they have now diversified their role into a state-wide monitoring team that patrols airports, major transport hubs and special events, and they have become an integral part of the state's anti-terrorism unit.

Northern Territory

The Northern Territory Police Dog Operations Unit is the youngest dog squad in Australia, commencing operations in December 2004 with two drug detector dogs and handlers located in Darwin. Since this time, the unit has expanded to seven drug detector dogs.

Since its beginnings, the drug detector dog unit has had over 600 seizures of cannabis, methamphetamine and ecstasy. These were the main target odours for the dogs. The main focus of the drug detection work is the remote community strategy, which targets illegal substances being transported out to the Aboriginal communities.

In December 2008, three general purpose dogs joined the drug detection dogs in the Dog Operations Unit. The dogs were born and raised in Queensland. The three German shepherds were trained by the Queensland Police Service Dog Squad puppy development program at 12 months of age. The dogs, named Prowler, Xanto and Stinger, completed a 14-week intensive course where they learnt tracking, search and rescue, obedience and skills in providing operational support. The dogs were a valuable addition to the Dog Operations Unit, increasing police operational capability in a variety of situations.

The Dog Operations Unit has expanded in order to protect the community and police in the Northern Territory to, at the time of writing, ten operational dogs, including both general purpose and drug detection canines. It has grown in leaps and bounds since its inclusion into the service.

Alice Springs has a new drug detector dog unit on the south Stuart Highway. Two dog handlers have recently completed eleven weeks training in Canberra and Brisbane and are now working with their labradors Nugget and Misty.

One of the handlers has been with the NT Police for 22 years. His last posting was at Kulgera near the South Australian border.

It is not unusual to have 40 degrees days so often the dogs are inside their air-conditioned vehicle while the humans are out in the heat. The two dogs in the Alice will mean the practice of transporting dogs from Darwin will be discontinued.

Queensland

The Queensland Police Service (QPS) Dog Squad began in 1972 when two police officers were sent to RAAF Base Drayton (Toowoomba) and received training in the skills of dog handling. An additional two handlers travelled to Trentham Police College, New Zealand where their training was completed. The four handler/dog teams returned to Brisbane where they commenced active duties. In March 1975 a further four police officers received training, in Brisbane, from the founding members of the squad and so began the QPS Dog Squad.

The QPS currently has 57 general purpose, 5 EORT and 9 Drug Detection police dog teams operating throughout the State. Developing from a Brisbane-based squad the QPS Dog Squad has expanded and now operates in every region from Cairns in Far North Queensland to the Gold Coast and Ipswich. The number of operational handler/dog teams is constantly increasing as the demand for the dog squad's specialised services increase. In addition to the General Purpose dog teams the QPS Dog Squad also have a Specialist Drug Detection Unit at the Brisbane Dog Squad that is available for drug search duties as required throughout the state. The EORT also has dogs available to search for explosives and firearms throughout the state.

Currently the QPS Dog Squad obtains dogs through donation from members of the public. The dogs are assessed for their potential as police dogs before the service accepts them. The QPS also has its own breeding program. Dogs are fostered out until over 12 months old before returning for assessment and suitability; after selection they are allocated to handlers for training.

As of early 2005 the service has opened the Puppy Development Kennel Complex at the Brisbane Dog Squad and is undertaking a Puppy Development Program which develops puppies identified by the state co-ordinator as suitable for police work.

The QPS Dog Squad is not restricted to using only German shepherds; in the past labradors have been successfully trained for specialist detection roles. Rottweiler and Belgian shepherds have also performed operational duties in the squad.

The basic reason dogs are used and are effective in police work is their superior senses, particularly smell and hearing. The dog's senses are adapted for operational work to provide specialised support for police.

A general purpose dog is trained to perform multiple functions. These are:

- Obedience exercises. This is an important function as handlers must have and be able to maintain control over their dogs at all times

- Tracking (following a person's scent) offenders and missing persons if they are moving on foot

- Searching buildings, enclosed areas and bushland. Here the dog searches for scent drifting in the air and follows it to locate the person

- Searching an area of ground for recently discarded property or evidence

- Apprehending violent offenders

- Performing perimeter security on raids where there is a likelihood suspects may decamp from the premises

- Searching for the dangerous drug cannabis and its derivatives

- Assisting with control of crowds threatening the safety of the general public

Specialist police dogs are trained to perform specific tasks requiring exact training. Teams from the Drug Detection Unit of the Brisbane Dog Squad are trained to search for illicit drugs including, but not limited to, cocaine, amphetamines, heroin, ecstasy and cannabis. These handler/dog teams can be used for interior and exterior searching of dwellings, vehicles and vessels. The explosives/firearms detection dogs are trained to search for all types of explosives. These include firearms and ammunition. The explosives/firearms detection dogs are attached to EORT and are based in Brisbane. These handler/dog teams are used before major events or VIP visits, or if a bomb threat is received. These handler/dog teams are also trained in locating hidden firearms and/or ammunition.

Other specialist dogs have been trained for cadaver searches and locating evidence of fire accelerants at fire scenes.

The QPS police dogs have a great life. At the end of the shift the dog is taken home with the handler and spends its time off with the handler and their family. The dog and handler work exclusively as a team from start to finish.

The dogs receive the best attention, food and vet care, ensuring their health and happiness. At the conclusion of their working life the 'retired' police dogs can sit back and relax as a normal backyard dog. Handlers generally retain their old police dogs.

No experience or outside qualifications are required to train with a new police dog as training is undertaken by suitable applicants on an internal three-month Police Dog Training Course conducted by the State Coordinator (Training) Police Dogs. Naturally applicants must have a love of animals and possess the ability to work alone and at times unsupervised. The training is a combination of theory, from the *Police Dog Training Manual* and practical exercises. At the completion of the training course the new handler/dog team is partnered with an experienced operational team to integrate them into the working environment. Every 12 months of the dog's operational life every handler/dog team is assessed and certified 'Competent'.

New South Wales Police

The News South Wales (NSW) Police Dog Squad is a specialist state-wide resource whose primary role is to provide support to police in a wide variety of operations, from all types of searches to foot patrols, pursuits and rescues. The Dog Squad is on call 24 hours a day, seven days a week. The squad operates across the state and is divided into four police regions. Only a small number of German shepherds, a breed with intelligence and strength, are selected each year to train as police dogs. Each dog undergoes extensive training with its police handler. A strong bond is developed between the handler and dog. The training is at the Police Dog Training Centre in Goulburn. Established in 1932, the Police Dog Squad's role was originally very similar to its role today. The dogs were used for searches, rescues and apprehending offenders.

From 1954 to 1979, the squad was disbanded but with a renewed police need for dog squad support, two dogs teams were trained and qualified at the Victorian Police Dog Training Centre in 1979. These teams started working once again in New South Wales.

Each dog is carefully the evaluated to see if it has the necessary intelligence and temperament to become a police dog. It then undergoes and intensive training program with its handler, teaching the dog obedience, protection of its master and there police dog duties. After training, all police dog teams are able to track and find wanted offenders or missing persons in urban, rural or rugged bush land; search all types of buildings for wanted offenders in hiding or property connected with crime; search for illegal drugs that may have been hidden or buried; chase and apprehend offenders who may be escaping arrest; and may be armed and dangerous; act as a deterrent and back-up in dangerous situations such as brawls, sieges and domestics; and provide high profile foot patrols of places such as schools, industrial areas and shopping complexes.

There are 14 police dogs and handlers operating in each region and three located at the Police Dog Training Centre; a total of 59 teams.

Those dogs with the necessary intelligence and temperament undergo an intensive training program with their dedicated handler at the Police Dog Training Centre in Goulburn.

The training teaches the dog obedience, protection of its master and other police dog duties. As a part of this process, a very close, strong bond develops between the handler and dog. After training, all police dog teams are able to:

- Track and find wanted offenders or missing persons in urban, rural or rugged bushland areas

- Search all types of buildings for wanted offenders in hiding, property connected with crime or illegal drugs that are hidden or buried

- Chase and apprehend armed and dangerous offenders who are attempting to escape arrest

- Act as a deterrent and back-up police in dangerous situations such as brawls, sieges and serious domestic violence cases

- Detect illicit drugs, whether they be hidden, discarded or buried in and around buildings or in motor vehicles

- Provide high profile foot patrols of places such as schools, industrial areas, shopping complexes, railway stations, trains and car parks to deter crime and make these places safer for the community

Stinger Meets a Snake

In May 2009, one of the newest police dog recruits, Stinger, was bitten by a snake while performing tracking duties. Stinger and his handler were called out to track a driver and possibly passengers from a vehicle that had recently rolled and crashed. With fears the occupants may be injured, Stinger was sent into bushland to follow the scent. Unfortunately Stinger could not complete the job; as he was tracking in the dark, his handler heard a yelp. Quickly shining the torch to where the dog was, his handler saw what he thought was a snake. He said that he did not know what type of snake it was, but it was brown and a couple of metres long, making him think it was a deadly bite.

Stinger was bitten on one of his back feet and was rushed to the nearest emergency veterinary clinic and within 24 hours he was back on duty. Vets conducted a series of tests and observations of Stinger and cleared him of any serious venomous bites, and said that it was more than likely to have been a non-venomous reptile that had struck the young police dog.

K9 Chuck Captures Fugitive

Malcolm Naden, one of Australia's most wanted fugitives, having been on the run for seven years, was captured in a dramatic police operation in a remote area 30 kilometres west of Gloucester, New South Wales. Police from the Tactical Operations Unit, along with a dog dressed in military camouflage, swept on his hiding place early in the morning. Naden is alleged to have murdered a 24-year-old female, indecently assaulted a 15-year-old and attempted to murder a police officer. Some international media misguidedly called him the new Ned Kelly — another infamous cop killer.

Naden received stitches in his leg after being bitten by a German shepherd police dog called Chuck during the arrest operation. He was found putrid, dirty, thin and looking beaten. At his bail hearing he sat shoeless and motionless in the dock and limped from court at the end of the hearing.

Mr Naden's lawyer told reporters his client was 'very tired with serious bite wounds from police dogs on his legs', trying to gain sympathy — lost on the family of his victims no doubt. Two officers had tended to his bleeding ankle and strapped it with a bandage before he was led to a waiting police vehicle at the scene.

Assistant Commissioner York paid tribute to the Tactical Operations Unit and the Dog Unit. K9 Chuck, a three-year-old bred by the Police Department, has been operational since 2010, and is now up for an annual good work award for his part in capturing Naden.

West Australian Police Dog Squad

The Western Australia Police Canine Section was formed in 1993 with the initial intake of two police officers and two German shepherd dogs. Training was conducted in Trentham, New Zealand, as this was the best available training facility. At the completion of training, the section had one general purpose dog and one narcotics detection dog.

Even in the early stages, it was found that the dogs were of great assistance to police on the streets and it quickly became apparent that an increase in staff was needed.

Since that time the section has steadily grown. It now has one senior sergeant in charge, one training sergeant, eleven general purpose dog teams and five narcotic and two explosive detection dog teams, providing services state-wide. All training is now carried out in Perth at the WA Police Canine Training Section at the Police Complex, Maylands. Police dogs are mainly German shepherds, Rottweilers and labradors, which have been found to be best suited to policing.

The Dog Squad also conducts joint training and operations with other government agencies such as the Australian Customs Service, Australian Federal Police, Department of the Attorney General, Special Air Services and the Australian Defence Force. The Dog Squad is always looking for potential dog recruits. German shepherd or Rottweiler (male or female)

Each dog is assessed by experienced police dog personnel. If the dog is suitable for further assessment, subject to agreement with the owner, it will be thoroughly assessed by the WA Police Dog Squad. The dogs come from all walks of life. One of the current serving dogs was rescued from a local pound when training officers saw his potential and saved him from being destroyed.

Victoria

It was decided that Victoria Police should form a Dog Squad in 1975. The Dog Squad plays an important role in operational policing in Victoria. Dogs can often crawl or jump onto places where it would be impractical or impossible for police members to go. The Dog Squad also provides operational support. It works with the Special Operations Group during siege situations or when searching for explosives, and utilises the Air Wing when they require transport in a time critical situation. However, most of their support is given to local operational police.

Police dog handlers respond to complaints of intruders on premises, break and entering offences, sexual attacks, brawls, prowlers, lost persons and many armed or violent situations. The dogs are trained to specialise in one of three disciplines; general purpose, narcotics and explosives.

General purpose dogs are skilled in the areas of tracking, searching and protecting life and property. Handlers and their dogs often work from home within an allocated police district. The dogs used are male German shepherds and labradors as they are physically strong, are of a good size and often need to be aggressive. The greatest demand for dogs is at night when a dog's acute sense of smell is most needed. However, there is a 24-hour roster for general purpose dog teams to ensure there is always at least one team on duty.

Narcotics detection dogs search houses, cars or personal belongings. Female German shepherds and labradors are preferred for this type of work, as their smaller frame is more suited to work in confined spaces. Handlers and dogs predominantly work on an appointment basis for stations or specialised units requiring the expertise of a dog. Consequently, they can be called upon night or day.

Explosives detection dogs and handlers search for bombs and other explosive devices in buildings, cars or personal belongings and often work alongside the Special Operations Group and bomb technicians. They also regularly visit schools and railway stations at night in the course of routine patrols. Female German shepherds and labradors are used. The Victoria Police Dog Squad train and deploy canine teams (handler and dog) to help operational policing. The dog's natural instincts and nose ability, which cannot be copied by science, provide a very efficient tool for police.

The Dog Training Centre is in Attwood, Victoria. Police dogs and handlers are trained by qualified Dog Squad personnel. As part of their training, dogs use an agility course, which includes hurdles, ladders and planks, tunnels, fences and other obstacles that the dogs may confront when they are on the job. Canine teams are available and deployed to tasks 24 hours a day, seven days a week.

The training course for general purpose dogs takes approximately 18 weeks. During the course, dogs are trained in obedience, agility, retrieving, searching for property, searching for people, tracking and criminal work.

A detector team dogs training takes approximately ten weeks. Labrador retrievers are used for detection work and during the course the dogs are trained to detect various smells linked to narcotics, explosives/firearms or human remains.

Some people think that narcotic detection dogs are addicted to the drugs they are trained to locate. In fact, the dogs are rewarded with food when they find the smell they are trained to find.

Victoria Police Dog Squad has had a breeding program since 1990. At nine to 10 weeks of age, pups are placed in the care of carefully chosen civilian puppy-walking families who receive lessons on how to raise pups in preparation for their training by the Dog Squad. At 12–14 months of age, the pups are returned to the squad and are ready to start full-time training as police dogs.

The Victoria Police Dog Squad is currently staffed by 38 specially trained teams. The Dog Squad receives calls every day of the week around the state. Victoria Police canine teams respond to planned operations for searches and reports of offenders in premises, burglary offences, sexual attacks, fights, prowlers, lost people and armed and violent situations.

South Australia

The South Australian Dog Operations Unit provides support to operational police 24 hours a day seven days a week through the deployment of highly trained mobile dog teams. Each team comprises a handler and trained dog, with German shepherds used for general police work and labrador retrievers used in specialist roles. These dog teams are based in metropolitan Adelaide but are able to respond to calls for assistance throughout the state. Police dog teams are trained to carry out duties involving tracking, searching, criminal apprehension, drug detection and explosive detection.

The Dog Operations Unit is part of the Special Tasks and Rescue Group (STAR). The STAR Group is designed to handle problems and situations which require more concentrated attention than can normally be provided by general patrol police. Its members are highly skilled in the use of firearms, anti-terrorist tactics, crowd control, crime prevention techniques, and underwater recovery and search and rescue operations. Dogs play an important role in assisting to keep the community safe in South Australia.

German shepherds are the preferred breed used by South Australian Police, which has mostly relied on donated dogs from members of the public but now uses dogs from the Queensland Police Dog breeding program.

Cleaning Up the Streets

Police dogs are cleaning up the streets in South Australia — sniffer dog drug seizures have plummeted, even though police have more than doubled their searches.

Police say this shows fewer drugs are on the streets, with 462 dog searches seizing 150 ecstasy tablets, 4 kilograms of cannabis, 40 grams of amphetamine, 10 grams of cocaine and 40 pieces of drug paraphernalia last financial year. Operations led to 11 arrests, 400 reports and 94 people being sent to drug rehabilitation programs.

During just 205 searches the previous year, drug dogs netted a staggering 540 ecstasy pills, 8 LSD and 28 dexamphetamine tablets, 7.3 kilograms of cannabis, 62 grams of amphetamine, 3grams of ketamine, 38 grams of cocaine, 20 millilitres of GHB, 6 grams of heroin and 47 pieces of drug paraphernalia.

Police do not comment on the specific methods people use to hide drugs from patrols due to operational reasons, but have warned users they are aware of the extreme methods some take.

South Australian Police late last year boosted the number of drug detection dogs in the Dog Operations Unit, which they say is due to their 'continual success' against the illicit drug trade. A spokesperson said: 'The public needs to know that if they are going to carry illicit drugs, there is a good chance they will be caught by our dogs.'

BELGIUM

It is doubtful that these original dog handler pioneers had any idea that the concept they originated in 1899 would still be a vital part of world law enforcement over 100 years later. Every citizen who has ever had his stolen property recovered by use of a police service dog, every parent who has ever had a lost child found by a police service dog, and every police officer who has ever been protected from serious injury by a police service dog, owes an everlasting debt of gratitude to these 10 men who had the fortitude to initiate a concept, which, at the time, was unheard of in the law enforcement field.

The Belgian Police work on two levels: the federal and the local level. These two levels are autonomous and come under the authority of different departments. Together, the Local Police and Federal Police perform the integrated police function. The Federal Police are composed of operational services (judicial police, traffic police, railway police, air support unit, dog support unit, cavalry, etc.) as well as of administrative services (material means, human resources, etc.). The Federal Police also provide support to the administrative authorities and the local police services. They do so, for example, by lending them staff and special material (helicopters, dogs, etc.) to help them maintain public order.

The Canine Support Group has 35 teams that are trained in various specialities. Some detect drugs, while others detect human remains or fire accelerants. Over a third of them are trained to locate missing persons and are often deployed to earthquake zones. Additional to these canine teams some explosive detector dogs from the Federal Police are attached to the CGSU.

The Dog Support Unit was established at the special school of the former Gendarmerie in 1968. It was responsible for the training of the dogs and handlers that were engaged in the Gendarmerie. In the late 1960s, the dog training moved to the mobile legion in Brussels, and moved to Sint-Joris-Weert in the 1970s. The unit changed location twice in the following years (military domain of Leopoldsburg, Leuven), and finally ended up on the military domain of Neerhespen in 2004.

The Dog Support Unit consists of an operational division and a training division:

- The operational division sends out specialised dog teams at the request of judicial authorities and local and federal police services. This division also provides a minimum of dog teams 24 hours a day outside normal office hours.

- The training division is responsible for the training of all police dogs and handlers of the federal police. As far as the training of the local police dog teams is concerned, the trainers of the Dog Support Unit provide the training of all patrol dog teams through the police schools.

At present, the Federal Police have about 80 specialised dog teams. Half of these teams work in the Dog Support Unit. The other teams are employed in other federal police services, such as the Special units, the Railway Police and the Waterway Police.

Each dog team (dog and dog handler) that is trained by the Dog Support Unit can specialise in one specific discipline.

Tracking dogs work on the basis of the smell of living persons. The tracking dog can be used for several tasks:

- It can pick up and follow one person's specific human smell. In this way, the tracking dog can be of extra value to the police services, especially in the case of worrying disappearances and escaped offenders.

- In a certain zone, this dog can look freely for the smell of a random person who would be (or would have been) present there.

- The tracking dog can also trace small objects carried by a person and containing the smell of that person.

- It also traces living persons that are buried under the rubble. It indicates where the rescue workers have to start digging and may save lives in that way.

- Some tracking dogs also carry out identification tests. The dog tries to link an object found on the crime scene to a suspect. The dog handler asks the suspect and a number of neutral persons to each rub four tubes. The dog then compares the smell of the tubes with the smell of the object found. If the dog chooses the tube rubbed by the suspect twice, this means that there is a positive identification.

The passive drug detection dog searches for illegal drugs on individuals and sits down in front of the person whom it notices has a suspicious smell. This dog is mainly deployed to check big groups of people including in schools, prisons, discotheques, airplanes, trains and during festivals.

The active drug detection dog searches for illegal drugs in open and closed spaces and in cars. It barks when it notices drugs or the smell of drugs and is deployed in house searches and road checks.

A Belgium Special Response K9 team. Now one of the most modern users of K9 teams, Belgium led the way in police dog deployment.

The human remains detection dog is used to trace dead persons, physiological liquids and blood. If there is a chance that the person is still alive, a tracking dog is deployed during the first 72 hours.

The accelerant detection (arson) dog is deployed to trace fire accelerants in case of fires that were probably started deliberately.

The patrol dog is an all-round police dog that is deployed within the scope of community policing. It is used to patrol and to maintain law and order during football matches and big events. Both the Federal Police (Waterway Police and Railway Police) and the Local Police make use of this discipline.

The explosive detection dog is part of the Special units and searches for explosives, ammunition and used firearms.

The attack dog, which is part of the Special units, is considered a weapon and is deployed to neutralise dangerous persons.

The migration control dog is deployed to trace illegal immigrants in buildings and in large means of transport. It belongs to the Waterway Police.

The dogs that work with the police belong either to the Federal or Local Police, or to the handler himself. The Dog Support Unit has close contacts with several countries like the Netherlands, France, Germany, Switzerland and Poland. Information and knowledge is exchanged, new training methods and techniques are analysed and various dog specialisations are examined and evaluated.

In principle, each dog between nine months and two years qualifies for training at the Dog Support Unit. When the dog is purchased, certain characteristics like social behaviour and courage are appraised, but also certain urges and special talents like searching and retrieving, are considered.

Before a dog is purchased, it is extensively observed and evaluated. If the dog gets a positive evaluation afterwards, it is finally purchased by the Dog Support Unit after a medical examination by the veterinary service of the Federal Police.

A number of conditions have to be fulfilled to become a dog handler. For instance, the candidate dog handler must have the grade of police inspector and must be highly available for service. A permanent interest and motivation to raise, train and maintain a police dog and a good team spirit are also important.

A dog handler is expected to be very flexible in the work organisation and to be honest and collegial. It is also essential to be able to work independently.

As the dog teams from the Dog Support Unit are deployed throughout Belgium, knowledge of the second national language is a plus.

The selection procedure is split up into four steps: a written test, an interview, a medical test and a traineeship of one week. When a candidate dog handler is accepted at the end of the selection, he can start his training in the Dog Support Unit.

The Training Pillar provides the basic and continued training of all dogs belonging to the Federal Police. It also gives support at the police schools' request for the basic training of patrol dogs.

If the Local Police wish to employ a police dog team, this team always has to be trained in a police school. The basic training takes 5 to 26 weeks. Afterwards, the dog team receives continued training every year to confirm the level reached and further develop. This training mainly focuses on social behaviour and the possibility to deploy the dog team without stress (during football matches, concerts, etc.) at any time.

If a Federal Police directorate or service wishes to employ a dog team in its formation, it has to address its training request directly to the Dog Support Unit. Depending on the discipline of the dog team, the basic training will take six months to two years. Continued training is provided here as well.

CANADA

Toronto Police Dog Services

The Toronto Police Dog Services was formed in 1989. At present, the unit consists of 21 handlers and dogs. Most teams comprise one handler and one general purpose police dog. There are currently three exceptions to this where one handler has both a general purpose police dog and a narcotic/gun detection dog. There is also one handler with an explosives detector dog. Every handler is responsible for the care and maintenance of his or her canine partner(s). The dog not only works with the officer but becomes part of the officer's family.

Each dog has been chosen for its good health, temperament and training ability. Once selected, the dog is assigned to a handler who must also meet certain requirements. The officer must be a first class constable, have a good work ethic and pass a rigorous physical test.

Both the general purpose handler and the dog form a team and embark on a 15-week training course. During this period, the dogs and handlers are taught obedience, agility, tracking, property/evidence searches, area searches, building searches, handler protection and criminal apprehension.

The service presently uses German shepherds and Belgian shepherd (Malinois) for general purpose police dogs and currently use a labrador, springer spaniel and Malinois breeds for the detection of narcotics, firearms, ammunition and explosives. All are purchased after testing and are usually between the ages of one to two years.

When the teams graduate, they are assigned to general patrol work and respond to a variety of calls, such as lost or wanted persons, searches for stolen property or evidence, break and enters into stores or factories, or any other situation where a suspect has fled or may flee from the police or a crime scene.

Police Dog Services is now located in a new facility in East York.

Since its short history Police Dog Services has been responsible for hundreds of arrests and the laying of hundreds of criminal charges. it has also located thousands of dollars of property and pieces of crucial evidence including numerous firearms and other dangerous weapons.

In Canadian winters, the Mounties initially used husky breeds for transportation instead of horses. Today the RCMP uses German shepherds as general patrol police dogs.

The Original Police Dogs

Chief Van Wesemael, Ghent Police Chief from 1888 to 1915, even then was faced with the same problems which plague most police administrators today: a rising crime rate, numerous unsolved major crimes, and a lack of funding to hire additional personnel to combat this rapidly deteriorating situation. When the Ghent burgomaster (mayor) refused him additional funds, Van Wesemael made the statement, 'If you can't give me more policemen, then give me some dogs.' The mayor agreed, since the cost of the dog program, as outlined to him by Van Wesemael, was substantially less than the funding of an additional 100 policemen, as was the original request.

It remains unclear just how Van Wesemael had gained experience in training dogs. It can only be assumed from what little information is available on Van Wesemael's personal life that he was at the time actively engaged in breeding and training Belgian herding dogs and felt that if such dogs could be trained to herd cattle and sheep, they could likewise be easily trained to 'herd' criminals. Perhaps he had been experimenting with this theory in private and was convinced that his concept would work. So, in March of 1899, three dogs of the Belgian herding variety, resembling our present-day Bouviers, were acquired for Chief Van Wesemael by the Ghent city veterinary officer, and the training of these dogs, along with that of their policemen handlers, was personally begun by Chief Van Wesemael, who eventually turned this training task over to qualified subordinates. Shortly before

Christmas of 1899, ten dog and handler teams were at work. The dogs were initially utilised at night in the city's high crime neighbourhoods, along the waterfront, and in the wooded outlying sections of the city. Their success in diminishing the problem at hand was nearly instantaneous. Night crimes, previously both numerous and serious in these sections of the city, fell by two-thirds.

After ten months of trial, the most conservative members of the Ghent City Council became enthusiastic over these new police 'recruits' and voted additional funding for more dog patrol teams to be used in other areas of the city. Chief Van Wesemael wasted no time and soon there were 30 big, powerful dog 'policemen' on duty and working with surprising efficiency. They would take a new handler over his night beat with a zeal, a thoroughness, and a relentless, systematic vigour that would kill a lazy officer. They knew their work and could and did correct many an officer who was a novice at this type of assignment.

As far as their off-duty time was concerned, the animals were given every care. They were given baths once a week and their kennels were disinfected regularly and periodically whitewashed. For the first 15 days new recruits were kept in their kennels and taught merely obedience. Military brevity, combined with unvarying kindness, marked all orders. In fact, any human member of the force striking a dog was subject to instant dismissal. In due time, certain training officers would take the recruit dogs out on patrol with chosen veteran dogs.

All dogs began duty at 10 pm and ended their shifts at 6 am. They were never allowed to leave their kennel/training compound, located in the heart of the old city, during daytime, and on no account were they allowed to become acquainted with outside personnel or civilians. They were fed twice a day. During patrol duties at night, each dog received a large slice of bread, and so carefully were their needs and capacities studied, that the animals never appeared tired or spiritless upon returning to the kennels after a lengthy and often dangerous tour of duty. When a recruit began to show aptitude under training, the handler/trainer to whom he was assigned took him out on patrol, giving him scraps of meat and an occasional bone, and in this way emphasis was placed on the lesson the dog was intended to be taught, namely, that only people in police uniforms were to be trusted. All other humans were to be eyed with suspicion, if not with positive ferocity.

During this time, the recruit was also led to every nook and corner of its future beat for the purpose of familiarisation. For one month this work was conducted three or four hours a night under all weather conditions, the hours of duty being gradually increased to the standard eight. The final stage of the recruit's training involved the attack, or rather pursue-and-hold, training. The dogs were taught by means of dummy figures made to resemble thieves and other characters the dogs would be likely to encounter. Great patience was needed as the dogs had to be taught to seek, seize, and hold a suspect without hurting seriously.

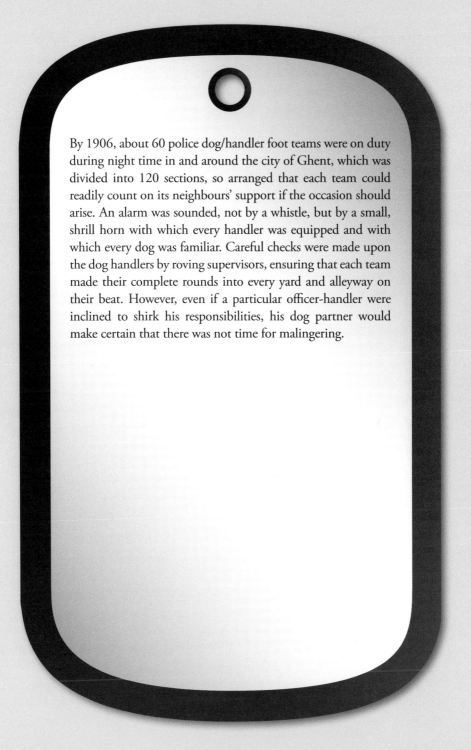

By 1906, about 60 police dog/handler foot teams were on duty during night time in and around the city of Ghent, which was divided into 120 sections, so arranged that each team could readily count on its neighbours' support if the occasion should arise. An alarm was sounded, not by a whistle, but by a small, shrill horn with which every handler was equipped and with which every dog was familiar. Careful checks were made upon the dog handlers by roving supervisors, ensuring that each team made their complete rounds into every yard and alleyway on their beat. However, even if a particular officer-handler were inclined to shirk his responsibilities, his dog partner would make certain that there was not time for malingering.

Royal Canadian Mounted Police (RCMP)

Canada has a long history of using dogs — law enforcement dogs were first used instead of patrol vehicles or horses for that matter when terrain and snow made other forms of transport useless. When the days of the great Northern Patrols ended, the need for the famous huskies was also gone. But the Mounties were still using dogs for new purposes. Even in the early years, dogs were used for some search and rescue by the North-West Mounted Police. Bloodhounds and other tracking dogs would be borrowed from local citizens to help find criminals or lost people.

From 1908 to 1935 members occasionally used privately owned dogs to assist them in their investigations. The Royal Canadian Mounted Police (RCMP) dog section was formed in 1935 with the acquisition of three German shepherds: Black Lux, Dale of Cawsalta and Sultan. In 1937, Commissioner MacBrien, satisfied with the value of police dogs, ordered an RCMP training school for dogs and handlers to be established at Calgary. In 1940, the RCMP won its first case involving dog search evidence. The RCMP Police Dog Service Training Centre was established at Innisfail, Alberta in 1965. The training staff comprises one officer in charge, one staff sergeant program manager, one staff sergeant senior trainer, five sergeant trainers, one acquisition sergeant, two corporal pre-trainers and a support staff of six public service employees.

In 1999, the RCMP started a pilot breeding program to produce a working strain of dog most suitable for law enforcement duties. One pup from this program has already graduated to field service and a number of others are currently in training. With 125 police dog teams across Canada, the RCMP needs up to 35 replacement dogs every year. With a recent infusion of $1.18 million in funding, the centre will now be able to expand its breeding program, relying less on dogs they buy on the open market. The Police Dog Service Training Centre in Innisfail, Alberta has a higher success rate and a higher retention rate with dogs personnel breed and train themselves.

To ensure its dogs are on the path to perfecting these skills, the centre begins training within two days after a puppy is born up until it is eight weeks old. It is then tested to determine if it has the potential to become a police dog. If the puppy passes, it enters the imprinting program, where prospective handlers must raise it before it returns to the centre for the final stages of training. The increased funding will allow the centre to improve the imprinting program as additional staff will be able to monitor the animals more closely, weeding out unsuitable dogs at an earlier stage.

Canadian Mounted Police K9s need to be able to work in all climates and environments, including snow.

The breeding and accompanying imprinting programs have even reduced the time it takes to train a dog handler, from 80 days down to sometimes just 40 days. This is because handlers are raising and pre-training their own puppies themselves. Because the breeding process is a science, an expert is necessary to examine blood lines and isolate which animals have the genes that will produce the best police dog candidates. With additional resources, the centre can now dedicate one person solely to this task. Currently, one in four dogs the centre breeds goes on to become a police dog. By breeding its own, the centre eliminates the unpredictability that can come with dogs it buys from brokers. Brokers are sometimes unable to provide dogs that meet the RCMP's strict standards and skill requirements.

Most other police forces around the world generally look for dogs that can serve one or two functions. But RCMP dogs mostly German shepherds must be multipurpose, able to perform a minimum of four profiles, or tasks, including tracking, searching, guarding, locating drugs or explosives and apprehending criminals. Some of the dogs are even able to fulfil search and rescue duties during avalanches and other disasters. The responsibilities of police services dogs include locating lost persons; tracking criminals; searching for narcotics, explosives, illicit alcohol and stills, crime scene evidence and lost property; VIP protection; crowd control, in conjunction with tactical troop; hostage situations; avalanche search and rescue; and police/community relations.

Only purebred German shepherds are considered for the RCMP Police Dog General Duties Services. Male dogs are favoured but some females are chosen. In addition to being in perfect physical condition, they must have particular personality traits which make them suitable for police work: even temperament, hunting instinct and sound character are essential. All RCMP dogs are taught to protect their handlers, themselves or to apprehend upon command. Any that display reluctance to do so are not accepted. Other breeds may be used for Specialty Detection teams.

The German shepherd breed displays the versatility, strength and courage that makes it eminently suitable for Canadian police work. Their heavy coats allow them to work under extreme climatic conditions. In addition, their presence seems to have an inhibitive psychological effect on potential wrongdoers. German shepherds trained to apprehend will invariably make a successful arrest despite the fact they are trained only to hold, never to be savage.

The Police Dog Service Training Centre also understands the importance of working closely with its partners. By training teams from outside agencies, both domestic and internationally, 'bridges' can be built and allow all parties involved to better serve the communities of the world that engage us for their protection. Agencies around the world are beginning to recognise the quality of RCMP dogs including the Royal Australian Air Force (RAAF), which visited the centre in 2002. RCMP dogs had the traits that they wanted to further enhance their own dog program. The centre has since provided the RAAF with semen from its own breeds, which has already produced a few litters of puppies. The RCMP is going to see a lot more international collaboration with other agencies looking to exchange genetic material.

The security team for the 2010 Winter Olympics in Vancouver, Canada, included a special group of dogs who work with the Royal Canadian Mounted Police. The RCMP Police Service Dogs used their special training to provide protection no human or machine could match. The Police Dog Service Teams at the Olympics worked in teams with other police professionals in the detection of explosives. They also prepared to deploy in any other type of role that was necessary to protect the public who were at the games or visiting the area at the time. There were more than 50 teams deployed during the Olympic Games with many more working outside the venues. The main function of the dog teams at the Olympics was to ensure the safety of guests and to work as part of a specialised team to ensure all areas are safe and secure.

Dog handlers are regular members who volunteer for this particular duty. Candidates must go through a staffing selection process, which involves meeting certain criteria. Although expertise is acquired through training and experience, a dog handler should have a tolerance towards animals and be capable of appreciating the known dog instincts. There are currently over 400 names on the waiting list for police services dog training. The Police Dog Service Training Centre is staffed by some of the most experienced and best Police Dog Handlers that the RCMP has to offer. No other organisation or agency in Canada has more fully trained and operational police dogs. The RCMP has well over 100 Police Dog Teams, and is therefore in a position to maintain and further develop programs relating to enforcement.

The RCMP Police Dog Service Training Centre has three core functions:

- Dog acquisition

- Training of dog teams

- Annual validation of dog teams

To meet these core functions, they have a number of interdependent programs.

- Dog Acquisition program

- Potential Police Dog Imprinting program

- Potential Police Dog Pre-Training program

- Dog Handler Training program*

  - Narcotic Detection

  - Explosive Detection**

- Dog Handler Retraining program*

- Narcotic Detection

- Explosive Detection**

- Avalanche Search & Rescue program

- Advanced Techniques Training program

- Assistance to outside agencies

- Breeding program

- Specialty Narcotic Detection program*

* These training programs have a mandatory six-month follow-up component.

** All teams trained in explosives detection have a mandatory two-week on-site explosives training.

All teams trained are subject to annual validation(s) of each of their working profiles. Failure to meet the prescribed levels mandate remedial training with follow-up validation.

The Edmonton Police

The Edmonton Police Service (EPS) Canine Unit has a long and proud history which began with a gifted and ambitious man named Maynard 'Val' Vallevand. In 1955 Val joined the EPS with an already great devotion to the training and raising of dogs.

In 1963 Val's dog Sarge became a member of the Edmonton Police Service and Val became the first EPS canine handler. This was after they were called to a drugstore break-in where the members on scene could not locate the culprit. Moments after arriving Sarge located the culprit hiding among some cardboard boxes. Subsequently, Val and police dog Sarge were utilised on a call-out basis.

The Canine Unit was officially formed in 1967 and consisted of three teams. At this time the police service dogs were kennelled at Val's residence. Members would start their shifts by picking up their police dogs at the beginning of the shift and would return them back to Val's at the end of their tour.

In 1977 the unit moved into a central kennel facility near the Municipal Airport. The unit eventually expanded to nine teams and was responsible for the entire City of Edmonton seven days a week, 24 hours a day. Val retired in 1978 as the sergeant in charge of the unit and remained a close friend to the members for many years afterward.

On 14 November 1997 after dedicated and exhaustive efforts the Canine Unit, now ten teams strong, moved into a new state-of-the-art facility. The building was fittingly named the Vallevand Kennels in honour of the unit's founder who passed away on 1 August 1994.

The Edmonton Police Service Canine Unit was officially formed in 1967 by Val Vallevand. Presently there are 12 handler and dog teams and one sergeant, who are stationed at one of the finest kennel facilities in North America. The 11 dogs currently in the unit include 12 general purpose dogs, of which two are cross-trained for narcotic detection.

Members of the Canine Unit provide the citizens of Edmonton with 24 hour a day, seven days a week service. The teams respond to calls that involve tracking, criminal apprehension, area/building searches, evidence searches, and narcotic/explosive detection.

The Edmonton Police Service Canine Unit has a long and proud history with both members and their dedicated partners committed to taking a 'bite out of Crime' in Edmonton.

To become a member of the Canine Unit constables must have a minimum of eight years on the job. During that time constables who have an interest in becoming a dog handler begin training with the unit on their time off as quarries or what you might call potential bad guys.

They learn to lay tracks, take dog bites and hide in the most difficult and uncomfortable places. Quarries with enough seniority may then apply to be puppy holders of potential police service dogs. Due to the high standards set within the unit only the most qualified and dedicated applicants and dogs are accepted. When the puppy reaches one year to one and a half years old the dog and handler enter into an extensive training period.

During training the teams learn to become proficient in the areas of tracking, criminal apprehension, searching, obedience and agility. Presently, Police Service Dogs and their handlers can remain in the unit for up to seven years, which is considered the most productive years of a police dog's life. The primary function of the Canine Unit is to provide support to the patrol officers on the street. The teams respond to any or all crimes in progress where suspects are fleeing on foot or possibly hidden. The unit has expanded its services and now also uses trained narcotic detection and explosive detection dogs.

Bravery Award

On the morning of 31 August 1989, a devastating gas explosion rocked a building in Ottawa, creating considerable structural damage. Much of the building still standing was unusable and in danger of collapsing. Although most of the tenants who were in the building at the time of explosion had been safely evacuated, there were still some people trapped inside.

Rescuers worked quickly and carefully searched for trapped victims, while under the threat of a second explosion.

Constable Joseph Guy Denis Amyot, Dog Handler at A Division (Ottawa), Ottawa Airport Detachment, was off duty when he heard the news reports of the explosion. Volunteering his services and those of police service dog Jocko, he entered the building accompanied by Captain Gerard Patry of the Ottawa Fire Department to search the debris for victims trapped beneath the rubble. Despite the dangers, they searched the most heavily damaged portion of the building for a missing boy, who was later found alive in the rubble.

In recognition of his courage and professionalism, Constable J.G.D. Amyot was awarded a Commissioner's Commendation for Bravery. Captain G. Patry of the Ottawa Fire Department was awarded a Commissioner's Commendation to a Civilian for his courage and assistance to Constable Amyot.

CHILE

The Police Canine Training School of *Carabineros de Chile* (Chilean National Police Force) has had an outstanding trajectory over more than 50 years. The school, called Training Center for Police Dogs, commenced operation 4 July 1956. It was incorporated into the police service with the aim of preparing guides (handlers) and dogs for the completion of support missions for police operations. As a result, this noble animal has become an integral element in the tasks of preserving order and the prevention of crime. Today Chilean police dogs are a true icon in the field of cultural extension, demonstrating their excellent qualities throughout diverse public exhibitions.

In 1991 the training centre became part of the Non Commissioned Officer School of Carabineros de Chile (constituting the seventh police dog training squadron). Then on 30 January 2007 it advanced to the category of Canine Training School, becoming separate from the Non Commissioned School. The objective of this measure was to give better support to the tasks relating to order and security, drug and explosive detection and finding missing persons. Police force members here are focused on the care, reproduction, maintenance and training of the dogs.

Training for the dogs' guides includes knowledge of canine breeds and their characteristics, the proper use of techniques for utilising the animal in police activities and first aid for their faithful companion. For its part the animal is trained in the detection of drugs, searching and signalling, attacking criminals, protecting their guides, locating missing persons, deterrence through visible presence and public exhibitions.

Public demonstrations are often held for varied sectors of the community. They are an opportunity to appreciate the level of training and the perfect synchronisation that the dogs have with their guides.

The history of the program shows that police dogs exhibit an effectiveness of 100 per cent and in certain tasks are indispensable. Their brilliant sense of smell and unique training make these dogs a key aspect in the pursuance of criminals and the detection of explosives and drugs.

The outstanding participation of the police dogs of the *Carabineros de Chile* in continental championships has brought numerous sporting achievements to the institution and has proven the centre to be one of the best in Latin America.

The dogs make fine work of their exceptional abilities of comprehension and execution of orders, which are given by whistles, voice and gesture. The high level of preparation has prompted their inclusion in programs developed by the *Cuadro Verde* (cavalry unit). The excellence of these police dogs is widely recognised in the continent and has generated theoretical and practical exchanges with foreign institutions.

The *Policía de Investigaciones de Chile* (PDI) (Narcotics Brigade) has dogs trained to search for drugs. These dogs are mainly used in anti-drug smuggling operations along the borders and on police drug raids.

The Canine Brigade of Servicio Agrícola y Ganadero (SAG) was implemented in 2005, with the intention of strengthening vigilance for certain points of entry into Chile for organic products which pose a potential risk to the public health.

The dogs are trained by the PDI, which takes three months. It consists of strengthening their natural abilities that are necessary to carry out their work. This is mainly done through a kind of 'play training' where the dogs are rewarded for successfully completing their tasks. During training the dogs are always accompanied by their guides, with whom they will share all of their years of service.

The brigade consists of 36 working teams, each with one guide (handler) and one dog. The years of service of a dog can depend on the area they work in. The breeds used in SAG are labradors and Golden retrievers. These dogs are capable of detecting the scents of 45 different products which enter the country, and have been a part of the operations that saw 17 tons of goods seized in more than 30,000 interceptions during the last four years. Through this work they have prevented the entry of vegetable plagues and animal illnesses.

CHINA

The Chinese Police use dogs for law enforcement and security functions which includes border patroland some military use. At present, there are 4000 police dogs, 408 units with police dogs and 4300 police dog technical personnel all over the country. Police dog techniques are widely used in public security such as searching narcotics, tracking, scent identification, searching and apprehending suspects, searching for explosives, controlling and preventing violence and patrol.

At the foundation of new China the public security organisations took the lead to set up police dog divisions, taking over the police dogs of the police organisations of the Japanese Puppet Regime and of the Kumintang Administrations.

In 1957, the Ministry of Public Security built up two teaching and training teams of police dogs, and introduced some excellent breeding dogs from the former Soviet Union, Democratic Germany, and North Korea.

In 1961 the Ministry of Public Security dispatched a circular on using police dogs, affirming the contributions made by the dogs to solving criminal cases, pursuing escapists, and guarding the frontiers and coastal borders, etc. and stipulating definitely the scope, principle and sanction of police dog uses. By the end of 1965 there were about 1500 police dogs all over the country and during this same period of time China began supplying police dogs to foreign countries.

During the Cultural Revolution, police dog technical work was criticised and was finally stopped in 1968. In 1972 the Ministry of Public Security proposed in that dogs could be used when needed in frontier, coastal and remote areas. This was a step towards resuming police dog work and by 1979 two police dog bases had been re-established.

In 1984 the first National Conference on Police Dog Work was held issuing the Provisional Regulations of Police Dog Work. It was proposed that police dog work be developed as an important part of criminal investigations.

In 1996 the Committee of Police Dog Division of China Criminal Scientific and Technological Association was set up. At the same time there was also a faster development of police dog work in the Chinese People's Liberation Army, Armed Police Forces, customs, railways and forestry canine units.

By 1999 the Ministry of Public Security stated that police dog work is an important component of criminal technical work and has a role that cannot be replaced by other technical means and therefore must be greatly strengthened. As a result, some professional rules and regulations were worked out, such as Rules of Police Dog Breeding, Operating Rules of Police Dog Breeding Management, Rules of Police Dog Selection, Rules of File Management of Police Dog Work (Trial), Stipulations of Propagating Introduced and Original Domestic Breeding Dogs, Methods of Police Dog Earmark Management, Methods of Grading B-level Units of Police Dog Breeding, Rules of Training Police Dogs, Rules of Using Police Dogs, Criterion of Assessing the Training of Breeding Dogs, and Criterion of Assessing the Training of Young Dogs.

In general, the ministry-affiliated police dog bases, research institutes and police dog technical schools take responsibility for directing their corresponding regions in police dog technical work. There are 253 breeding dogs of 6 breeds introduced from Germany, France and Britain for police use, including German shepherd, labrador retriever, Rottweiler, Belgian shepherd (Malinois), Doberman pinscher, and English springer spaniel.

In China, possibly due to its Communist government system, law enforcement is quite complex and frequently duplicated to ensure one department does not have too much authority over another. The main law enforcement agency, the People's Armed Police, known as PAP, is responsible for law enforcement. Internal security comes under the joint control of the Central Military Commission and local police departments. In wartime PAP performs border defence and other support functions to assist the army. A special police unit called the Snow Wolf Commando Unit (SWRU) is tasked with counterterrorism and other special tasks including riot control and bomb disposal, making extensive use of explosive detection dogs. Both PAP and SWRU were seen conducting security at the 2008 Olympics.

Chinese Railway Squad Police patrol along railway stations throughout China with police dogs. These dogs search for narcotic and explosives and prevent crime on transport facilities.

COLUMBIA

In several South American countries there is regular cooperation between military and civilian police dog teams to fight against narcotics. Tracker dogs have been used by specialist police units in the fight against the leftist terrorist organisation , The Revolutionary Armed Forces of Colombia (FARC), which at one stage controlled up to 40 per cent of Columbia. Since President Uribe took office terrorist attacks have gone down by 75 per cent and the area FARC now control has been reduced to jungle areas. US support has assisted Columbia since the 1980s in the fight against cocaine production. The focus now is on anti-terrorist activities and dogs are used to track down FARC camps and supply dumps throughout the jungle.

Dog units are highly specialised and units are inserted via either parachute or helicopter into suspected terrorist occupied areas.

Columbian Police dog training — jumping through fire. Many South American countries make extensive use of dogs to track down terrorist and criminal groups hidden in jungle areas and to locate drug labs and narcotics.

CZECH REPUBLIC

The first police dog handlers in the Czech Republic were service dogs during the Austro-Hungarian monarchy period. In the 1920s the first courses were organised by police dog handlers in the district of Hrady, Czechoslovakia; in subsequent years the school for police dog handlers was based in the village of Pyšely. In 1952 the school moved to the district of Býchory.

The cyncology department provides training to dog handlers and police service dogs (it is also the official horse training centre). It also manages the breeding of dogs, and determines the focus of education and training of police dogs and horses. The department provides breeding dogs for restocking and replacement of police dogs and horses, according to the requirements of the Czech Republic Police departments throughout the country. It also organises the national competition for handler and service dogs and organises canine competitions for individual police departments. Plus it provides the basis of contractual relations, training and other armed forces in the Czech Republic.

Originally dogs were bought from civilian breeders for police work. Given that civilian breeders focused mainly on what the dogs looked like the police decided to breed their own offspring, aiming at perfecting the behavioural characteristics of dogs required for the service. A breeding station was established in 1953. Located in the protected landscape area of the Czech Central Mountains on the left bank of the river Elbe it contains a hospital and the breeding and veterinary dispensary. All dogs that are born here today have the name of the kennel (Plzen) as part of their name.

Initially they started with one female dog; from its inception until now mostly German shepherds have been bred, but the Czech Republic Police have also used Dobermans, beagles, bloodhounds, labrador retrievers and for a short time two wolves. Recently the station has bred litters of Belgian shepherds (Malinois). The maximum capacity was reached at the breeding station in the 1990s with over 200 breeding dogs. Currently there are 12 breeding females. On average, the breeding station each year breeds about 80 puppies. These puppies face rigorous selection criteria in order to become suitable dogs for the police.

Another important part of the Department Staff Cynology is the training centre. Dog handlers are trained and prepared to perform their important tasks. The training centre provides the versatile training program and a special training program. Versatile training is divided into the disciplines of tracking, obedience and defence work. Special training focuses on training dogs to identify and detect certain substances: odour identification, search for drugs and narcotics, search for explosives and improvised explosive devices, weapons search, finding human remains and the detection of accelerants. Handlers in the different types of courses receive varying periods of training, from14 days to 20 weeks.

There are several police dog training centres throughout the Czech Republic. Býchory is the oldest centre. Dogs are trained to be multi-skilled. After completing the course and passing the examination they are categorised as pátracího or patrol dog. The Service Dog Training Centre in Dobrotice was rebuilt in 1993–1994 from the former border troop dog school. The first courses for handler and service dogs started in September 1994. The resort has a scope for 80 dog pens. The centre mainly focuses on training handlers of police dogs. Based on an interdepartmental agreement, it also trains service dogs for the local (municipal) police and prison services. Dogs are trained to be multi-purpose. Some dogs are specially trained to find people hidden in vehicles. These specialists are involved in the Aliens Police. The Alien Police service dogs are used to support the activities of checking the validity of movement of foreigners within the Schengen area, the control of aliens and monitoring compliance of illegal employment of foreigners.

The police dog training centre at Plzen in the White Mountain district was founded in the late 1960s as a service dog training centre for armed railway police. The centre has undergone many changes and is a two-storey building with a capacity of 18 beds for trainees. Currently it specialises in the training of young dogs to supplement the needs of individual police departments.

The Police Department Pyrotechnics is for the protection of constitutional officials and provides security services to protect VIPs. Forty-eight handlers and dogs perform special tasks within the service including explosives detection and patrol work.

Currently the government uses a total of 823 police dogs. Operationally there are around 450 patrol dogs and 160 specialist dogs.

The Czech Republic has used Rottweilers for over a century in its military and police forces and still favours the breed.

DENMARK

The National Police Dog Centre has 425 police dog teams that serve in the Danish National Police, in Greenland, in the Faroe Islands and in the 12 police districts that cover the whole country. The NPC has the responsibility for all national and international tasks concerning police dogs.

The predominant breeds used are German shepherds, labradors and springer spaniels. German shepherd dogs are used for the general purpose role – named patrol dogs. The labradors and springer spaniels are used for drug and explosive detection.

All police dog handlers are experienced police officers who need at least six to eight years of police service before they join a police dog unit. The dog handler buys the dog from private kennels and can be granted financial support from the NPC. It is a requirement that the dog lives at home with the handler.

Training courses and education of the dog handlers and their dogs are conducted at the Danish National Police Dog Training Centre in Farum, north of Copenhagen, and in the districts.

A few months after joining a police dog unit all new recruit handlers receive basic training at the National Police Training Centre. The training philosophy used by the police is based on positive reinforcement. Dogs are required to be highly socialised, strong in any environment, with a high prey and retrieve drive. All dogs have to pass a mental and medical test before they are recruited.

The police dog team (dog and handler) must pass a basic test before being employed in the service. After passing the first test, annual tests are conducted to ensure that the police dog teams are able to manage and solve the tasks they face at work.

The training centre creates specific training programs for dogs working in the police districts according to their needs.

Police dogs are divided into three categories:

- Patrol dogs

- Drug detection dogs

- Explosive dogs

The patrol dogs are divided into three groups: the young dogs in group 3, the more experienced in group 2, and the highly experienced dogs in group 1.

All the patrol dogs are trained in:

- Searching for missing persons, dead or alive

- Searching for escaped suspected persons

- Apprehending suspects

- Defending their handler and other police officers

- Locating a crime scene and/or finding traces and items on a crime scene

The patrol dogs in group 3 are not used in searching for missing people or attend crime scenes. When the dog has been in group 3 for a year it has to pass a test in order to be placed in group 2. The dog can stay in group 2 till it retires.

It is voluntary for the dog handler to take the dog to the level of group 1. It demands much more skill from the dog and handler. There is high demand for the dogs and their dog handlers that are able to support officers at the crime scene. These dogs have proven their value by finding bodies, body parts, hair, human blood, seminal fluid and small items.

Drug detection dogs are an efficient tool used to locate any kind of illegal drug. The dogs have a preventive role and are used daily as support to the criminal investigators working with drugs.

Explosive detection dogs are trained to indicate the presence of explosives in a passive way – looking at the source of the scent. The dogs are used as a preventive measure and to locate explosives at crime scenes.

In order to respond to the needs at the crime scene some police dogs are trained to locate items and human remains that have been buried in the ground for a long period of time.

The Danish K9 Association was founded in 1909; its purpose is to:

- Create interest for breeding and training of police dogs, their practical use in police work and for civil members

- Test civil dogs and keep the police dog pedigree up to date. The tests of the civil dogs are to be seen as a work dog test

- Organise competitions related to practical police dog work

- Seek cooperation in competitions and police dog work with similar associations domestically and abroad

The association is divided into 7 areas and 51 local associations. The local associations are spread all over Denmark. At the end of 2006 the Danish K9 Association had 2101 members. In section 1 (police officers with K9s in duty) there are 184 members, with 1766 in section 2 (civil and police officers with K9s not trained for police work). In addition to these the association had 151 associate members. The association has its own magazine called *Politihunden*.

ESTONIA

In 1923, the Estonian Service Dogs Training Centre Training Facility was established. The dogs and dog handlers were trained in guarding and protection work as well as in searching skills. Within four years, there were 15 fully trained service dogs and handlers on the border. The border guard training sector was established in the summer of 1930 in the Petseri sector in Irboska where the work with service dogs has continued. The training of the service dogs was taken very seriously.

After Independence in August 1992 the border guard dog training commenced at the Neeme Border Guard Dogs Training Centre (BDTC).

In 2006 BDTC was joined to the Public Service Academy (Academy of Security Sciences) and the official name became the Service Dogs Training Centre of the Public Service Academy. The Estonian Public Service Academy is a public security and safety educational and research institution. At the academy, it is possible to get a higher education in one of the seven regular curriculum specialties of public service: police, border guard, rescue service, customs, tax administration, corrections and public administration. The academy has six colleges — Police, Border guard, Rescue, Judicial, Public Administration and Financial Colleges — with more than 1500 students.

The academy trains dog handlers and the border guard dogs as patrol dogs, drug dogs and rescue dogs. The patrol dogs must be able to detect a track after various time intervals and environmental conditions. The drug dogs must find the drugs wherever they are such as in cars, in luggage, in travellers' clothing or in houses. The rescue dogs search for people who have disappeared in a forest or the same dogs must be able to search at a checkpoint for people who have hidden themselves in vehicles – illegal immigrants.

The Service Dogs Training Centre of the Estonian Academy of Security Sciences was established in 2005 as a training service for dogs and dog handlers under the Border Guard Board. In 2007, the school moved to the newly built centre in the premises of the then Muraste Border Guard School. In 2008, the Department of Criminal Cynology of the Personal Protection Service was merged into the Service Dog Training Centre and now police and border guard service dogs and handlers are all trained in Muraste. In addition to training, service dog assessments and professional championships are organised. Service dogs have three duties:

- Searching for human scent

- Drug detection

- Use-of-force training

Responsibility for training service dogs is shared between several departments including the Tax and Customs Board, the Prisons Department of the Ministry of Justice and with the Explosive Ordnance Disposal Unit Board. Cooperation with foreign countries includes having regular training with the Swedish, Danish and Finnish police dog training centres and the Finnish Marine and Border Guard School. The centre also has a strong relationship with Latvian and Lithuanian centres for training border guard service dogs.

FINLAND

There are about 240 police dog handlers in Finland; however, the Finnish Police have about 300 dogs at any one time. The German shepherd and Belgian shepherd (Malinois) are the most widely used breeds of police dog. Certain local/native hunting dogs have also been given special training.

The Police Dog Training Centre comes under the Police College of Finland. The task of the Police Dog Training Centre is to train the dog handlers, acquire all the police dogs needed and develop police dog operations. In addition to this, the Police Dog Training Centre monitors the standard of police dog training and the professional skills of the dog handlers, and maintains contact with various authorities and other stakeholder groups.

Police dog operations in Finland started in 1905, when the first police dog was brought to the Helsinki Police Department from Germany. Officially the Police Dog Training Centre started operations in 1909. It has been located in its present location in Rinkelinmäki in Hämeenlinna since 1927. The Police Dog Training Centre comprises training areas, a training building, an obstacle course, classrooms and accommodation facilities, an office and a kennel. There is space for 41 dogs. The Police Dog Training Centre has a staff of 13.

Most of the dogs are bought from private individuals or breeders. The dogs are usually acquired as puppies or at the age of about one or two years. Dogs are bought both from Finland and abroad. The Police Dog Training Centre acquires all the dogs that are trained as police dogs.

Every year, about 50–70 dogs are acquired, half of them as puppies. The Police Dog Training Centre is constantly buying dogs of breeds that are used as service dogs. Dogs that are to be trained as police dogs must be healthy and receptive to training. The dogs may have a background in service dog activities or as family pets. Adult dogs offered as police dogs are subjected to an entrance examination and, if they pass, remain with their new handler for a trial period of about one month. The dog starts in training if it is healthy and has the makings of a police dog.

The dogs live with their handlers as members of their families and they work with their handlers. The dogs enjoy their work, especially as it gives them plenty of stimulation and things to do. Their physical condition is also maintained with great care. They are fed on high-quality dry feeds and their health is monitored continuously. Police dogs retire at the age of ten, when they usually continue to live with their handler and enjoy a well-earned retirement.

Police dog training consists of basic and special training. The basic training of patrol dogs is made up of five main elements: obedience, use of force, tracking, search and rescue, and article and crime scene searches.

The patrol dogs are trained for multiple tasks: obedience, tracking, search and rescue operations, searching for articles and crime scene searches, as well as protection, where the dogs are trained for use in situations where the police have to use force. The patrol dogs are also trained in one special area, either searching for narcotics, explosives or cadavers (human remains). The special police dogs are trained in obedience and one special area, e.g. searching for narcotics, explosives, or searching for traces of flammable liquids or scent identification work.

Most patrol dogs are trained to search for narcotics. The dogs are capable of finding substances (or their derivatives) in various circumstances and conditions.

The requirements for becoming a police dog handler are a Diploma in Police Studies from the Police College in Tampere and about three years' work experience, ideally in both security work and investigation.

Dog handlers are expected to make a long-term commitment to their line of work, as they should ideally continue in their position until their dog retires. It is important that they are responsible and calm, since they will be working with a dog. Good physical condition and initiative are also important. Finally, a sense of humour and playfulness are never a bad thing when you are working with a dog.

The position of dog handler is highly rated and very popular. There are about 230 police dog handlers in Finland, and about 15 new dog handlers graduate every year.

It takes one and a half years to complete the training program for a police dog handler, and 12 weeks of this time are contact hours at the Police Dog Training Centre. Before starting the basic training, the student dog handler will have had the dog for some months.

During the training program, the dog takes the official behaviour test for police dogs and the official stamina test.

The work of a police dog handler differs in essential ways from other special police duties, since dog handlers must work on the dog's terms. A dog patrol team consists of a dog handler and a single dog. They perform tasks that are relayed to them by the emergency centres. The police dogs are the property of the Police Dog Training Centre, which places them with the police districts, specifically with individual dog handlers. Dog handlers are responsible for training their dogs and maintaining their skills level.

Dog handlers train their dogs in their spare time and during special times reserved for dog training and practice. At best, the work of a dog handler is a lifestyle choice that is a seamless combination of work and leisure-time activities.

Police dog handlers are allowed to pursue various leisure-time activities with their patrol dogs, and many handlers and their dogs compete in civilian life in competitions for service dogs, rescue dogs and skijoring competitions (where a dog in harness pulls a cross-country skier), for instance. Dog handlers may also enter their dogs in dog shows.

The police dog handlers have their own registered association, The Finnish Police Dog Association. Together with the Police Dog Training Centre, the association arranges annual championships for police dogs. The coveted title of overall champion is won by the dog-and-handler team that gets the best total result in all four sections of the competition: obedience, protection, tracking and searching.

There is also an annual event where all the Nordic countries compete; each of these countries takes turns to arrange the Nordic championships for police dogs, and the participating countries send three-man teams to compete. Police narcotics dogs also compete in Finnish and Nordic championships.

French Police Special Response Team dogs are dual trained to locate explosives and to attack offenders.

FRANCE

The French National Police or *Police Nationale* is the main civil law enforcement agency within France with its primary jurisdiction in cities and large towns, while the Gendarmerie has jurisdiction in smaller towns and rural and border areas.

The (French) National Gendarmerie has a canine unit called the National Centre for Canine Section of the Gendarmerie (CNICG). It was established in December 1945 and is located in Gramat. The Gendarmerie operates approximately 41 groups of dog teams totalling 645 dogs.

The CNICG Centre at Gramat is responsible for:

- Recruitment and medical care of dogs

- Selection, orientation, team-building and initial technical training

- Education and training of dog handlers

- Technical and statistical monitoring of operational teams

- Training of military personnel and civilian agencies

The CNICG provides 14-week training courses, refresher courses, training for foreign delegations and specialised training of the Gendarmerie, and specialist training in:

- Defence

- Tracing

- Avalanche rescue

- Guard patrol

- Assault (GIGN)

- Search for human remains

- Search for arms and ammunition

- Search for drugs

- Search for explosives

- Search for accelerant products

Within the French police or Gendarmerie, the National Gendarmerie Intervention Group, commonly abbreviated to GIGN, operates various specialist units for its hostage rescue and anti-terrorist roles including elite canine teams.

GERMANY

The success of dogs in curbing gang violence led to their use in Germany in 1896. It was in Germany that the first scientific and planned development in this field took place with experiments in breeding, training and utilisation. Through their experiments with dogs in police work, the Germans selected the German shepherd as the breed best suited for the assigned duties, and the Doberman pinscher as second choice.

Police dogs were first used in Germany in 1901 in the town of Schwelm. It was a German mastiff named Caesar. As early as 1910, the Berlin Police had 100 police dogs and in 1909 the Prussian school for police dogs in Grünheide in Berlin was established. It was the first training school for dogs to be used in the field of law enforcement. Here the dogs were trained in basic obedience, tracking and searching. From this school came the plans and criteria for those to come and much of the training system used in modern dog section operations has been taken from Grünheide.

Police dogs deploy from various modes of transport including police air and maritime assets. Here a German Police dog leaps from a helicopter and secures a high risk criminal.

The school operated under the guise of training German civil and railroad policemen, so as not to publically violate the WWI Versailles Treaty. A small number of army K9 units were also trained, but not in large numbers that would arouse the Western powers' attention. The National Socialists then formed their own training camps, and K9 units were formed under the guise of being public work units. In 1936 all police forces within the Third Reich were formally consolidated under the control of the SS. Throughout the war police dogs were used on the home front as crime still existed; however, to many the lasting image is of police dogs being used to guard concentration camps.

Dogs were also used by the German Railway Police as early as 1923 to patrol train stations, waiting rooms and railway cars. Each of the 700 teams of dogs and handlers underwent yearly examination by Reichsbahninspektor Langner, and teams that were incompatible were disbanded. The K9 training methods developed by Langner became recognised worldwide.

In 1948 Berlin was divided politically and two independently working police authorities were established in West and East Berlin. In west Berlin training continued at the Tegal facility while the guide dog service from Berlin (East) moved into the 'teaching and Abrichteanstalt for service dogs' at the S-Bahn station Wuhlheide. In 1953 the police needed to expand its service dog numbers. The increase in staffing levels from 90 to 120 service dog teams required space for a larger kennel so a new facility was built in the police compound in Schulzendorf.

In 1973 there were major police reforms and many police stations were closed. The service dog came under the Directorate of Public Safety/Traffic. The service dog command was divided into four platoons. They were housed in different locations and motorised accordingly. In the same year the first training of narcotics search dogs started. This was necessary because drug crime greatly increased in the early 1970s. Also in the context of police reform, the cadaver dog search of the criminal investigation units were turned over to the service dog command. The next several years were marked by rising crime, so service dog units were enhanced by numbers and various roles. Dogs for narcotics search, cadaver search and explosives detection dogs were established. The preparations begin for the training of their own explosives detection dogs in 1986. Up to this point, explosive search dogs arrived in Berlin from West Germany or service dogs in the US armed forces were used.

In 1985 a new, larger kennels for housing service dogs was completed. The plant in Schulzendorf was abandoned. In 1989 with the merger of the service dogs of East and West Germany many dogs from East Berlin and other provinces were transferred (around 248 teams) to the Federal Police, to the training facility of Falkenberg/Hohenschönhausen. In 1996 the service dog training again moved back to Ruhleben.

Approximately 500 working dogs are used in the Federal Police at present. Most of the dogs are German shepherds. Other dog breeds are also used such as Dutch shepherd, German wirehaired pointer, giant schnauzer and Rottweiler. They accompany their handlers on daily missions in railway facilities, at airports, at the border or in physical security. Most working dogs live with the families of their handlers. Basic and advanced training is performed under the supervision of the Federal Police Academy at the Federal Police canine schools in Bleckede (Lower Saxony) and Neuendettelsau (Bavaria) where dogs and handlers go through patrol dog and explosive detection courses.

The Bundespolizei is the primary federal law enforcement agency in Germany. Other and more numerous policing agencies within Germany are administered at the state level and are known as Landespolizei. They use dogs similar to any police force worldwide to aid investigations and to fight crime.

Today in Germany police dogs are trained to export to foreign countries as well as supplying untrained pure breed dogs for breeding or that countries own training regime. In 2010 Germany supplied specialist detection dogs to Pakistan. A special unit of sniffer dogs trained to help trace terrorists and hidden explosives has been handed over to the special branch of the Sindh police.

The Sindh police has also imported 12 dogs, aged between five months to one year, from Germany. The Pakistan Army will train the dogs at Garden Police Headquarters, where a special unit has been set up.

GREECE

The Hellenic Police assumed its present structure in 1984 when the Gendarmerie (Chorofylaki) and the Urban Police Forces (Astynomia Poleon) were merged. Hellenic Police comprises both central and regional services. In its continuous mission to serve and protect citizens, the Hellenic Police has responded to the times by improving training, adopting a modern crime prevention policy, better utilising science and technology and by exploiting international law enforcement cooperation. As such it maintains a unit of police dogs. In recent months the image of Greek police in riots using dogs has somewhat tarnished their image; however, it is in these very circumstances that dogs are worth their weight in gold.

The Hellenic Police uses specially trained dogs in order to guard or identify people or items as well as to detect drugs and explosive materials. Each police dog has its own handler, who is a specially trained policeman. The dog is an integrated part of the handler's family. The police mainly use Malinois or German shepherd dogs to guard and identify people or items, and German shepherds, labradors, Malinois or golden retrievers to detect drugs and explosive materials.

HONG KONG

The Police Dog Unit (PDU) in Hong Kong was established in 1949. Members work in collaboration with other departments in anti-crime operations. During this time and up until the recent British withdrawal the Royal Army Veterinary

Corps jointly conducted border patrol operations using military working dogs. The PDU in Hong Kong today operates both explosive and narcotic detection dog teams as well as general purpose patrol dogs.

In 1949 when it became apparent that dogs would be useful in policing the border area, four German shepherd breed patrol dogs were purchased and a civilian trainer recruited. These dogs were used solely in the New Territories, and were kennelled in Fan Gardens located at the old New Territories Police Depot, Fanling.

After the scheme was proved to be successful, a decision was then made to expand the unit and establish a headquarters at the Pat Heung Police Station, Yuen Long in 1956. The unit subsequently moved to Ping Shan Police Station in 1964 when further expansion required additional facilities. There it stayed until 1995 when it was relocated to the former British Army barracks in Queen's Hill Camp, Fanling. In 2001 the PDU moved to its Provisional Headquarters to Cheung Yip Street in Kowloon Bay and at the end of 2003, the PDU finally moved into its new Headquarters in Sha Ling in the Northern District, complete with an office block, a medical centre for police dogs and training grounds. The extensive grounds allow all police dogs to undergo the widest possible range of the latest training techniques. From its humble beginnings of only four police dogs, the PDU has developed into a mature unit with more than 100 police dogs in active service today.

In the early years, like police dog units elsewhere, the fledgling PDU consisted mainly of German shepherds, also known as Alsatians. German shepherds are loyal, brave and their martial bearing is a great asset to policemen on patrol or riot control duties. However, springer spaniels and labrador retrievers are used in searches for narcotics and dangerous explosives because of their superior sense of smell compared with other breeds.

In recent years the PDU has recruited Malinois as police dogs. Over the past few decades the Malinois breed has been improved, through cross-breeding with Dutch shepherds, German shepherds and great danes, and it is now a medium-sized dog with greater agility. Malinois are also longer-lived, with an average life span of 13 years, and are more able-bodied and less susceptible to diseases and injuries. Apart from being a loyal and friendly dog, it is also very intelligent, highly obedient and easy to train, which is why it is widely used as a working dog nowadays.

'Puppy Outwalk' is a program designed to ensure that puppies bred by the Hong Kong Police Dog Unit receive the care and support necessary for the development of sound character and working temperament. At the tender age of between seven to eight weeks, police puppies are placed under the care of carefully selected host families whose members are willing to devote their time and energy to raise the puppy properly. After about a year, the full-grown puppies are then returned to the unit to commence their formal training.

Apart from undergoing training and performing their daily duties like patrols and police searches, police dogs also take part in community and public relations events like District Fight Crime Carnivals and Crime Prevention activities, to assist in disseminating information on crime prevention and crime fighting to members of the public.

The Hong Kong Police have long used dogs in policing. The British originally used K9s to stop illegal immigrants and as narcotic detection and general police dogs in the cities. Today the New Territories Government has taken over many of the British dog programs and facilities.

HUNGARY

In Hungary, the deployment of service dogs was widespread by the armed forces — the police, the gendarmerie, and the border guard — between the two world wars.

From 1926, the centre of police dog breeding and training was at the Kispest Police Office. They were very proud of their four-year-old puli that won the working dog competition held in Vienna in 1934. By the end of the 1930s, there were 28 trained police dogs deployed at the Újpest Police Office, 20 at the Pesterzsébet and 30 at the Csepel Police Office.

The police service dog training and deployment was started by the Kispest Police Office in January 1945, with eight dogs. The Kispest Police Office wasn't large enough for accommodating and training the dogs so the construction of a new building was started in 1947 in Budaörs, with dog training courses starting in 1948.

The first six-month patrol dog handler course started on 15 February 1949 under rather harsh circumstances. The aim of this course was to train the dogs in patrol and observation — searching various areas and landmarks, capturing, escorting and guarding a fleeing person. The course consisted of obedience, obstacle, protection exercises and nose work.

Dogs were purchased and breeding began in 1949 at Törökugrató; its purpose was to increase the number and improve the quality of service dogs. Those dogs that performed the best became breeding animals.

The law enforcement agencies urged the increase of the service dogs. In 1950, the armed forces needed 220 dogs and dog handlers to be trained. These demands couldn't be met at Törökugrató. After having gathered the necessary information and designs, a so called dog yard was constructed in Dunakeszi-Alag. Training and supply staff were employed enabling the training and dog breeding in Dunakeszi to commence by April 1951. In 1952–53 the training palette was broadened with the police patrol dog, tracking dog handler, and military and prison guard dog handler courses. Modification of the organisation and the expansion of the staff were also necessary.

In 1971, the Dog Handlers Training School was an educational institution of the Ministry of Interior with special training tasks. In those days, the principal task of the Dog Handlers Training School was to provide the basic and periodical refresher training of patrol, guard, tracking and other specialist dogs and dog handlers working in several kinds of services of the Hungarian armed forces and bodies as well as surveillance organisations. The aim of the school was that with all of the skill collectively in the centre they would be able to teach many roles in the defence of law and order as well as in other professional fields.

Almost all of the old buildings were renovated and modernised between 1971 and 1982 and the area of the school was enlarged to 20 hectares and some new buildings were built. The syllabi were updated in 1989, in order to modernise the training and raise standards in:

- Scent identification dog training

- Patrol dog training and deployment (for border guards)

- Patrol dog training deployment (for police officers)

- Explosives searching dog handler training

- Animal health

- First aid

The training of mine rescue dogs and search dogs arose as new tasks and an explosives detection dog handler course was held for the Ministry of Interior of Czechoslovakia.

In 1997, the school started crime scene investigator training and the Central school of instruction Training Centre was established. The yearly training plans were prepared according to the requests and demands of the Hungarian law enforcement agencies. Per annum, the educational institution is able to provide the basic training of 400 dog handlers and dogs, and the refresher training of 500 dog handlers and dogs.

Mostly the following dog breeds are trained for police service purposes: German shepherd, Rottweiler, Schnauzer, Doberman, labrador retriever and spaniel.

In 2006, there was a restructuring process within the police structure and the school was renamed as the Hungarian National Police HQ Directorate of Education. There was another restructuring process in 2011 and the institution got a new name: Hungarian National Police HQ Dunakeszi Training Centre. The centre provides training in nine main fields of expertise:

- Dog handling (tracking, explosives searching, drug searching, scent identification, patrol, SWAT, cadaver searching, general purpose, guard)

- Crime scene investigation

- Traffic accident scene investigation

- Duty commissioned officers and non-commissioned officers, prison officers, escort officers

- ADR (International Carriage of Dangerous Goods by Road), AETR (European Agreement concerning the Work of Crews of Vehicles Engaged in International Road Transport), ADN (European Agreement concerning the International Carriage of Dangerous Goods by Inland Waterways)

In the past 63 years, Hungary has developed active international relations in the field of dog and dog handler training. They have been contributing to the training of dog handlers and police dogs in recent times for the following countries: Slovakia, Czech Republic, Poland, Estonia, Romania, Uzbekistan, Mongolia, Bosnia and Herzegovina, Austria, France, Belgium, Finland, and Netherlands. They have contributed to the establishment of the training school for dog handlers of Uzbekistan as well.

Due to its international presence, Hungary was asked to contribute to the United Nations Office of Drugs and Crime project, involved in the project 'Developing effective drug searching dog programmes in Central Europe'. The Regional Implementing Agency of the project was the Hungarian National Police Headquarters Dog Handlers Training School (now Dunakeszi Training Centre). One of the high priority projects was the preparation of training materials regarding the training of drug searching dog teams. The package consists of a video educational film a teacher's handbook and a manual.

INDIA

Police dogs in India are well established and are employed in most of the many law enforcement agencies throughout the country. Most police dogs in India are employed in riot suppression role or the detection of explosives.

The security scenario in the country calls for employing diverse equipment and methods to provide adequate security to vulnerable places and persons. The loyalty and sniffing qualities of a dog, combined with its ability to receive training and act according to the orders of the master, has given this animal a position of great importance in all Indian security systems. Experience and time have proved that a well-trained dog is the most reliable and efficient component of any security apparatus. However, there is a shortage of centres for training of dogs for security duties in India.

To fill this gap between demand and supply, the Punjab Police Academy, Phillaur, has performed the dual role of 'Dog Breeding-cum-Training Centre' since January 1999. It was formally inaugurated by the then Director General of Police Punjab, on 4 April 2000. This centre is situated on the campus of the Punjab Police Academy and is run by a team of highly trained and committed dog-trainers. The centre specialises in training dogs for various purposes related to security and general training of dogs of all breeds. Highly pedigreed dogs/pups of the champion/imported class are procured from German shepherd, labrador, Dalmatian and Doberman Pincher breeds and are trained at the centre.

In New Delhi, dogs definitely added teeth to the Commonwealth Games security. They were used to sniff out explosives, conduct anti-sabotage duties and vehicle checks and help sanitise the Games village, stadiums, hotels and parking lots. Seventy-five more canines were added to the dog squad of the capital's police to provide foolproof security during the 2010 sporting extravaganza. With this, the total number of dogs with the New Delhi Police has gone up to 123.

The dogs were trained to provide security at all the Games venues, city markets, parking areas and VIP routes. The dogs, which include German shepherds, labradors and Dobermans, have been undergoing training at the paramilitary Border Security Force — academies in Tekanpur in Madhya Pradesh and Hoshiarpur in Punjab.

It was decided that the 48-odd dogs with Delhi Police were not enough for a city with a population of 17 million as most of these were deployed on VIP routes. According to police, the home affairs ministry sanctioned a piece of land at Saket for the kennels. However, the future of the dogs after the Games is not clear as the construction of permanent kennels in Saket is in a limbo.

Seven well-trained dogs from the Indian Army's veterinary corps were also acquired by the police over the Games period.

The ramped-up dog squad will also ease the pressure on the existing overworked squad which attended to 12,429 calls last year, including 709 tracking calls and 11,009 explosives calls. It also performed anti-sabotage checks during several VIP functions and visits. Each district has a dog squad.

The Gujarat Police will soon have an independent cadre of dog handlers, which will be unique to the state. The aim is to professionalise dog handling in the police force. As many as 100 dog handlers will be recruited for this specialised cadre, and nearly 100 canines of breeds like labradors, Alsatians and bulldogs will be acquired by the state police. The department has 70 dogs at present and plans to increase the strength to 150 dogs.

State police chief SS Khandwawala said this about the special Dog Handling Unit that will be set up by this year: 'In this cadre, constables and assistant inspectors would be recruited as dog handlers and would gradually rise in the hierarchy. State police forces across the country have deployed constables as dog handlers in Dog Squads and other police services. This will give them a chance to rise to a senior level in this specialised unit. After being recruited here, they will not be transferred to any other department or unit. We will choose candidates carefully and only recruit those who have a genuine liking for dogs and other animals.'

INDONESIA

POLRI, the Indonesian National Police, was incorporated into the armed forces in 1964 during the Sukarno era. As part of the army, the Police Force assumed all aspects of military structure, including ranks, budget, duties and even wage structure. On 1 April 1999, POLRI was separated from the Indonesian armed forces. Although POLRI has been separated from the army, it remains under the jurisdiction of the Defence Minister, General Wiranto.

The present K9 Police directorate is also responsible for the Horse Mounted branch of the police. Their vision is the realisation of a K9 unit and mounted police that is reliable, professional, moral and modern to support the INP in its operational function, protecting, caring and serving the community.

The inspectorate for K9 and mounted police was established in 1952 in East Java, which was commanding the use of dogs to assist police tasks. The early strength was four dogs from the Bouvier de Flanders and one German shepherd.

A veterinarian from the army was also assigned to the dog brigade and to command the K9 unit. Senior Inspector R Soedhono and Police Senior Inspector RJ Soedarjanto were appointed; both had completed special training overseas (Italy, West Germany and Austria).

However, the use of dogs in police work raised some doubts because many people in this predominantly Muslim country believed that man's best friends were *haram*, or forbidden under Islam. (Even as late as 1986 when I trained some drug detection dogs for several South East Asian countries including Indonesia and Brunei, the handlers they sent to the training school in New Zealand were none-Muslims.)

The ministry issued a decree in 1956 stating that based on verses from the Koran and the Hadist — a collection of sayings by the Prophet Muhammad — the use of trained dogs is allowed for hunting food and activities for the greater good of society.

With that decree as support, the K9 Brigade — its original name — was formally established on 4 July 1959, with the formation of a special canine training unit at Kepala Dua. In 1966, the name was changed from K9 Brigade to Animal Brigade and horses and carrier pigeons were added to the squad, although the use of the latter was discontinued in 1980. In 1985, the unit was renamed the Animal Police and assigned as a sub-directorate of the National Police.

Since its establishment, the unit has assisted the police and the Armed Forces in operations against insurgent groups, drug trafficking and DVD counterfeiting, and taken part in security sweeps for foreign dignitary visits and international events.

Breeds recruited for the unit are German shepherds, Weimaraners, Doberman pinschers, Rottweilers, Belgian shepherds (Malinois), golden retrievers, labrador retrievers and beagles. The last three breeds are used for the special detection group, mostly to sniff out drugs and explosives, while the former are part of a general detection group that tracks criminal evidence. This includes two Weimaraners that work as cadaver dogs, detecting human remains.

When considering a particular dog, a recruitment team that comprises a vet, a handler and instructors judges the dog's ability and aggressiveness.

Training for the dogs includes detecting substances that have been carefully hidden or planted, so they must learn the scents of drugs and explosives that are commonly circulated and used. The dogs were exposed to 40 explosive substances, including trinitrotoluene (TNT), research development explosive (RDX), pentaerythritol tetra nitrate (PETN) and plastic explosive Composition 4 or C-4.

'A dog can actually detect and distinguish up to 19,000 chemical substances and explosives used to assemble a bomb,' says Djoko, the unit's veterinarian.

Molly, a male beagle and the only small- to medium-size breed in the pack, detects illicit drugs with her handler, Second Brig. Didin Rosidin, who uses English as his language of instruction with the dog. The 18-month-old dog is the first beagle — known for their keen sense of smell — the squad has had, and is trained to scratch a spot or package if it detects illicit drugs.

A rookie handler and dog must undergo basic training for three months at the K9 police training centre in Gunung Putri, Bogor, before the officer earns the title *pawing*. Then they go through another three months of specialist training in detecting explosives, drugs, criminal evidence, human remains or even polycarbonate optical discs such as DVDs to track down bootleg recordings.

Once a dog is selected and assigned to a handler, they become permanent partners, even after the dog is retired because of age or injury.

'A handler cares for his canine partner until it dies, before he is assigned to a new dog,' Djoko said. Retired police dogs cannot be adopted as family pets because they are classified as state inventory. Djoko says that recruitment for would-be handlers also includes psychological testing to determine if they like animals. 'However, we would be glad to accept a police officer that shows genuine interest [even if they are unfamiliar with dogs] to join the squad. To like animals is a special quality that not all people have.'

IRAQ

For years, US military commanders have been urging the Iraqi forces to incorporate more dogs into their security program. The Iraqi security forces first formed a K9 unit in the 1970s, but they scarcely used them. As in many Muslim countries, Iraqis generally see dogs as unclean animals; some of the religiously devout point to the teachings of the prophet Mohammed that prohibited believers from keeping the animals in their homes.

The streets of the capital are filled with mangy canines, but dog owners are few. But in a country where bombs and explosives are an everyday threat, Iraqis may start learning to love man's best friend. Iraq's newest weapon against the ever-evolving improvised explosive device may be the guest never invited indoors: the dog. It is said among Iraqis, however, that if a dog touches a serving dish, the dish must be scrubbed with sand and set in the sun for 40 days. Pet a dog after washing for prayer, and you must wash again, and scrub your whole body too. Dogs considered 'inside dogs' are kept in the yard or garden or upstairs on a third floor with no furniture. They don't really see the inside of the house.

When I was in the military under the United Nations Forces in Mogadishu, Somalia (also a Muslim country people) people were so terrified of our patrol dogs that one team could quell a riot just by being present.

Iraqis, however, recognise that dogs' keen sense of smell makes them invaluable weapons in thwarting terrorists whose calling cards are roadside bombs and explosively rigged vehicles. The effective use of the K9 teams provides a deterrent impact, as well as the ability to 'clear an area' prior to a major event such as a conference.

Today the canine program is run by the Ministry of the Interior. Some of the newest students walking around campus at Baghdad's police college have special skills, an important mission and four legs. A 45-day training program that teams K9 service dogs with Iraqi police for explosive detection operations has proven so successful the program is growing by leaps and bounds. So far, dozens of dogs are hard at work in 12 provinces around Iraq. The Iraqi police force hopes to introduce 1000 bomb-sniffing dogs and their handlers on the streets of Iraq within five years. That's not a lot of dogs for a country of 29 million people, but in Iraq it is. There was some concern before starting the program that there wouldn't be enough police officers interested in training as dog handlers; however, for the last selection program 60 volunteers applied for 25 spots. And 120 more bomb-sniffing German shepherds, Malinois and labradors are scheduled to be incorporated into Iraq's police force by the end of 2010, nearly all imported from the USA.

In the next few months the US is sending 145 more K9 students from Indiana along with veterinarians and experienced American police K9 advisors. 'There is no better investment to countering the threats of bombs and explosives,' said Col. Randy Twitchell, chief US military adviser to the Baghdad Police College. 'The Iraqi security forces are recognising how useful a role dogs can play in securing the country.'

The recent embrace by Iraqi security officials has been welcomed by the US military, which is paying $12,000 for each dog. The vast majority of bomb-sniffing dogs being used at Iraq's airports are owned by foreign contractors. Over time, those contractors will be phased out and replaced by Iraqi government-owned dogs and their police handlers.

The Ministry of the Interior's curriculum includes training more veterinarians and police who can lead K9 units. Credit for Iraq's police dog initiative is largely due to Iraqi Brigadier General Mohammad Mossheb involvement in the program. The commander of the K9 unit at Baghdad Police College was the one and only veterinarian working for the ministry since the mid-1980s. He has led an assessment team to do the pre-checks on the kennel facilities in each province scheduled to receive explosive detection K9s and reviews the qualifications packets on *shurta* (Iraqi police) nominated to become dog handlers. Additionally, BG Mohammed has arranged contracts for dog food and medicines needed for the wellbeing of these new Iraqi assets.

One of Iraq's newest K9 units, a five-man Anbar unit, stood up in 2010 after the handlers completed a 45-day course at the Baghdad Police College. This new Iraqi unit often trains with a US Army Military Police K9 unit attached to 1st Advise and Assist Brigade, 82nd Airborne Division, at Camp Ramadi. Within three days they found their first explosives cache. Another local story of success from this one unit, a 15-year-old boy had walked up to an Iraqi Army checkpoint and handed over a suicide belt to the soldiers. He told them he could lead them to the two women who gave him the belt, along with instructions on how and what to blow up. Kennel master Maj or Mohammad Ali Hamadi explained what happened next: 'The dog picked the woman out of a 10-woman line-up many times. Then I had her move to another place in case the smell was in the ground and she was innocent, but the dog kept indicating that the scent was coming from her; not only one dog, but three.

'They brought another older and younger woman in. He sniffed around them but came back to the first woman. She changed clothes, but the same thing happened,' he said. 'I [feel] like the wealthiest man on earth because of what we have achieved and the innocent lives we saved.'

The dogs of the Anbar K9 Unit are typical of those used in the Iraqi K9 program. Handler Hussein's dog, Arko, is a boisterous, energetic German shepherd whose personality, his handler says, is 'heroic'. Anbar is scheduled to receive an additional 21 dogs and handlers.

ISRAEL

Israel has a countrywide national police force that is subordinate to the Minister of Internal Security. Its two main areas of responsibility are law enforcement and public service. The work of the police includes the war on crime, enforcing traffic laws, maintaining public order, preventing road accidents and attending to problems pertaining to the quality of life (environmental hazards, conflicts between neighbours, etc.).

Army and Border Police use dogs in attack and detection roles. The police operate the smallest unit ,most of their dogs have been purchased directly from the USA, usually fully trained.

In Israel police dogs were not initially embraced due to the image of guard dogs from the concentration camps. But now the Israeli Police Force has a troop of dogs that come to the aid of the various units in the criminal and security fields. The police are assisted by dogs to sniff out missing people, drugs, explosives and bodies in buildings destroyed by fire. They also assist in foiling and preventing hostile sabotage attacks within the country.

The Border Police (which counts for a third of the police force) performs internal security assignments on the borders of the country. In Israel the total number of Border Guards is believed to be about 6000 soldiers and officers. Because of their combat training, Border Police are employed in areas where there are greater risks for riots, violence and even terror. They serve mainly in the countryside, at Arab villages and towns such as the West Bank (along with the regular police) and near Israeli borders. Serving three years as a border policeman is equal to three years as an Israeli Defence Force soldier. The best candidates are selected to specialise in and receive training to become dog handlers.

The Israeli Civilian Police also operate a selected number of dogs. These were obtained from US sources initially. Once solely a male-dominated area, military and paramilitary dog units now include female handlers.

In today's era, when fighting crime and global terror is on the top of the public agenda, the use of trained dogs in the security and policing field both in Israel and abroad has become more and more common and efficient. The dogs are trained to detect drugs and any other contraband substances that can be used in a terrorist attack or criminal acts.

Due to the growing demand for trained dogs for security purposes across the globe, it has become difficult to find high quality purebred dogs fit for the nature of this work. In order to overcome the difficulty, it was decided by the Ministry of Public Security and Israel Police to promote the subject in Israel. In order to do so, the Ministry joined forces with the Rural Education Administration in the Ministry of Education and created a dog breeding and training program on the grounds of the Manof Youth Village, involving the students in the program.

Israeli Border Police make extensive use of dog teams to track persons attempting to cross the border, and to locate hidden explosives and during riots at vehicle check points.

The purpose of the program is to breed and train dogs from a very early age to take part in the operational service of the Israel Police and Israel Prison Service. An added value to the program is the rich educational program it offers to the students in the youth village, with an emphasis on agriculture education and working with animals.

The Chief Scientist of the Ministry of Public Security, along with the Israel Police, defined specific criteria required for the selection of the youth village, the pedagogic program, the breeding program and the kind of training the dogs will receive. The following requirements were defined:

- The kennel grounds will meet the highest standards, including the quality and number of cages, an isolation room and training facilities

- The program will employ only professionals with appropriate knowledge, experience and background

- The program will use a newly designed software program documenting every stage of the dogs' development

- Lesson plans were prepared for the youth village, designed to meet the student's needs

- The Manof youth village was carefully selected by a committee within the Ministry of Education due to its high professional and administrative standards

The program is running under the on-site supervision of the Chief Scientist of the Ministry of Public Security and the Israel Police. With the completion of every stage of training, the dogs are being tested by the Israel Police specialists.

ITALY

The *Polizia di Stato* (State Police) is the civil national police of Italy. Along with patrolling, investigative and law enforcement duties, it patrols the Autostrada (Italy's Express Highway network), and oversees the security of railways, bridges and waterways. It is a civilian police force, while the *Carabinieri* are military. While its internal organisation and mindset is somewhat military, its personnel are civilians. Its headquarters are in Rome, and there are Regional and Provincial divisions throughout Italian territory.

The first Police Dog Training Centre was established in the aftermath of World War I. In 1924 German shepherds were purchased from Germany and used primarily by the border police stations in the activity to counter illegal immigration and smuggling along the Alps.

The Carabinieri Kennel club was established in June 1957, based in Florence, in order to ensure the use of police dogs and conductors of police activities, research, life in sensitive areas and all operations in which such action was considered a valid support.

Dogs that are selected for police work come from national and European countries such as The Netherlands, from Central and Eastern Europe breeders and are aged between 12 and 30 months.

The human candidates must pass accurate medical and psychological aptitude tests, and are subjected to clinical examinations, X-rays and a series of tests to see if they meet the requirements and psycho-physical traits necessary to perform the duties. After a period of medical observation, successful candidates are assigned to an instructor of the training centre for further evaluation to assess their attitudes and aspects of character that are compatible with that of being a dog handler.

German shepherd dog breeds are used because of their all-round skills in certain areas. Labradors are particularly gifted in the search for drugs, weapons and explosives areas. Belgian shepherds (Malinois) are highly appreciated for their exceptional olfactory gifts and for their great temperament. The Rottweilers are valuable aids in the protection area. It is not essential to have a pedigree; dogs from public shelters have been successfully trained.

There are several formations in Italy that are responsible for various aspects of law enforcement. The Guardia di Finanza Corps, which comes under the control of the Minister of Economy and Finance, is responsible for policing financial and economic crimes like tax and drug violations, including anti-Mafia operations.

Dogs in border areas are of particular importance; they are involved in anti-smuggling operations and are a valuable aid to the police in the capture of traffickers without making use of firearms.

Avalanche dogs are used in the mountains, led by environment specialists who are part of the mountain rescue units of the Corps.

A Tight Four-Dog Team

Senna, Patsy, Lazslo and Millie were immediately put on their leashes when news of bomb attacks at two downtown luxury hotels reached the quiet and leafy headquarters in Kelapa Dua, Depok, where they are based with their handlers. The dogs and handlers headed quickly from their base on the outskirts of Jakarta to the South Jakarta crime scene.

'We arrived at 9.20am at the scene with 12 policemen and four dogs,' Djoko Sutikno, head of the special tracking unit of the K9 Police, said from in front of the Marriott Hotel just a few hours after the bombings. 'However, we couldn't enter the crime scene as broken glass was scattered everywhere and it could hurt the dogs.'

The group had been ordered to remain on alert until the police forensic team finished examining the bomb scene. The team remained in the area searching surrounding locations and vehicles entering the vicinity to ensure no further attacks occurred. This is a typical routine function of explosive dog teams across the globe, they are usually the first at a scene. Their job is to secure it and ensure no other explosive devices are present prior to other emergency services such as fire and ambulance crews attending.

The same four dogs also gave final clearance that the area was secure before US Secretary of State Hillary Clinton stepped off her plane at Halim Perdanakusuma airport when she visited Jakarta in February 2010. 'These canine cops and

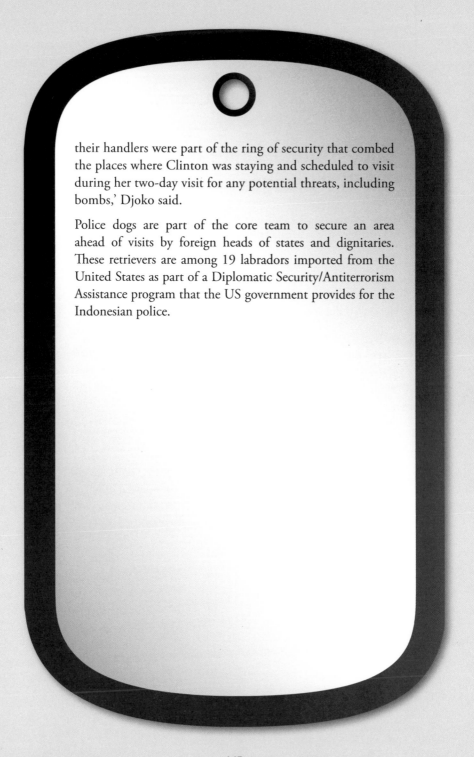

their handlers were part of the ring of security that combed the places where Clinton was staying and scheduled to visit during her two-day visit for any potential threats, including bombs,' Djoko said.

Police dogs are part of the core team to secure an area ahead of visits by foreign heads of states and dignitaries. These retrievers are among 19 labradors imported from the United States as part of a Diplomatic Security/Antiterrorism Assistance program that the US government provides for the Indonesian police.

Good Things Come in Small Packages

Does size matter in a police dog? Well, a long-haired chihuahua named Momo has passed exams to become a police dog in Japan.

Momo (Japanese for peach) went through an examination to become a police dog in Yamatokoriyama, western Japan. The brown-and-white dog was one of 32 successful candidates out of 70 dogs, passing a search and rescue test by finding a person in five minutes.

'Any breed of dog can be entered to become a police dog in the search and rescue division,' a police spokesman from the western Japanese police stated.

He also admitted that news a chihuahua had been entered may still come as a surprise to many. 'It's quite unusual,' he said.

Momo will be used for rescue operations in case of disasters such as earthquakes, in the hope that she may be able to squeeze her tiny frame into places too narrow for more usual rescue dogs, which tend to be German shepherds.

JAPAN

Many Asian countries have a distinct dislike for dogs due to cultural or religious reasons. Japan is one exception. Traditionally Samurai warriors (who in their time also acted as a type of police force) were often seen with a dog companion, which we now identify as an Akita. These dogs acted as a guard at night as the Samurai slept. During the Russo-Japanese war Akitas were used to track down Russian POWs and sailors who had swam to shore after naval engagements off the coast. In World War II the Imperial Japanese Army used dogs as guards and scouts. Since then the Japanese Police Forces throughout the country use dogs in general police criminal work and specialist detection dogs at the airports to detect explosives and illegal contraband. Police dogs are very highly prized; most often today the Akita has given way to the more versatile German shepherd.

The Metropolitan Police Department in Tokyo held a biannual memorial service for deceased police dogs in a cemetery for animals in Tokyo's Itabashi Ward. About 30 officers from the police canine unit and other MPD sections took part in the ceremony in heavy rain in front of the cenotaph for sniffer dogs the MPD built in the cemetery in July 1968. A total of 200 police dogs are buried there. The MPD is in charge of maintaining security in one of the world's largest cities with a population of 13 million.

'The longevity of police dogs is somewhat shorter than ordinary dogs due to their harsh working conditions,' said Kazufumi Ryu, chief of the identification section, after the ceremony. 'I want the dogs (buried in the cemetery) to rest in peace,' he said.

Among the 200 dogs is one named Clark, which died in June this year at age 12, after receiving the Superintendent General Award for discovering in a forest at the foot of Mt Fuji the severed leg of a man who was murdered in 2004.

JERSEY

The use of police dogs in Jersey dates back to the early 1950s when a bloodhound called Rollo was borrowed from its owner when required for police duties. This arrangement unfortunately stopped when the dog fell off the breakwater while taking a walk (off duty) and had to be put down. In the early 1960s three officers from this force became dog handlers after receiving periods of training in the United Kingdom. By the 1970s there were four dog handlers: PCs Dave Bolton,

Charles Holmes, Bob Roscouet and Jon Faiers. The dogs were general purpose dogs, and all were Alsatians.

This number of handlers and dogs continued until the 1980s when the first drug detection dog was obtained and trained as a proactive drug detection dog. This dog was a springer spaniel.

From around 2003 to the present day, the number of police dog handlers has been reduced to three. In the early 2000s the dog handlers were re-deployed to work under the line management of the Community Services Department and work their own shift pattern independent from the normal shifts. There has been the acquisition of another drugs search dog and both these dogs (springer spaniels) are also trained in explosives/firearms detection, while one is also a cash detection dog.

In the last 12 months, there has been the acquisition and training of a passive drugs detection dog (labrador). There has also been a restructuring of the force: the dog handlers have now been re-deployed to work under the operational management of specific shifts.

At this stage there is talk of recruiting a further two dog handlers to bring the strength up to five. However, this has yet to be ratified.

The dog handlers undertake initial training at Surrey Police Dog Training School, where they return for refresher training. An instructor from Surrey also travels to the island when the handlers and their dogs require re-licensing.

JORDAN

The Tracking section of the Jordan Police Service was established in Amman in 1956 with eight male dogs and one female. The section duties at that time were limited to tracking, but now has K9 dogs for:

- Detection of explosives

- Detection of drugs

- Safeguarding and hostage rescue

- Riots dispersion

- Terrorism combating

The section name was changed to K9 Inspection Unit and offer the following training:

- Participating in specialised courses outside the country e.g. in the USA, France and Germany

- Conducting a 'Train the Trainer' Program

- Delivering basic and specialised relevant courses to the new staff

German shepherd dogs are the preferred dogs, and are used in tracking fugitives and dispersing riots. Labrador retrievers are used the detection of explosives and all types of firearms. The Belgium shepherd (Malinois) is used in combating terrorism and hostage rescue situations. Springer spaniels are used in the detection of drugs.

KENYA

The Kenya Police Service provides reliable support services using police dogs to provinces and other formations to fight crime and for general law enforcement. The core functions of the dog unit are:

- Care and maintenance of police dogs

- Training of personnel to work with police dogs

- Training of police dogs

- Procurement of dogs for police work

- Breeding of dogs for police work

- Deployment of trained officers and dogs in crime prevention and investigation

The Kenya Police Dog Unit was started on 5 October 1948 in Nanyuki as a section of the Criminal Investigation Department (CID). It was known as the CID Dog Section, and was manned by two officers, C.I Bill Warner and I.P Montgomery, with only five dogs. They were assisted by six officers. The section was later moved from Nanyuki to Nairobi Central Police Station by then, Kings Way Police Station. The dog handlers were housed at Mathare Depot. Later on, it was again moved to the Army Kennels near King George Hospital, currently Kenyatta National Hospital.

On 2 October 1980, the section headquarters was moved to its present location at Lang'ata next to Lang'ata Women Prison. The Kenya Police Dog Unit Headquarters is located within Nairobi Area Provincial Dog Unit premise. In 1988, the section was separated from the CID and became an independent Police Formation, under the command of Mr Marimba Mugambi, SP as the first Commandant.

Types of police dogs used by the Kenya Police:

- Patrol dogs
- Tracking dogs
- Firearm detectors
- Drug detectors
- Explosive detectors
- Show dogs

The Kenya Police started using German shepherds in the early 1950s. It is currently the mostly used dog breed by the Kenya Police. Dogs are trained for tracking and patrol work. German shepherds have proved to be resilient and successful at work. They have been posted to all provinces and other Police Formations for protection duties.

Labrador retrievers were first used by the Kenya Police in the mid-1980s. They are mainly trained for weapon, narcotic and explosive detection. Black and yellow labrador retrievers have been introduced into the Kenya Police. Rottweilers are solely trained for patrol work and have proved to be very effective. The use of Rottweilers in the Kenya Police has increased rapidly since 2004.

English springer spaniels are trained for explosive and narcotic detection. The Kenya Police first introduced this breed in 2006. Their numbers have grown remarkably since then. They have proved to be agile during searches.

The Kenya Police acquires its dogs from breeders locally and abroad. The K9 Unit also breeds dogs for police work from selected stud dogs and brood bitches. Acquisition and breeding of dogs is demand driven. The unit has established three breeding centres in Nairobi, Nakuru and Nyeri.

The unit embarked on a kennel expansion program during the 2004–08 Kenya Police Strategic Plan implementation. In conjunction with other formations and provinces kennels have been put up in various police stations. The Kenya Police have a long-term plan is to have a police dog in every police station in Kenya.

A Nose for the Job

Bobby is one of two drugs detection dogs who are making a vital contribution in the ongoing effort to stifle the illegal drugs trade in Jersey

The criminals who are behind the mugs trade on the island are becomingly increasingly sophisticated in trying to cover their tracks whilst profiteering from the exploitation of those who become dependent on drugs. That means a major investment of police time and resources into gathering the intelligence required to put a stop to their work and that of their distributors. Primary responsibility for tackling the major dealers rests with the Drugs Squad. Their work is supported by the Joint Intelligence Bureau, staffed by Police and Customs personnel, who collate the intelligence received from national agencies, local operations and other departments such as the uniform shifts and Crime Unit. The public also plays a vital role in providing information.

The final outcome of the intelligence-gathering process is often a raid on a targeted property. 'This is when the dogs come into their own,' says Bobby's handler PC Bill Nelson. 'Drugs are often hidden in ingenious places but Bobby and Molly will invariably track them down. During the year we detected 48 drugs offences.'

LITHUANIA

During the interwar years in Lithuania official police dogs were used by the police and army for state border protection, investigating crimes and ensuring public order. After World War II Lithuania became the Republic of the USSR, and the dog training unit was disbanded. In 1950 the Ministry of Interior of the Soviet Socialist Republic of Lithuania started to create an official dog unit, which in 1956 was assigned to the criminal police division. In 1980 an official breeding program was established.

After Lithuania restored its independence in 1991, the official breeding program remained under the specialised Home Affairs unit. On 1 October 2004 the Lithuanian Police Dog Training Centre became an independent organisation. In January 2008 the Lithuanian Police Dog Training Centre was incorporated into Lithuania's police forensic science centre and became known as the Scent Examination Board.

Since the collapse of the Soviet Union many Baltic States have returned to the use of dogs to protect people and property due to fiscal constraints on buying technically advanced law enforcement equipment.

Currently, in Lithuania there are 81 police officers working with service dogs. Service dogs are specialised in drugs detection, cadaver and human remains search, explosives detection and objects with traces of scent, such as lost property.

The Lithuanian Police Forensic Science Centre's Scent Examination Board provides police agencies and other local law enforcement authorities with scientific and practical assistance in the preparation of dog training specialities in criminal investigation and crime prevention. The board is responsible for organising the official training programs, providing methodical training tools and providing practical assistance to police agencies. Service dogs are used by police and other law enforcement agencies in joint operations. The board is also responsible for organising and participating in service dog competitions. The Scent Examination Board's office is located in Vilnius.

NEPAL

In 1975 Nepal Police established a dog unit in Police Headquarters at Naxal in order to cope with the challenges of increased crime rate and pattern; the crucial role of dog in crime investigation. It was named the Central Police Dog Training School in 2007. Since then the Central Police Dog Training School has been successfully working in the field of crime investigation and security. Regional dog departments have since been established in all the five development regions. There is now a total of 50 dogs working for the Nepal Police.

The objectives of the Central Police Dog Training School are to:

- Produce pedigree dogs

- Train the thus produced dogs

- Prepare skilled manpower (handlers and trainers)

- Identify facts associated with crime and criminals, track down criminals and narrow down the horizon of investigation

- Search arms and explosives, and identify them to check losses before their activation

- Search drugs and thus help control the drug trafficking.

- Provide assistance for rescue at times of natural disasters, and look for persons

The training courses provided are:

- Dog handling basic training

- Arms and explosives identification dog training

- Tracker dog training

- Search and rescue dog training

- Drugs identification dog training

Dogs are used 24–7 at the international airport since 2009 for the security of passengers and to discourage and control activities like trafficking of illegal goods.

The Himalaya Rescue Dog Squad Nepal (HRDSN) was founded on 8 October 1989 by Dutchman Ingo Schnabel in the village of sundarijal, Baghmati Zone, in Kathmandu Valley. For the first two years this organisation was working under the umbrella of His Majesties Government of Nepal's Ministry of Home Affairs (SDU) as a special disaster unit and training centre for Nepalese search and rescue workers. A wolfhound breeding centre was registered attached to this project with the Ministry of Agriculture. The project also provided dogs to the Nepalese Police Dog Training Centre in Maharajgunj, Kathmandu.

In 1993 the Himalaya Rescue Dog Squad Nepal had to become a private limited company as there was no law prepared for registering any private NGO in the field of national disaster aid and search and rescue groups. Lack of vision and political interest in such volunteer organisations prevented the policy makers in Nepal from including these kinds of NGOs on their list. As a result and in order to go on with their work, HRDSN had no other option than to become a registered company. This has hurt its ability to raise funds for this vital work.

NETHERLANDS

The Dutch Police consists of 25 regional police forces and the National Police Services Agency (KLPD).

Each of the Netherlands' 25 police regions is headed by a regional police board, consisting of mayors and a chief public prosecutor. The KLPD is headed by the Minister of the Interior and Kingdom Relations (since 1 January 2000). The KLPD carries out national and specialist police tasks. It collects, files, processes, manages, analyses and distributes information, and carries out other support tasks. It guards the Royal Family and other important persons. And it procures police weaponry, uniforms, and other equipment.

Often the chances of success are much greater when using police dogs than when using technical equipment or police personnel. Furthermore, the same result can be achieved by far fewer police personnel. For example, a dog can sometimes complete a task within just a few hours that might have taken days for a mobile unit section or a large team of investigators. Often the deployment of police dogs at the scene of a crime can yield new clues, such as traces that contain a DNA profile or other new evidence.

At present the Dutch police have 94 sniffer dogs, 74 of which are the property of DLHP. Two regions — Rotterdam-Rijnmond and Amsterdam-Amstelland — have their own dogs. Most other regions have one or more handlers, but the dogs which these handlers use are the property of the KLPD.

The length of the training depends largely on the aptitude of the dog, the skill of the handler and the type of work for which the dog is being trained. For example, a minimum of eight months is needed to train a dog to locate human beings by their scent. This — together with narcotics training — is the most common specialisation for police dogs. Police dogs are of many breeds. But what is even more important than breed is the temperament and aptitude of the dog. The Belgian shepherd has these qualities in abundance and is often used as a police dog. Other breeds of shepherd dog, labradors, spaniels and even the German hunting terrier are trained as police dogs. Dogs that are not immediately recognisable as police dogs can be used by handlers in civilian clothes very effectively in public areas such as airports.

Dogs used for surveillance or apprehending criminals receive very different training. Most police regions have their own surveillance dogs. The Mounted Police and Police Dogs Service of the KLPD does not have such dogs, but does play a central role in quality assurance and certification.

The Dienst Levende Have Politie (DLHP, which stands for Mounted Police and Police Dog Service) dogs are trained to recognise a single specific scent and specialise in the following areas:

- Identifying scents (identifying the scent shared by an object and a person)

- Narcotics (sniffing out drugs in homes and outdoor locations, or in large crowds such as airports, stations and football stadiums)

- Explosives and firearms

- Detecting human remains

- Locating drowning people

- Detecting fire accelerants

Dogs are trained to operate under unusual conditions and for specific purposes, where it would otherwise be more or less impossible to conduct a search or carry out instructions.

The Royal Netherlands Marechaussee is one of four departments of the Dutch armed services. They perform both civil and military policing functions. There specialist detection dogs are used in the protection of borders while their general duties police dogs are used in both military and civilian police roles.

NEW ZEALAND

The New Zealand Police service has 21 dog sections comprising approximately 110 general purpose police dog teams. In addition, the section also operates ten narcotic detector dog teams and three explosive detector dog teams. Police train German shepherd dogs for the general purpose role, and predominantly labradors for the specialist roles. All police dog handlers are experienced police officers with approximately five years policing experience behind them before they join the Dog Section.

All training courses are conducted at the Police Dog Training Centre at Trentham (Wellington). The quality of the training provided by the centre is well recognised in both New Zealand and overseas. Assistance has been provided to set up dog sections in several Australian states. Another important part of the centre's operations is providing training to other Pacific countries. Police also train drug detector dogs for the New Zealand Customs Service and Department of Corrections, and Explosive Detector dogs for Aviation Security Service. The Dog Training Centre has also trained New Zealand's first accelerant detector dog for use in arson investigation. The training philosophy employed by the Police is based on positive reinforcement. The type of dog the police look for is one that is well socialised to people, places and things, is even-tempered and has a high retrieve drive.

The general purpose dog is mainly used to track and search for people. Unlike Australia with its heat and many US cities due to population density, New Zealand has a relatively mild climate with a sparse populace thus NZ police dogs are well known for their skills in tracking criminals over long distances in the middle of the day. The training of a general purpose dog is based on a three-stage qualification process and takes approximately eight months. Dogs live at home with their handlers. Police use German shepherds because of their size, temperament and trainability. Half of the dogs trained are gifted or bought from the public. The Dog Training Centre also has its own breeding program, which provides the remaining dogs needed.

Police mainly use labradors for the specialist role of locating illegal drugs. They also train many of their general purpose dogs to carry out other roles. These include:

- Search and rescue work including avalanche rescue

- Deployment with the Armed Offender Squad

- Firearm detection work

- Drug detection in smaller centres that do not have a specialist dog

Explosive detection dog handlers in New Zealand seen wearing full EOD equipment, most countries handlers wear the bare minimum of kit replacing protection for agility. A handlers job is to locate a device not defuse it.

In 2008/2009 a working group investigated the use of vests for police dog and a trial was conducted using a vest used by Australian Police. The investigation found that the vests would not have offered any protection to any of the dogs killed in New Zealand or any of the serious injuries suffered by dogs in recent years. Over 80 per cent of patrol dogs in New Zealand are involved in tracking (often long distances) and in all weather conditions, and injuries to police dogs occur when least expected.

The investigation found that vests would seriously compromise the effectiveness of New Zealand Police Dog Teams due to the conditions that they work in. However, they will continue to look into advances in protective equipment and practice for dogs and their handlers. A dog's best defence is its natural speed, agility and strength accompanied by safe deployment practice by the handler.

The safety of police dogs in New Zealand is of the utmost importance, and this is reflected in the very low numbers of injuries and deaths to our dogs when compared to the very high number of incidents they are involved in.

New Zealand police dogs, in 2009/2010, responded to over 36,000 calls for service and apprehended more than 7000 suspects. Police detector dog teams were also deployed to assist police operations in narcotic, explosive and firearms detection. A comparison of statistics shows just how far the Dog Section has come: in 1958 dogs were called out 55 times; by 1968, call-outs had risen to 1645.

Over the years the Dog Training Centre has developed an enviable record for its expertise. The quality of the training provided is recognised internationally. In 1972, training was given to police officers from Victoria, Australia to help them set up a dog section. Since then, training and assistance has been provided to other Australian states and to Asian countries.

The past 24 years have also seen dogs trained for specialist work, with the first drug dog training course being held in 1976. This was closely followed by the introduction of explosive detection courses in 1977. More recent developments have seen the introduction of the armed offenders squad dog course (1992), accelerated detection (1997) and search and rescue (1998).

The Dog Training Centre has developed from its humble beginning to a million dollar complex, which was officially opened in 1996 to mark the 40th anniversary of police dogs in New Zealand.

History of the Dog Section in New Zealand

A history of the dog unit in New Zealand begins in September 1956. Sergeant Frank Riley of the Surrey Constabulary disembarked from the vessel *Hinekura* after making the long voyage from England. What brought him halfway across the work was the desire of the then New Zealand Prime Minister, Sid Holland, to have a police dog section after he saw the Surrey Constabulary police dog school during a state visit to England.

Sergeant Riley arrived with his fully-trained police dog Miska, a nine-month old dog named Dante, bitches Karen and Silver and twelve two-month-old puppies born during the voyage. Constable Colin Guppy, who handled Dante, joined Sergeant Riley to become New Zealand's first police dog handlers.

A Dog Training Centre was set up in Trentham in conjunction with the Police Training School. were it remains today. Although today the dog section is an integral part of the New Zealand Police, the first ten years were a struggle. Vehicles and equipment were hard to come by for the dog section and there was no uniform. And, at one point the entire dog section came within two minutes of being scrapped. Constable Guppy and his dog Dante were instructed to carry out a tracking exercise in the hills behind the Dog Training Centre. Guppy was told where the 'offender' was last seen, cast his dog and picked up a scent. They tracked the offender for two hours before finding him at 10.58am. It was only later that Guppy found out that if he hadn't located the offender by 11.00am the dog section would have been disbanded.

NORWAY

The first official training of police dogs at Sæter farm was in 1989. Sæter farm is the National Police Academy's course centre for police dogs and their handlers. The education from start to finish is done here. Some of the education is local, but most of the training before the dog is approved is done at Sæter farm.

Dog roles in Norway include:

- Patrol dogs

- Narcotic dogs

- Bomb dogs

- Avalanche dogs/ruin dogs

- Crime scene dogs (fire)

- Various combinations of those mentioned above

Police dogs in Norway are mainly privately owned under contract to the Norwegian Politihundelag, but remain the handler's property. Some dogs, including bomb dogs, are owned by the state. Police dog handlers are full time and are under contract.

Dog handlers or guides as they are called in Norway have for years not been compensated for being employed as a dog handler and most training is carried out outside of working hours. This has improved in most places, but it is not wages that attract people working with police dogs in the service. They are enthusiasts, which is absolutely necessary to work with dogs in the police profession.

The police dogs in Norway are distributed throughout the country. Most of the dogs are from Helgeland and Sørvoer and number as follows

- Patrol dogs: 123

- Drug dogs: 64

- Bomb/explosives dogs: 4

- Total number of police dogs: 191

Police dogs are trained to cover all types of terrain and in all climatic conditions. Here a Norwegian Police dog hunts down an escaped prisoner.

The most common dog is the patrol dog. It is approved for track, wind scent, search for objects and criminal work. The dog handler has to have excellent control of his dog. They can be used for almost everything and are considered to be the all-rounder among police dogs. The most commonly used breed is German shepherd dog, followed by Malinois and Rottweiler. Basically, most breeds could be used as long as they satisfy the basic criteria necessary for a patrol dog.

In some police districts where winter conditions and landslide hazards are common patrol dogs are duel trained as avalanche detection dogs, trained to search for missing persons in arctic conditions. More recently dogs are trained to be combination dogs; this means that some patrol dogs with very good skills can also be trained as a drug dog or arson detection dogs.

Both males and females dogs can become patrol dogs. Patrol dogs may be accepted at the age of 2 years and retire at 10 years and every two years must undergo a quality control test to ensure operational readiness.

Narcotics detection dogs are the most common police specialist dog. Most are German shepherds and labradors but other breeds are used. Both males and females can be used as a drug dogs. A dog handler who has a drug dog can either work in the order of service or work specifically in the field of drugs. A dog handler must of course have a good knowledge and interest in the field of work.

Some drug dogs in Norway have been duel trained as avalanche dogs. Avalanche dogs are trained at Rjukan in Telemark. The dogs can find people who are several metres below ground. The dogs are also trained to find people lost in the mountains. The dogs can be transported to the landslide area by helicopter, snowmobile or by small sledges pulled on skis/snowshoes.

In addition to these two most common service dogs, Norway also has a small number of bomb dogs, firearm detection dogs, accelerant detection dogs, avalanche, and urban search and rescue dogs. They are fewer in number in these roles and are scattered throughout Norway.

A recent decision by the Supreme Court established that violence against a police dog is as bad as against a police officer. This is a great victory for the Norwegian police.

Norwegian Politihundelag publishes the magazine *Police Dog*. The magazine is the main body of the police dog service in Norway and has six issues a year. The magazine is distributed in addition to its own members, a good number of subscribers, all the advertisers and partners in Norway and Scandinavia. The magazine contains articles and reports of police dog handlers and their canine colleagues, mission and actions, subject matter dog, training, meetings, competitions, debates and more. Norway also has several associations which actively promote police dogs.

POLAND

The Polish Police today are part of the Ministry of the Interior and are administered by a general inspector out of the national headquarters in Warsaw, Poland. The national headquarters supervises 16 province headquarters known as *voivodships* that are essentially regional police similar to the various provincial police forces in Canada. It also is directly responsible for the Warsaw police headquarters.

The 16 voivodships supervise the nation's 392 county police agencies (Poviat), and these county police have under their control the local police stations (komisariaty), of which there are approximately 1800. Although Poland still maintains a chain of command from local police to the national headquarters, the provincial, county and the government administrations at their specific levels. Therefore, there is an element of local control over the local police.

An interesting advancement in Polish policing is osmology, or scent identification, which is considered to be one of the newest yet most effective areas of forensic science investigation. Osmology uses specially trained dogs controlled by specially selected and trained police officers for the trace scent identification of suspected criminals. Human beings leave trace scents on every surface they touch, which means that criminals leave trace scents at crime scenes. The most popular breeds of dogs used for forensic investigations in Poland and other European countries are German shepherds, Belgian shepherds, Polish shepherds, labrador retrievers, and German schnauzers.

Both the dog and the handler, usually a police officer, must undergo continuous annual training and evaluation. Initially, both the dog and his trainer attend a seven-month training class at the Polish Canine Training Centre. Dogs that are initially selected must possess, among other things, a keen and decisive sense of smell. After this initial training, a dog can only obtain certification after successful completion of a short-term probationary period in a police unit. These certificates are renewed each year, and the dogs are either permitted to continue working or are simply disqualified due to unsatisfactory results.

Either a crime scene investigator or the actual canine officer can carry out collection of trace scents. The scent collection process involves several steps and calls for an acute attention to detail. First, pieces of cotton swabs, known as absorbers, are placed on a particular area or object. Aluminium foil is then used to cover these swabs for roughly 30 minutes. Afterward, the investigator uses tweezers to remove the foil and collect the swabs and subsequently places each swab in a glass jar with a screw on lid. The jars are logged into evidence and photographed then taken to a lab where they are labelled, Next, an evaporation vacuum method is used to further extract scents from surface absorbers and place them on new neutral absorbers. Each of these cotton absorbers is then placed back into its labelled container and sealed until the appropriate scent comparison can be extracted from the suspect. Once a comparison is taken from a suspect, the officer and the canine can conduct an official laboratory examination.

The canine officer then conducts an assessment in a controlled laboratory environment to see if a suspect can be linked to scents taken from a crime scene. First, the officer places numerous glass jars filled with different human scents in a row on the floor of the examination room. Usually the officer will have three or four comparison jars along with the actual scent taken from the crime scene. Next, outside the examination room, the canine is permitted to smell the scent taken from a suspect who is implicated for that particular crime. Then, the officer takes the dog into the exam room and verbally instructs the dog to locate the identical scent of the suspect. The dog will then systematically inspect each scent until the dog indicates to the officer that a match has been made (usually by sitting in front of the container). If the dog does not sit down, then it is considered that the scent of the suspect in question is most likely not the same as the criminal's scent that was collected from the crime scene.

Although Polish criminal justice officials acknowledge that osmology is in its infancy as a viable forensic tool, it should be noted that other European countries have also started to employ these same techniques for crime scene investigations.

Two Polish police officers patrol a beach near one of the country's main border crossing points, the breed of dog is a spitz breed. There is no ideal breed in policing, any dog that is brave and intelligent will do, pedigree does not count.

REPUBLIC OF IRELAND

An Garda Síochána is the national police service of the Republic of Ireland. Following the establishment of the Irish Free State in 1922, the Dublin Metropolitan Police merged with the recently established An Garda Síochána in 1925. An Garda Siochana in the native Irish language translates into Guardians of the Peace. A police officer or constable is called a *garda*. The Canine section is called the Garda Dog Unit.

The Garda Dog Unit was established in 1960 and initially it was made up of general purpose dogs only, which were all German shepherds. In 1984 when drugs started to take a serious hold in Dublin, the first drugs detection dogs were introduced. In the late 1980s some of the general purpose dogs were trained in the detection of explosives and they operated as dual purpose dogs. The unit remained like this until about ten years ago when in line with ACPO (Association of Chief Police Officers) Guidelines in the UK the practice of having dual purpose dogs ceased. So now most of the handlers have two dogs; a GP dog and a specialist search dog.

Twenty-three dogs, including German shepherds, labradors and springer spaniels, are based at Kilmainham Garda Station in Dublin although not attached to it, being part of the Operational Support Unit which also includes the Water Unit, the Mounted Unit and the Air Support Unit. There are four other handlers operating in the south of the country in the cities of Cork and Limerick but they are not attached to the main unit.

The Garda Dog Unit has grown over the years and has become an integral part of policing through the assistance of its canine partners.

Potential Garda dogs are assessed for 3 to 4 weeks and if suitable they undergo a 14-week training program. The dog and its handler will then start operational duty. Specialised dogs (drug and explosive) will train for a further 6–8 weeks before becoming operational. Ongoing training is undertaken on a very regular basis. Garda dogs are also familiarised with working alongside personnel in the Garda Mounted Support Unit, Garda Air Support Unit and Garda Water Support Unit.

Breeding Wolves to Serve

Russian scientists were the first in the world to train wolves to serve as police dogs. The Institute of Interior Forces has interbred a she-wolf and a dog and as a result created a unique breed of wolfdogs. This new breed has an exceptional nose from the wolf and the love of people from dogs.

Russian researchers were lucky with the initial material of the experiment. She-wolf Naida was wonderfully friendly. And this is in spite of the centuries-long genetic wolves' fear of humans. During the interbreeding, Naida rejected a male wolf and chose a male dog. It is thanks to the she-wolf Naida that unique puppies came to the world and will soon become wonderful police dogs.

Another unique experiment on interbreeding the jackal and Eskimo dogs (huskies) was conducted in Russia. Author of the experiment Vyacheslav Klimov called the new breed of puppies *shakolaika*. The small dogs had exceptional noses and were used for detecting drugs and explosive at airports. Unfortunately, the researcher failed to fight the natural cautiousness of jackals and the new breed of shakolaika turned out to be awfully cowardly so the police could not employ the new dog breed in their work.

REPUBLIC OF SERBIA

In Serbia the Utility Dog Guides Unit is part of the Third Battalion of Police Brigade, Police Directorate in the city of Belgrade, and its core role is training and working with utility search/tracking dogs, attack dogs and specialist dogs for the detecting explosives and drugs.

The use of dogs began in 1923 at the school for utility dogs, which opened in the village of Delovo in Banat. The Ministry of Interior founded the Department for Dog Training in 1948. At that time utility dog guides (handlers) were located within the Militia Detachment.

The training took place in Jajinci and then in Zuce, near the Avala Mountains. The dogs were used in the investigation role or what many call general duties police role.

Today the unit is in Bezanijska kosa in Belgrade, where the following breeds of dogs are currently used: German shepherd, Belgian shepherd (Malinois), Rottweilers, labrador retrievers, Breton and German short-haired pointer.

A Serbian Police dog — in this case a Belgium shepherd — takes down an offender. Many Eastern Bloc countries have a long tradition of using dogs and many of these countries still breed the best examples of the breeds.

After basic police training, police officers who express the will and who have the abilities to work with dogs are posted to the Utility Dog Guides Unit. Initially an instructor follows their work for a month and if they pass this selection phase they will start their official work in the unit, where they continue training for four more months.

There is a club called 'Policajac' in the unit made up of dog handlers, civil dog owners and dog lovers that gather to meet. The club members organise a school for dog guides two times a year, for three months each time.

RUSSIA

The Regional Centre for Dog Services belongs to the Main Department of Internal Affairs. The first centre for police tracker dogs appeared in St Petersburg in 1909 and later it became the first cynological department of the Ministry of the Interior. Now it is situated in the centre of the Moscow Region. The centre has 240 enclosures where they keep 120 dogs. The enclosures are clean and neat and the dogs are kept warm.

The main breed used in Russia is the German shepherd. These dogs are better adapted to the Russian climate.

Russian Police patrolling on foot have used attack dogs off and on for a long time, usually exceptionally large German shepherds. These are kept on a leash at all times and required to wear muzzles that are removed only when the dog is needed to pursue and detain suspects. The dogs are trained to remain calm, docile and unfazed by crowds or noise, remaining perfectly calm when on public transportation. Such dogs may react to any and all stimuli only if ordered to do so. They are a common sight in cities and are rarely if ever perceived as unnerving by the general public.

Crime scene investigation units and patrols seeking dangerous fugitives have also been known to use dogs for tracking. Interestingly enough, these units also use German shepherds, which were chosen as the all-purpose police and army breed. These practices have remained common in most of the Soviet Union's successor states. The police buy the dogs in for $2000 and after they have trained them they are worth $5000.

Russia uses various breeds including mixed breeds. Here are a German Shepherd cross and a Rottweiler; both are large and trained to be aggressive.

SINGAPORE

In 1911, the Singapore Police Force (SPF) first experimented with the use of dogs with the purchase of an Airedale terrier by a British army officer to track down escaped prisoners. Unfortunately, the dog died the following year and the use of dogs ceased.

In 1954, following the successful use of police dogs in the United Kingdom (UK), Chief Inspector Frank C Pestana attended a three-month Dog Instructor Course at the Metropolitan Police Dog Training School. He returned with four German shepherds in 1955. The dogs were based at the Police Academy together with four trainee handlers and after five months of training, these handlers and dogs formed the nucleus of the SPF's Dog Unit. Dog teams, then, were mainly used to suppress secret society activities and disorderly crowds, perform anti-housebreaking patrols and tracking of criminals.

In 1956, the British Army Guard Dog Unit donated four German shepherds to SPF. The then total dog strength was eventually increased to 16 but a severe epidemic of aplastic anaemia in 1968 wiped out all but three dogs in the unit. In 1969 and 1970, the Australian Government and the British Army donated four and nine dogs to SPF respectively.

In 1970, the dog section was shifted to the Mowbray Camp along Ulu Pandan Road. It shared common dog training and kennelling facilities with the Singapore Armed Forces Provost Unit Dog Wing, with a complement of 35 dogs and 48 police officers. In 1987, it took over the assets and functions of the Customs Dog Unit together with the established strength of 48 narcotics detector dogs (NDD) and NDD handlers posts. In 1995 it also took over the assets and functions of the Prison Dog Unit together with the established strength of 64 security dogs (SD) and SD handlers posts.

In May 2002, the unit embarked on an explosive detector dog (EDD) program after the September 11 terrorist attack in the United States. The pioneer batch of six handlers attended the Initial Explosive Search Dog course in UK in August 2002. The PDU has since grown to over 250 dogs today. Its mission is to uphold the law, maintain order and keep the peace in the Republic of Singapore.

Officers and their trained canine sniffer dogs are deployed at all major entry points to prevent the smuggling of controlled drugs into Singapore. They are also deployed to screen in-coming mail and parcels for narcotics at the Singapore Post Centre. Occasionally, the dog teams also attend to service calls to assist other law enforcement agencies in the search for concealed drugs, large quantity of cigarettes or firearms in vehicle, vessel, building or cargo.

Officers assigned to general purpose dog Teams complete the Police Land Divisions for anti-crime patrols. The general purpose dogs are trained to sniff and detect humans hiding in buildings, vehicles and even in tracking down potential criminal fleeing into forested areas. Apart from these tracking exercises, the dogs are trained to perform 'criminal' or 'attack' work where they will chase and bite any fleeing criminal at the command of the handler. The teams are trained to perform crowd control duties at popular football matches or pop concerts. The dogs are also trained to detect cadaver.

The explosive detector dog teams are deployed randomly to search selected or suspicious looking vehicles for concealed explosives at the Woodlands and Tuas

Checkpoints, Changi Airport and ferry terminals. The teams are also required to attend to service calls to assist in the search for explosives in different types of operating environment.

The Security Dog Team officers and their canine partners are trained in basic obedience and 'attack' work. As a team, they are deployed at our penal institutions. Their main duties are to patrol the perimeter fencing and assist in guard and cordon duties in the Prisons Department 'riot', 'escape' and 'fire' exercises. The K9 Unit introduced cadaver detection in 2007 to enhance its search operations. Its cadaver detector dogs (CDD) are specially trained to detect decomposing body or body parts. The CDDs have successfully detected even very small traces of human remains in a number of cases. In one such operation, the dogs were able to sniff out two finger bones at different locations.

SLOVENIA

In Slovenia, the first to use service dogs was the Ljubljana Police between the two world wars. Their dogs were purchased from the Vienna Police. Immediately after the liberation in 1945, the People's Police, as it was then called, played a special role as an operations body, since it was entrusted with maintaining law and order, as well as the detection and prevention of criminal offences. In addition to all the more advanced technical means they also used police dogs in the performance of their duties.

In 1948 a Service Dogs School was formed to select dogs with appropriate characteristics and train them to help police officers in the performance of their tasks, with the support of the Police Administration. Soon after the formation of the Service Dogs Schools, the initial enthusiasm was put to the first test, since the personnel skilled enough and capable of taking over the work of instructors was simply not available. However, the demanding working conditions did not lessen the enthusiasm of the pioneers in this field.

At that time, dogs were mostly trained for general tasks. They were trained in obedience, defence, tracking and search for missing persons and objects. Dog handlers attended courses in criminology and dog psychology, communication between man and dog, theory on tracking, etc.

Until 1959, the school brought up its own dogs in dog kennels. Some male and female dogs, mostly for the school's own needs, were purchased in Germany. Since it proved to be too expensive to breed their own offspring, in 1959 it was decided that the school would no longer breed its own dogs but would purchase the required number of dogs from private breeders. In 1976, the school again started to breed its own offspring but after ten years again decided to stop doing so.

The Service Dogs Training Section, as the police dog school is currently called, has been operating under various names for 62 years, and until 1991 was the leading institution for training of police dogs for the needs of the entire country. In its long and varied history, the school has trained many handlers and an enviable number of service dogs for other state authorities such us the Customs Administration of the Republic of Slovenia, Slovenian Armed Forces, the Ministry of Justice of the Republic of Slovenia and the Ministry of the Interior of the Republic of Croatia. Testifying to the high quality and professional work of the school are in particular the high qualifications and outstanding results of service dogs in police field work and their superior results obtained at the international level.

The recent years have been very dynamic for the school. The school has seen an intense development in the use of service dogs and improved quality and recorded an increase in the scope of their work. The professional skills and the equipment used by dog handlers as well as the skills of their four-footed assistants have improved considerably. As a result, handler/dog tandems have become indispensable in the performance of certain tasks. To many, the role of service dogs in police work may seem out of date, even exotic. The technological development over the recent decades has, indeed, left its mark on police work as well. However, despite the technological development and introduction of various technical aids, handlers and their four-footed friends are still indispensable in police work.

At present, the Service Dogs Training Section is an independent section within the Police Academy organised for the training of service dogs and their handlers for the Slovenian police. It is responsible for the training of handlers and service dogs for general and special tasks. The section also performs many other tasks, which are closely related with its field of work, such as training of dogs through play and a system of rewards for a job well done. Dogs are seldom corrected and only in case of specific exercises. Hitting dogs is not allowed!

One of the special characteristics of the Slovenian police dog school is the veterinarian clinic, which in other police forces is rather the exception than the rule. The veterinarian clinic is responsible for preventive and curative treatment as well as food and accommodation for service dogs.

On 17 April 2008, the Service Dogs Training Section of the Police Academy moved into new, better and larger facilities at Gmajnice in Ljubljana, thereby solving long years of difficulties for instructors and dogs. In the period since

2007, dog handlers in almost all police administrations have been given new or renovated facilities; in a few cases, the renovation or construction works have not yet been finished. The new facilities provide better working conditions and improved accommodation for dogs as well as their handlers.

In order to maintain a high level of professional skills of handlers and their dogs, a test for handlers of service dogs is organised every year. Handlers and service dogs for general tasks test their mental and physical condition and skills in four disciplines: tracking, obedience and a field test in which they have to master a 3-kilometre trail with 12 obstacles, shoot, and perform a defensive exercise without a muzzle. The fourth discipline is different every year and is chosen by drawing of lots. This decides which of the three additional disciplines (search of a facility, search of a forest and free tracking) will be included in the test.

The purpose of the annual competition for handlers of service dogs is to test the physical and mental abilities of handlers and their dogs. The results, which get better every year, show that the skills of handlers and dogs also improve every year, which results in more efficient operations of handlers and their charges.

Handlers of service dogs from the Slovenian Armed Forces, the Customs Administration of the Republic of Slovenia, the Prison Administration of the Republic of Slovenia and the Croatian police participate in the competition almost every year.

Service dogs are trained for general and special tasks. Dogs which are trained for general tasks are mostly used for traditional police tasks. In other countries, they are also called patrol dogs. Special task dogs are trained in particular for search of illicit drugs and explosives.

The tasks of handlers of service dogs do not differ from the tasks of other police officers. They only differ in the method of operation and the location. Due to their work with a dog, handlers of service dogs are more visible than other police officers. By its presence alone, a service dog has a preventive effect on potential perpetrators or violators and often prevents them from committing a criminal or other offence.

All police officers are authorised to perform certain tasks specified by law, regardless of whether they are trained for any of the special fields of police work (e.g. traffic police, handlers of service dogs, mounted police etc.). So a service dog handler can fine you for a traffic violation (drink-driving, failure to use the safety belt, etc.).

One of the tasks of handlers and service dogs is prevention and promotion. Because service dogs are attractive, they attract a great deal of attention, in particular with children. Children are also the most enthusiastic about them, so that police officers are able to use their dogs to make children familiar with their work.

General tasks for service dogs:

- To ensure the safety of people and property
- To ensure and maintain law and order
- To search for missing persons
- To track and detect perpetrators of minor offences and criminal offences
- To protect state borders

At the Service Dogs Training Section, service dogs for general tasks are trained in obedience, tracking, defence and attack, both with a muzzle and without it, search of terrain and facilities and free tracking.

Special tasks for service dogs:

- Searching for illicit drugs
- Searching for explosives

Service dogs for special tasks are trained in searching for illicit drugs or in searching for explosives on the terrain, in facilities, vehicles and luggage. Practical experience teaches that the training of service dogs for special tasks requires two different methods of work and, consequently, has to be adjusted to the special requirements. The difference between the two methods lies in the way the dog shows that it has found the object that it has been searching for. Whilst a service dog for searching for illicit drugs shows the find actively by barking or scratching (there are certain trends to change the method of training in order to avoid a lot of material damage that a service dog can cause while searching for illicit drugs), a service dog specialised in searching for explosives indicates its find passively, i.e., by lying down and keeping still. The dog must not bark because barking could activate the explosive device.

The breeds chosen by the Slovenian police for service dogs for general tasks are the German shepherd, Belgian shepherd and Rottweiler. Service dogs for special tasks (searching for illicit drugs, searching for explosives) are usually German shepherds, Belgian shepherds, different hound breeds such as terriers (fox terrier, German terrier), German pointer, spaniels, etc.

Technology and Dogs Combined

Sniffer dogs in South Africa are being trained to help the fight against poachers of endangered species in a new way. Dogs have long been used to help police find contraband substances, including ivory and rhino horn. However, there are times when it is not practical to use dogs on the ground, as the tarmac at border posts gets too hot for them during the day, or if there could be a danger to the animal.

Now researchers at the South African company Mechem are adapting their Explosive and Drug Detection System to the fight against poachers.

The technology involves using a vacuum device to suction air from a suspect area. The filter in the vacuum is then given to the dogs to smell, disguised among blank control filters, and the dog's nose does the rest. Mechem says this technology helps to get round all the problems that sniffer dogs traditionally face by 'taking the odour to the dog rather than taking the dog to the odour. Mechem's Explosive and Drug Detection System was first developed in the 1980s to detect landmines, weapons, ammunition and drugs. It has now been improved and adapted to detect illegal substances taken from protected species.

Inspector TC Oosthuizen, of the South African Police Service, said: 'When we work at Komatipoort for instance, the tarmac is so hot, it starts melting so you can't get a dog to work from 12 o'clock in the afternoon. And the smugglers,

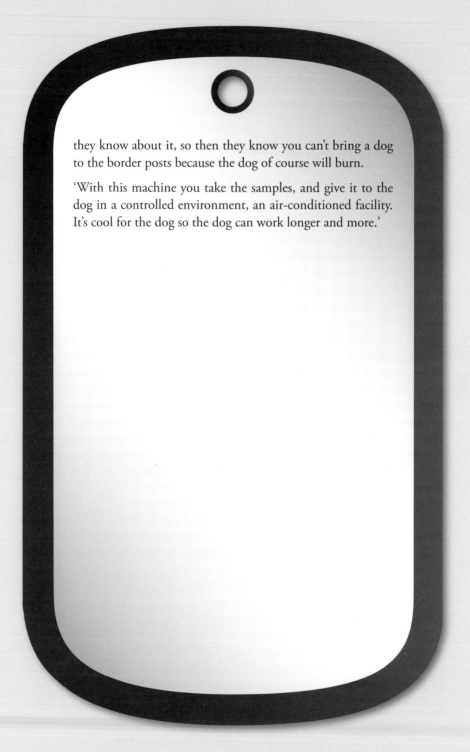

they know about it, so then they know you can't bring a dog to the border posts because the dog of course will burn.

'With this machine you take the samples, and give it to the dog in a controlled environment, an air-conditioned facility. It's cool for the dog so the dog can work longer and more.'

SOUTH AFRICA

There has been allot of media controversy in relation to the use of dogs in South Africa; many people can remember images of 'land sharks' savaging screaming black Africans during the 1980s.

When the change of regime occurred the dog service declined due to the stigma; however, it did not take the new government long to realise their value. Initially they were simply re-employed, this time with native African police not white police holding the leads.

Now police dogs in South Africa receive training to provide both proactive and reactive police services, including narcotics, explosives, protected species detection, tracking, fire investigation, patrol, and search and rescue operations. South Africa police have specific breeds of dogs they use and have specific requirements for police dog trainers and handlers.

The South African Police Service (SAPS) requires dogs accepted into its training program to be between the age of nine months and three years. The breeds accepted for police service dog training include: border collie, German shepherd, Belgium shepherd (Malinois), boxer, Doberman, labrador, cocker spaniel, bloodhound and Rottweiler.

In South Africa, the dog handler receives training in the care, training and handling of the police dog, and handles the dog during the prevention, combating and investigation of crime. The handler must be physically fit, healthy, non-allergic to dog hair, retain good motor and observation skills, complete basic training and have at least two years' experience in uniform duties.

An ever-growing need exists for the service of police dogs at special events such as general elections and world sporting events like the Soccer World Cup of 2010. Thus, SAPS launched a campaign in 2007 encouraging the public to donate dogs in order to increase the working police dog capacity.

To prevent public criticism of possible ill treatment to any dog found unsuitable to be trained by the SAPS, the service hands the failed candidates to the society for the prevention of cruelty to animals, which finds new homes for the ex-police dogs.

In 2000, an investigation examined SAPS dog trainers and handlers throughout South Africa for their style of dog training because of an incident that horrified people all over the world. A canine training unit videotaped a training session in 1998 of the unit using black prisoners for the targets of the dogs in training. In the one-hour taped training session, four dogs repeatedly savaged the prisoners as they screamed and begged for their lives. State television in South Africa aired the video, and it has since surfaced on the Internet.

Dog handlers use police dogs in the prevention, combating and investigation of crime. Handlers must qualify in the Basic South African Police Service entry requirement test and Completed Basic Police Training.

The Tactical Dog Handling Course and specialised dog handling course are some of the training offered. Police dogs in South Africa receive training in narcotics, explosives, detection, tracking, fire investigation, patrol, and search and rescue operations.

The South African Police only used tracker dogs, bloodhounds and Dobermans, or a cross between the two, until 1962, when other uses for the police dogs were introduced. The patrol dog section has always been the largest section in the South African Police Services, Canine component. Because of the instantaneous success which was achieved with the German shepherds in 1962, the training of these dogs as patrol dogs was then initiated. In the SAPS mainly German shepherd dogs are used, but Rottweilers are also being utilised for patrol dog purposes.

Prior to 1979, all dogs in the service of the South African Police were donated by the public, until the development of a breeding program at the Dog School in 1979, initiated by Warrant Officer Harry De Bryn. Training and breeding of police dogs at the single facility at Kwaggapoort grew to such huge proportions that another facility had to be purchased for the exclusive use as a dog breeding centre.

Thus the current SAPS Dog Breeding Centre was established in 1990 at Roodeplaat, approximately 30km North-East of Pretoria. Facilities include a well-equipped veterinary hospital, nine different dog units with kennels for 1000 dogs and an administration building. The South African Police Dog Breeding Centre (SAPDBC) is the only one of its kind in Africa. At this facility, dogs have to be bred and socialised to suit the needs for police dogs country wide, in other African countries and overseas, when necessary.

The dog unit currently has 14 patrol dogs, 2 explosives detection dogs, 3 narcotics detection dogs and 11 multipurpose (patrol/explosives detection) dogs. There are 64 staff members consisting of 33 dog handlers and 21 crew with 10 administrative officials here.

For dogs to qualify as potential patrol dogs they must:

- Possess a high level of aggression which is shaped in such a way that they follow, visually or by scent, clearly identified assailants and apprehend them until the handler gets close enough to carry out the arrests

- Search for assailants hiding in dense bush, or forest and buildings

- Search for weapons or objects at the scene of a crime (squaring)

Prior to 1994, patrol dogs were also utilised for crowd control. This, however, has changed and became the function of the Public Order Policing Unit.

The use of force with police dogs has again caught the attention of the South African community via the media over the last few years. Perceptions of patrol dogs and the alleged violations of human rights, in terms of the Constitution of South Africa, have recently been the focus of many debates.

Due to this an inquiry was establish in the Johannesburg area to evaluate police dogs' success in contributing towards the fight against crime. The researcher also emphasised the positive role of the police patrol dog in the combating of crime as well as the proper utilisation of patrol dogs and patrol dog handlers. Instead of trying to decrease patrol dogs, because of the negative perception of the public and even police colleagues, it was decided to focus on current training techniques as well as the recruiting process in order to obtain more suitable candidates to train as dog handlers.

SPAIN

Today the Canine Guide Section of the Spanish Police has trained dogs in the fields of locating explosives, drug search, advocacy and support, rescue and fire accelerants detection.

The Canine Section was established in January 1945, with locations in Madrid, initially having an establishment of eight German shepherd dogs. Its purpose was to combat crime that existed in the city at the time. By 1946 dogs gradually increased until reaching a total of 45 animals. They start training in obedience, defence, attack and tracking under the direction of a captain assisted by the brigade of dog training service of the German Army.

In 1947, the School of Police Dog Training was established, with a captain, lieutenant, sergeant, seven corporals and several police officers, in proportion to the number of dogs. Their mission was the training of dog handlers, and the care, preparation and training of dogs, and to perform custodial services. At first it used German shepherds, and then incorporated other breeds such as Airedale terriers, Doberman pinschers and boxers.

During 1945–1949, dogs of this school were added to the headquarters of the Guardia Civil de Granada at Avila, Orense, Lugo, La Coruña and Oviedo. As a result, in 1950 the Civil Guard created its own training school, at the School of Armed Police and Traffic.

Spanish Police K9s assist with general policing as well as well as providing a Military Police function in times of war.

In January 1973, the US Military donated to the Spanish police a German shepherd trained in drug detection, and handlers were sent to the US Base to receive training. In 1975 the first services were performed in this field, since the traffic and consumption of drugs, mainly hashish, is a serious problem in the country.

Following the terrorist bombings committed in the early 1970s came the need to train dogs to detect explosive substances, and by 1976 a small contingent of officers and dogs were qualified in this field. As terrorist groups increased their activity, so too were EDDs gradually increasing numbers.

In 1994 dogs began to be trained in the specialty of rescuing people in rubble and over large areas of terrain. In 2003, in collaboration with the Commissioner General of Police Science, dog training in detection of fire accelerant substances that assist in fire investigation work began.

The effectiveness of specialty handlers is demonstrated in numerous services all over the country:

- Location of explosives: preventive services, and bomb threats, real or simulated

- Drug dogs are used preventively at train stations and bus stops, marine transport and at schools

- Deterrence of rioters at football matches or other mass events considered contentious or high risk

- Location of people buried under debris or natural disasters. Location of people over large areas

- Fire accelerants detection working with experts of Forensic Science in fire investigations

The dog training school holds various courses for officials who belong to the Canine Specialty Guides and other officers with whom the specialty is closely connected, such as those working in the area of narcotics, explosives and public safety. These courses are also designed to update dog handlers in drug, explosives and new training methods to increase their knowledge in operational use. The dog handler course requirements are aimed at officials of the National Police who want to join the Canine Specialty Guides.

In 1982 the Civil Guard Service Cinológica was created in order to support the operational units of the Corps by providing technical and specific support for such tasks as such as searching for missing persons, disaster intervention, drug interdiction and explosives search, mountain rescues and any other special mission. The primary objective remained Law enforcement and protecting the freedoms and guarantee of public security. Civil Guard dogs are distributed throughout the national territory, mainly located in ports, airports, prisons and in capitals of autonomous regions. The Civil Guard operate a total of 500 dogs used to detect explosives as part of the bomb disposal units. Drug detection units in airports and ports, and rescue units. There are also several cadaver detection dogs.

The Civil Guard is a military unit with similar police missions to the French Gendarmerie, the Italian Carabinieri, Portuguese Republican Guard. It has a dog training school and distributes handlers all across Spain which is responsible for teaching expertise to staff being integrated into canine operational units within their specialty such as SAR or Specialist search teams, in addition the School is tasked to train Instructors for teaching dog training. This centre instructs future handlers to be employed throughout the national territory.

SWEDEN

The Swedish Police Service consists of the Swedish National Police Board and 21 county police authorities. Most of the dogs have been trained to be *kombisökhundar* (combination search dogs) meaning they are useful for both narcotics search and tracking criminals. Other dogs have been trained to find for example explosives/weapons, or to be used in arson investigations or as general surveillance dogs (although these are more common with the *väktarna*/guardians).

In 1910 two police officers from Sweden went to Hamburg to purchase police dogs. They came back with the Airedale terrier Cora and the shepherd Leo. Those became the first police dogs in Sweden. Cora and Leo were trained as criminal dogs to be used to aid police investigations.

Today the number of police dogs in Sweden is 364. They are located all over Sweden. The Swedish Police Service decides how many dogs there should be in each county. The police dogs are owned by the service but some of the dogs are owned by the handlers themselves.

Switzerland is regarded as one of the world's most advanced technological countries. Yet regardless of all the modern police equipment, a dog on the ground is still regarded as the most effective piece of kit a police force anywhere in the world can have today.

SWITZERLAND

In the 1900s, dogs were introduced into various police cantons throughout the country to ensure the safety of officers who regularly worked alone. Over the years the missions of canine groups have changed considerably. Currently, the dog is used mainly for its special scent and its acceptance to work with a master.

A group of dogs began working with the Fribourg Cantonal Police in 1912. The following year, a federation of Swiss police dog handlers (FSCCP) was created. Each township has become a section of the federation. Since its creation, the committee chairmanship is assumed by the commander of a cantonal police.

In Fribourg, the number of dog units varies between 12 and 15. Handler's carry out general police missions and use dogs as needed. For their versatility and superior olfactory performance, mainly German shepherds are used for finding people. All handlers own their dog.

Police dog roles include tracing missing persons, searching for perpetrators, search for articles, search for bodies on land or water, searching for traces of blood, drug search, search for explosives and accelerant detection. Police dogs are also used in the defence of their handlers during interception of aggressive fugitives and prevention / deterrent presence.

Puppy training starts at the age of 12 weeks. It lasts between 24 and 32 months. Both handler and dog participate in weekly training after completion of the course. Handlers are also involved in training seminars nationally and internationally. Each handler must complete regular tests and if they do not meet the criteria they are excluded from operational status.

In Fribourg, 12 teams are currently operational to respond to incidents and three teams are in training. Of the 12 pairs operational, three are specialised to search for narcotics; two others are specialised for finding missing persons; another to detect explosives, and for other specialties dogs from other cantons are used. Dogs are used over 700 times a year.

Baron to the Rescue

In the district of Bern in Switzerland, a police dog team responded to a domestic violence incident. The offender was armed with a knife and had seized an infant child from his de facto wife during a domestic argument and threatened to kill her. He was also the father of the child but evidence and history pointed to the fact that due to his mental health he could harm the child.

Police pursued the offender in his vehicle for over 40 kilometres on the autobahn until they deployed 'stingers', a device that blows out car tyres. He remained in the vehicle holding a knife to the infant. Fortunately he had his windows down. Baron, a German shepherd of the Bern dog squad, was released. As other police took the offender's attention Baron ran 20 metres before leaping through the passenger widow. Amazingly the dog grabbed the arm holding the weapon so the offender couldn't use it. Baron is a powerful dog of some 45 kilograms, and he dragged the offender out of the car window, leaving the baby behind.

Less than 24 hours later Baron hit the headlines again. This time a child had wandered off from a school. The seven-year-old was last seen in a forested area that backed onto the school grounds. It was getting dark and cold. Baron was deployed and soon picked up the scent. After 15 minutes of trailing through dense brush Baron was heard barking. When Baron's handler arrived a short time later Baron was lying on the young boy, keeping him warm, while the child held him tightly around the neck. Not a bad day's work.

TAIWAN

The police dog unit of the Special Police Third Headquarter is under the jurisdiction of the Nation Police Administration, which has three sections from the north of Taiwan to the south, with headquarters located in Xindian City. The first corps is located in Keelung City, and the second corps is set up in Kaohsiung City.

The Police Dog Unit (PDU) was established on 15 September 2004. In 2007, the PDU moved to the second corps, and inherited the Pingtung County Fire Department training base. In July 2009, the PDU finally set up its own headquarter in Feng- Xiu south camp in Kaohsiung City. The large site allows all K9s to undergo the latest training techniques. The PDU has developed into a mature unit today.

The unit consists of one captain, eleven police and 29 dogs. The main mission is to assist police conducting container inspections.

The unit uses various breeds of dogs including German shepherd, labrador, Belgian shepherd, Czech Republic shepherd, and English springer spaniels.

After training by qualified instructors, dogs can operate in areas such as armed defender, firearm/explosive and drug detection work.

The CIS PDU has assisted in a variety of tasks, including important events security protection, criminal-controlling, and searching for narcotics and explosives. In 2009/2010 dogs from the unit successfully sniffed out marijuana seeds, contraband cigarettes, and ketamine drugs attempting to be smuggled into Taiwan.

All the dogs that work for the Special Police Third Headquarter are invaluable crime fighting tools.

TURKEY

The use of police service dogs in the Turkish National Police began in different units in 1990. In order to perform professional and efficient police dog training services, the General Directorate of Turkish National Police established a Dog Training Centre Branch Headquarters affiliated to the Department of Training in 1997, with the help of the United Nations Drug Control Program, and the European Committee of the Foundation for Supporting The Turkish Police Department.

Turkey uses police dogs in their fight against drug smugglers and in general policing work.

In 2002 the Dog Training Centre became associated with the Department of Anti-Smuggling and Organized Crime due to the necessity of the service and changing circumstances.

The process of training the type of police dogs that the police departments required commenced with narcotics detection dogs training. However, due to the various needs of police units, dogs and handlers commenced training in six different fields: narcotics, explosives detection, weapon smuggling, search and rescue, cadaver and patrol work. The Dog Training Centre also provides training programs for the other law enforcement agencies personnel and their dogs.

The Dog Training Centre carries out activities such as supplying appropriate service dogs by means of breeding, grant and purchasing, socialisation of puppies, selecting the personnel to work with those dogs, setting the working principles for dogs and their handlers, holding training activities, carrying out initiatives for appointment and relocation, evaluating the performance of service dogs and their handlers, supplying garments, training and other equipment, medical support, meeting the transportation needs, shipment, nutrition and accommodation.

The dog species that are best able to adapt to the climate and weather conditions as well as geographical and regional conditions of the country have been identified and evaluated by the expert dog trainers and veterinarians. Based on this evaluation, specified dogs are bred and trained in the centre. Tests conducted by specialised puppy trainers at the 7th, 8th and 12th weeks reveal first whether puppies will succeed as detection dogs, and second which fields they can best be used in.

The achievements in seizures by detection dogs trained in the Dog Training Centre have been many. Identifying this crime is an important role in revealing the smuggling of narcotics which today is an international crime. Turkey has an effective role on the international platform due to the transit position between regions where natural and synthetic drugs are produced, transported and consumed. Therefore narcotic detector dogs are increasingly used in the determined fight against illicit production, abuse and trafficking of drugs. The use of the police dogs has greatly decreased the time spent searching and increased the probability of finding a felon or an illegal substance. The number of the service dogs and the fields in which they are used may vary. This is related to the strategies developed according to the politics and needs of the country.

The narcotics detector dog training program is committed to continuing the fight against drug crimes within the framework of inter-agency cooperation and coordination. The course is undertaken by personnel from the Gendarmerie, the Air Force and Customs Enforcement. The program is also available to international services; so far eight countries have participated in the training.

Likewise explosive detection dogs are also trained by the Turkish Police, and cadaver search dog and handler training programs are also held at the Dog Training Centre of the Directorate.

Due to the Marmara earthquake in 1999, live human search dog training programs were initiated to meet the need. These dogs are trained and assigned to the General Directorate of Security and stationed in the various provinces and central units. After natural disasters the police force search and rescue teams also have a primary duty to ensure security of life and property.

The Anti-Smuggling and Organized Crime Department carries out activities in the fight against cyber crimes, as well as the prevention of laundering proceeds of. Banknote detector dog training methodology, review, evaluation and program development was completed in 2007.

Odour identification training for dogs in Turkey started in 2006. Forensic research and training is still going on, this method is used by some agencies in Germany, Hungary, Poland, Belgium, the Netherlands and the United States.

Explosive detector dogs and handlers are continuously monitored in their performance and qualifications. High standards are demanded due to the nature of their work; dogs trained in this field ensure security of lives and prevent possible terrorist acts, They search international meetings protection of state buildings, vehicles, searching of sports facilities, airports, large and populous areas and gatherings such as concerts and ceremonies.

Arms ammunition detector dog training started in 2004. Detector dogs are trained in this area, for the fight against organised crime and terrorist organisations in Turkey. Because of the successful work in this field, it is planned to increase the number of dogs in the future.

Special operation Dogs are used in areas of high probability of armed conflict, such as hostage rescue operations. Dogs were assigned to special operations units, increasing the capacity of the operation; they are an important contribution to high risk situations.

UNITED KINGDOM

The achievements of police dogs in Ghent, Belgium, spread to several continental countries prompting the Metropolitan Police to take an interest in using police dogs during the 1920s. An experimental school was established to examine training, to determine which breeds had the most aptitude for police work and to begin formally training dogs. After World War II more experiments were run, including a highly successful test in using dogs to accompany patrols in Hyde Park. On their very first night in the park one of the dogs foiled a purse snatching attempt, and the crime rate in the park plummeted. This success proved the value of the dog section and in 1953, a specialised training unit was set up. Various other police forces were experimenting with dogs and in 1954 a standing committee was formed to co-ordinate the breeding, supply and training of police dogs throughout the United Kingdom.

The popularity of the police dog increased all over England with police forces both large and small employing dogs and handlers on their strength and setting up dog training schools to cater for the ever increasing number of dogs being used.

Today the value of the police dog has been recognised to such an extent that there are over 2500 police dogs employed among the various police forces in the UK with the German shepherd still the most popular breed for general purpose work with the Belgian shepherd (Malinois) catching up fast, proven when a Belgian shepherd female called Metpol, handled by PC Graham Clarke of the Metropolitan Police, won the 2008 National Police Dog Trials with the highest score ever recorded.

England

All English police dogs, irrespective of the discipline they are trained in, must be licensed to work operationally. To obtain the licence they have to pass a test at the completion of their training, and then again every year until they retire, which is usually at about the age of eight when the majority settle into a life as a family pet with their handler. The standards required to become operational are laid down by the Association of Chief Police Officers sub-committee on police dogs and are reviewed on a regular basis to ensure that training and licensing reflect the most appropriate methods and standards.

Many English police services now source the majority of their replacement dogs from within specialised police dog breeding programs designed to ensure that the dogs are bred with strong working ethics and health as a priority. The Metropolitan Police has the largest police dog breeding program in the UK supplying not only the capital city, London, but many other parts of the UK and the world with police dogs.

In the United Kingdom dogs have always had a tactical use in police forces as for centuries the British Police have remained unarmed, only special units carrying firearms. Dogs have therefore been the main back up to the police officer on the beat, if a situation was to aggressive for them to handle a dog team was called in.

Metropolitan Police Dogs

In 1914, following experiments in Germany and elsewhere, the Metropolitan Police Service introduced 172 dogs of various breeds to accompany officers on patrol. That year an officer and dog were commended for saving a person from drowning in a lake (and the dog got a new collar!).

In 1938 two labradors became perhaps the first true police dogs patrolling in Peckham. Following World War II, six labradors were introduced to combat crime and in 1948 the first German shepherd dog was used by the Metropolitan Police Service. The dogs were very successful and numbers grew until in 1950 there were 90. The Dog section was then based at Imber Court, Surrey.

In 1954 the current Metropolitan Police Service Dog Training Establishment at Keston, Kent, was opened, where all dog training courses take place. Since then the Dog Support Unit has been at the forefront of police dog training, constantly looking for new ways to use the special abilities of dogs to improve officer and public safety, and detect and prevent crime. Today, around 250 dogs of various types are currently working across the Metropolitan Police Service.

The role of the Dog Support Unit of the Metropolitan Police Service is to provide police dog and handler teams to support their colleagues across London, and to respond to emergency calls where their unique skills to help make London safer. The dogs and handlers have a variety of skills including:

- Searching for suspects and missing people

- Locating objects dropped or concealed during a criminal incident

- Following a track left by a person on the ground

- Chasing and detaining a person who runs away when challenged to stop

- Disarming violent armed suspects and controlling hostile crowds

Some of the more specialist skills include:

- Line access work: Some officers and their dogs are 'line access' trained. The officers often have to get themselves and their dogs up and down the outside of buildings or even boats using abseiling skills. The dogs are trained to cope with being tied to their handlers, via a harness, during these operations

- Supporting Metropolitan Police Service Firearms teams

Some dogs, particularly spaniels and labradors, are trained to find specific scents:

- Drugs, both hidden and being carried on a person in public

- Cash, (banknotes)

- Explosives, of various types

- Firearms

- Human remains and blood

Some of the above skills may be combined in one dog team, but explosives search dogs only search for one thing.

Police dogs operate anywhere it is safe to do so, in London and sometimes outside. They work from bases in five boroughs, namely Hillingdon, Redbridge, Lewisham, Croydon and Wandsworth.

Metropolitan Police Dogs are trained to:

- Search crime scenes, buildings, open spaces, vehicles, vessels, and aircraft (transport infrastructure centres and checkpoints are all regularly patrolled)

- Assist in executing search warrants

- Protect people and places from terrorism

The Operations office deals with most general enquiries about dog services and deals with requests for pre-planned operations. Staff here will also provide statistical information to the management team on deployment of resources.

Each unit provides a 24-hour response. Numbers 1–4 units have general purpose (GP) dogs, usually German shepherds or Belgian shepherd, and drugs/firearms detection dogs. Number 5 unit provides an explosives search dog capability. Some GP dogs are trained to find hidden firearms or human remains, and others can work as part of a tactical firearms team. Many of the unit members are very experienced officers and are able to give expert evidence in cases concerning dangerous or potentially dangerous dogs. Staff may also be called upon to deal with dogs that need to be controlled during entry to premises or out of control in the street. Special equipment is available for this purpose.

Explosives search dogs are used daily to protect people and places in London against the threat of terrorism. High profile events, airports, government buildings, and prominent people are among those they protect.

All dog teams are trained at the Metropolitan Police Dog Training Establishment, Keston, Kent. Many of the dogs are bred there and other dogs are donated by members of the public who can no longer keep them. Courses vary in length according to the type of work involved.

Each dog lives at home with its handler for its working life and usually retires to become a pet with the same handler. Every dog and handler is subject to yearly testing (licensing) and is also regularly checked at training sessions, to ensure high standards of safety and efficiency.

A range of specially adapted response vehicles are available to all units, each with fitted kennel compartments, soundproofing and air-conditioning for the welfare of the dogs. Storage space for specialist equipment is also incorporated in the vehicles.

The first choice of breed of dog for police work is the German shepherd. Its characteristic expression gives the impression of sharp vigilance, fidelity, liveliness and watchfulness. The police-bred and trained German shepherd stays alert to every sight and sound, nothing escapes its attention, it is fearless, and has a decided suspicion of strangers, unlike some breeds which are immediately friendly. The German shepherd's highly developed senses are complemented by its high standard of intelligence.

By the time the dogs are born, bred, reared and finally operational they represent an investment of almost £6000 in time and money. When this dog is on patrol it is considered one of the Metropolitan Police's most powerful deterrents to crime. Yet these dogs should never be considered vicious. They have been very carefully chosen, evaluated and trained to have an even temperament and exert only the force required by any given police situation, and to be only as bold and brave as called for by their handler.

As a team, handler and dog are an extremely sensitive command unit with a level of understanding that often seems to go beyond words. Their temperaments have been matched as carefully as possible, and through living together they can often understand each other in a way that defies description. Both dogs and handlers have risked, and sometimes lost their lives to protect each other. They are a team, and each part of the team has been carefully selected.

A police officer who volunteers to become a dog handler must have completed two years street duty experience as a uniformed police constable and with settled home circumstances. Once approved by a board of senior officers, the prospective handler attends a two-week suitability course to make sure that he or she has the ability and temperament to work with dogs. If the candidate completes this course successfully, he or she is allocated a puppy, which is usually 12 weeks old. The puppy then goes to live in the handler's home and becomes part of his family, creating that level of trust that is the essence of a good working relationship.

At 12 months the dogs take a basic training course. If all goes well, the dog will then be fully schooled as an operational police dog. The training course at Keston is carefully devised to produce the best results by preparing the dogs for almost every situation they are likely to face in their normal round of duties. It is training based on praise, starting with obedience exercises. The training moves on to tracking, following a ground scent over different types of terrain in varying conditions. The dogs are taught to search different types of places such as open country, wooded areas and buildings for criminals and property, and give tongue or 'speak' as soon as they find what they have been seeking.

By the end of the final stage the dogs are completely trained in criminal work involving the chase and attack; standoff; chase in the face of stick, gun and other weapons; and how to control prisoners and crowds. But at all times the training emphasises only the use of enough force necessary to carry out their police duty. At the end of 14 weeks the dogs are ready to go on the streets as operational police dogs. They will be assigned to stations throughout the Metropolitan Police district and can expect their duties to vary widely, from keeping soccer hooligans in order to searching for a lost child.

Devon and Cornwall Police

Traditionally in Devon and Cornwall, German shepherd dogs are used because they possess a range of specialist search skills, but they're used mainly for tracking and stopping criminals. In this part of southern England police dog duties include:

- Tracking missing people

- Searching for missing suspects

- Locating lost or stolen property

- Chasing and detaining suspects

- Keeping order in crowd situations

Some dogs are trained as specialists:

- Firearms support dogs: These dogs work with the Tactical Firearms team and are often the first to enter and search a building, often with cameras attached to their heads, with the monitor held by a police officer

- Explosives dogs: Explosives dogs are trained to search, locate and indicate the presence of military, commercial and homemade explosives.

- Drugs dogs: Proactive drugs dogs are used to search premises, vehicles and areas for drugs and to let their handlers know when drugs have been found. Passive drugs dogs screen the air around individuals, and are often used at concerts and outside night clubs. As well as detecting drugs, they act as a visible deterrent

- Search dogs for tracking lost people: Devon and Cornwall Police are taking the lead in dog training, as the first police force in the country to train dogs specifically to search for people who are lost or who have gone missing

A 13-week course at the police dog training school in Exeter is undertaken by all police dogs, regardless of their handlers' experience.

The ultimate aim of police dog training is for a dog to react in the same way each time it hears a certain command, or sees a visual sign from the handler. To obtain this degree of response from the dog, the handler must be consistent in commands and manner.

Control is the major factor in training dogs; self-control on the part of the handler as well as control over the dog. Self-control requires that handlers must, at all times, have complete control over themselves. A handler who loses their temper during the training period will also lose control of the dog. Handlers must have 100 per cent confidence in both their dog's ability and their own in controlling his dog.

Training is very much reward-based, be it physically, verbally or with food. Each handler must find out what works best for his or her own dog and apply it in such a manner as to suit the particular dog. Once the dog becomes operational, similar techniques are employed on the job. Handlers use a 'trigger' such as a hand signal or voice command to let the dog know it is time to work.

Dog training is a continuous process; it doesn't start and end on the training field. Physical contact between the dog and handler is a vital ingredient in the chemistry of producing a successful team.

At the end of this intensive 13-week course, which covers the principles of tracking, searching for people and property, obedience training and criminal work, there is an assessment to ascertain whether the dogs are qualified to go operational. The dogs have to pass a Home Office inspection once a year to ensure they are safe and effective and can confidently carry out the tasks expected of them.

Being a police dog handler is a long-term commitment. Police dogs have an average working life of about seven years and live with their handler both throughout their working life and into retirement. Police dogs live with their handlers and must be sociable and family-oriented.

At eight weeks old, they place suitable puppies with a volunteer puppy walker whose job it is to look after the puppy in their own home for one year and expose the dog to a variety of experiences. The puppy walkers must have a settled family background and a secure garden. They will undertake to regularly exercise, groom and care for the dog whilst also giving it a good upbringing in line with advice from our dog school. The Police provide dog food and pay for any veterinary costs incurred.

The puppy walker is given a handbook in which to record the variety of situations the puppy has experienced, including: a bustling town centre; a busy road filled with traffic; walking on rough terrain; a beach; a grassy park; a shiny shop floor.

The aim of the puppy development scheme is for the puppy walker to hand over a well-balanced, confident and social dog at the end of the year. If the puppy has successfully completed this stage, it is then ready to begin a 13-week course with the handler to whom it has been assigned.

North Yorkshire Police Dog Section

The Dog Section has one sergeant, 20 constables, two dog trainers and 35 dogs, assisting North Yorkshire Police divisions on a 24-hour basis, seven days a week.

The core functions carried out by this Dog Section include crime prevention and operational patrols; searching buildings and open ground for missing and wanted people; searching and recovering evidence; drugs detection and explosive detection; tracking suspects; tactical firearms operations; supporting community-based initiatives; public order response and high-profile, proactive, intelligence-led patrols. All of these operational functions actively contribute to public reassurance, response policing and engaging criminality.

Newly recruited police dogs can donated by a member of the public or purchased at a nominal cost; other dogs are purchased from specialist breeders. They will vary in age from 12 months to three years old.

Before the new recruits are accepted they are carefully assessed. Each dog must carry out a series of tests, specially designed to help identify whether or not the animal possesses the necessary instincts and temperament required.

Puppies from an established line of working stock will be placed with experienced handlers or puppy walkers and be brought on through the 'puppy program'.

The dog is continually assessed and, if all is well and the dog passes all its assessments, it will be paired with a handler. Whichever route the dog has taken to the initial course, the end result is the same. The dog is trained in all tasks required in order to become a fully licensed operational police dog.

Both dog and handler are carefully selected and trained to ensure all the necessary skills are fully developed. A serving police officer must have successfully completed an initial two-year probationary period before they can apply to join the Dog Section. A potential dog handler attends a two week familiarisation course. At the end of the two weeks the candidates and the dog training centre staff must decide whether they are suitable.

The course is physically and mentally demanding: The handlers must quickly learn new and varied subjects ranging from legislation to veterinary practices and canine psychology. During the training the dog and handler form an extremely strong bond.

The training is based upon positive reinforcement and harnessing instinctive behaviour patterns. Throughout training the dog's natural abilities are identified, encouraged and enhanced. Training encourages an animal to use its instinctive drives in a controlled situation and on command. A dog's natural abilities form the basis for many of the exercises in police dog training. One of the most important natural instincts is the dog's willingness to please the pack leader. For the police dog, this is the handler.

The police dog is constantly rewarded and praised for its hard work and given good food, care, exercise and protection. On completion of the initial course, the dog and handler are assessed and if they have achieved the required standards they are licensed to become operational, as a team. Training will continue to be a vital part of the team, with emphasis on control, safety and efficiency. Re-licensing will occur annually throughout the working life of the dog, to ensure the required standards are maintained.

All of our dogs are kept at their handler's homes to ensure they remain bonded. All of the police dogs receive holidays alongside their handler. This will usually be spent at home with the handler or in the police kennels. General purpose dogs are usually retired around seven to eight years old. Specialist dogs are retired at around ten years old. The handler is allowed to keep their dog and many choose to do this. However, if this is not possible, the dog will be re-homed with a suitable family for the rest of its life.

All general purpose police dogs serving within North Yorkshire Police are German shepherds. The breeds of dog generally used for explosive detection are springer spaniels, labrador retrievers or springerdors, a springer labrador mix. It is vitally important that dogs selected for explosive search work are of sound temperament, well socialised, and able to search in a variety of venues and conditions.

Once selected, a specialist dog and handler undertakes an eight-week training course in the methods of explosive detection. The dog team, on completion of the course, will assist in any Royal or VIP visits within the North Yorkshire region and at divisions in the event of a bomb threat.

The main breeds of dogs used for drug detection are springer spaniels, labrador retrievers and springerdors. On completion of assessment, the dog and handler undertake a six-week training course in the methods of drugs detection. All dogs are trained to search open ground, commercial buildings, vehicles and private houses for various illegal drugs.

Dogs can be skilled in the method of 'body scanning'. This involves the dog and handler searching large groups of people within queues, premises or vehicles. When the dog detects the scent of drugs, it indicates to the handler by sitting quietly beside the person concerned.

Surrey Police

Surrey Police Dog Training School was the first EdExcel Foundation Approved Centre for Dog Training, with CENTREX (UK Quality Assured) status. It is one of the top five largest and busiest dog training schools in the UK.

To date they have trained eight customs explosives search dogs, and have ongoing partnerships with Singapore Police and Hong Kong Customs. Through their partnership with Euro-Customs Paris, they are working towards training passive drugs dogs for both Lithuanian and Latvian customs.

Surrey Police train dogs for clients all over the globe. This includes a yearly dog and handler exchange with the Australian Army. They use all kinds of breeds within the police service and Customs, mainly German shepherds, labradors, spaniels, border collies, Rottweilers and Dobermans.

Dogs are trained to be:

- Passive dogs: Detection of drugs on persons

- Proactive dogs: Detection of drugs in a specific area, such as a warehouse, airport baggage control, nightclubs, schools or offices

- Explosives dogs: Searches of suspect items at any location such as airports, in vehicles or at facilities were VIPs may attend. They also search for firearms at incidents

- General purpose dogs: Used for tracking, searching for persons or property, and the chasing and detaining of fleeing offenders

Dogs are trained at the Surrey Police Dog Training School for police, customs, prison service and security service work, and then exported to the client. An assumption is made that a handler is ready and waiting at the receiving end. The handler can undergo a brief period of familiarisation at the end of training if required.

Whether used in drugs, property and firearms searches, helping to find missing persons, or being involved in public, sometimes violent disorder, the Operational Dog Section has played an integral part of the Surrey Police's service to the community since the 1940s.

The Operational Dog Section is a county-based resource, supporting the four divisional policing areas within the county. This way Surrey Police ensures area responsibilities, creating stronger links to the local officers on the ground, and the local community. Information can filter quickly from the areas of crime and/or conflict to the local handler, who can therefore react efficiently to the problems on his/her patch.

The issue is not about how many arrests the dogs can help make, but about acting as a deterrent. For instance, the dogs are used to help disrupt the flow of drugs. A business, club or school that is aware of a problem but does not know how to resolve it can contact the dog section to take the intermediate step. With their extremely acute sense of smell, the dogs are trained to find not just people who are carrying drugs, but even those who have come into contact with an illegal substance.

German shepherds are the most popular general purpose dogs used by the Surrey Police (and most police forces), as they not only have the combination of size, controllable aggression, stamina and will to work, but they also accept training willingly.

Clever Clover

Hundreds of people are reported as lost each year, with the most common incidents involving elderly people wandering off from aged care homes or people becoming disorientated when walking on places such as the moors. Devon and Cornwall Police dog handlers have trained three springer spaniels and one Brittany dog to hunt for lost or missing people who might be in danger, with great success. The spaniels differ in skill because they are trained to bark when they find someone; they run backwards and forwards between the person and their handler, eventually leading the handler to their find.

Clover, a 15-month-old spaniel, has already found two missing people, including one young woman who had run away from a care home, and was scared of large dogs. Clover found her, making it far less traumatic than if a German shepherd had been deployed.

Police Dog Inspector Andy Lilburn said: 'Our existing general purpose dogs are fantastic at what they do but vulnerable people are often scared when confronted by a German shepherd dog. Spaniels have a very friendly temperament so are perfect for these types of searches. They work well with people and other animals. They have a lot of stamina and are keen working dogs, which is crucial when searching for long periods of time.'

Buster and Duke on Patrol

Two RAF dogs, who have served in Afghanistan, were recently on patrol with the City of London Police Dog Unit so that the two forces could learn from each other's experiences. With the increased threat of domestic terrorism the joint patrols help reassure the population that the streets are safe.

One of the RAF K9s, air dog Buster, is an arms and explosives search dog with five operational tours under his collar.

'Buster really is something special. He's shown courage under fire in both Iraq and Afghanistan, from small arms fire to mortar attack. Each time he stayed calmly by his handler's side, and after the enemy contact was over he would continue his job; leading foot patrols, keeping the team safe as he searched for improvised explosive devices.'

Accompanying Buster was air dog Duke, a vehicle search dog, and his handler Corporal Heather Lacey, who talks of the special bond they have, and the morale boost working dogs provide for the troops:

'In Iraq, Duke and I were together for 24 hours a day, with him sleeping on the bottom of my sleeping bag. He flew in C-17 aircraft and Merlin helicopters, as well as worked with the Danish Army and the Household Cavalry. He is also used to travelling in the back of armoured vehicles with whatever team we are assigned to.'

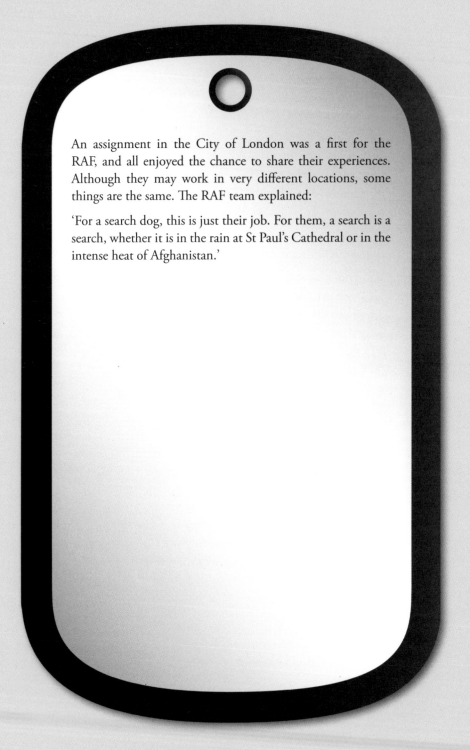

An assignment in the City of London was a first for the RAF, and all enjoyed the chance to share their experiences. Although they may work in very different locations, some things are the same. The RAF team explained:

'For a search dog, this is just their job. For them, a search is a search, whether it is in the rain at St Paul's Cathedral or in the intense heat of Afghanistan.'

SCOTLAND

Strathclyde Police

The Strathclyde Police Dog Branch is based at Pollok Country Park, Pollok, Glasgow. From headquarters they deploy police dogs throughout the Strathclyde Region. The centre is also designated as the Scottish Regional Police Dog Training School for all Scottish forces. Strathclyde Police was created on 16 May 1975 from the merger of several police services. It is the largest of the eight Scottish police forces.

The Dog Section consists of one sergeant and five constables, who are centrally based in Inverness and form part of Operational Support. Each officer handles a general purpose dog (German shepherd) and a specialist drugs or explosives search dog (springer spaniels/labradors). All the dogs live with the handlers and their families.

The dog branch specialise in training dogs for a range of policing support roles including:

- General purpose

- Drugs detection

- Explosive detection

- Offender detection

- Tactical firearms support

Handlers and dogs perform a range of valuable policing roles including:

- Crowd management at major sporting events

- Searching buildings and open ground for missing and wanted people

- Searching for evidence

- Drugs detection and explosive detection

- Tracking suspects

- Recovering victims

- Tactical firearms operations

- Supporting community-based initiatives

- Public order response

- High-profile, proactive, intelligence-led patrols

All of these operational functions actively contribute to public reassurance, response policing and engaging criminality.

 Dogs can come to the force through the general public as a donation or purchase, or through specialist puppy programs.

Every dog has to undergo extensive training. The general patrol dogs (German shepherds) have to complete a 12-week course with their handlers at a training school. This training involves basic skills, obedience and agility exercises. If this course is successfully completed, the dog and handler will be able to start patrol work.

The 12-week course is for all general patrol dogs, regardless of their handlers' experience and is held at the Strathclyde Police Dog School. The ultimate aim of police dog training is that a dog will react in the same way each time it hears a certain command or sees a visual sign from the handler. To obtain this degree of response from the dog, the handler must be consistent in commands and manner.

Training is very much reward based, be it physically, verbally or with food. Each handler must find out what works best for his own dog and apply it in such a manner as to suit his particular dog. Once the dog finally becomes operational, similar techniques are employed on the job. Handlers use a 'trigger', such as a hand signal or voice command to let the dog know it is time to work.

The course covers the principles of tracking, searching for people and property, obedience training and criminal work. At the end, there is an assessment to decide whether the dogs are qualified to go into operational work. Continuous assessment is very much a part of dog policing. The dogs also have to pass a Home Office inspection once a year to ensure they are safe and effective, and can carry out the tasks expected of them.

Also, to ensure the dogs are fully trained, both dog and handler have to attend regular training days and local refresher courses. The aims of these courses are to continually learn new skills and improve those already learnt on the initial course. Police dog training is a continuous process, it doesn't start and end on the training field.

Fife Constabulary Dog Section

Fife Constabulary Dog Section was instigated in July 1958 by the chief constable, who tasked two officers to research and purchase two German shepherds from Surrey. Both officers later attended an Initial Dog Training Course at Guildford, Surrey.

In January 1959 the Chief Constable issued a memorandum making the Dog Section official from this date. By April 1964 the section had grown to six general purpose handlers. Three handlers were based in Kirkcaldy and three in Dunfermline to provide the county with dog cover.

The present strength of the unit is a sergeant and seven constables, each handling a general purpose dog. The section also has dogs capable of drugs, cash or explosive detection. On the staffing are two Association of Chief of Police Officers (ACPO) accredited police dog instructors who are responsible for the training of both the dogs and handlers.

In the past Fife Constabulary obtained their dogs from members of the public. Suitability to become a police dog was then assessed prior to being allocated to a handler for training. Currently all the general purpose dogs are purchased as pups or young adults from some of the larger forces who run specific breeding programs.

All general purpose dogs within the section are currently German shepherds. The specialist dogs used to detect drugs or explosives are still acquired as gift dogs from members of the public. Spaniels and labrador retrievers currently undertake these roles.

The primary role of every member of the dog section is to handle a general purpose police dog.

General purpose initial courses take up to 12 weeks to complete. All instruction is carried out by ACPO accredited police dog instructors. The teams are thereafter required to continue to show development and pass a relicensing assessment on an annual basis

The main functions of the general purpose dog are

- Obedience

- Tracking

- Person search

- Property search

- Apprehending violent offenders

- Crowd control

The section has specialist dogs that are trained in passive/scanning drugs detection. Some of the dogs have also been trained to recover cash. The training of the dogs and handlers takes up to six weeks and is carried out internally. They are trained to search in different environments such as vehicles, buildings and outside spaces.

The section also has an explosive detection capability. It takes up to ten weeks to train both dog and handler. Training takes place at the Scottish Regional Police Dog Training School in Glasgow. The dogs are used at major events, VIP visits and as operationally required.

At the end of each shift the dogs go home with their handler. The dogs spend all their off duty time with the handler and their family. The dogs and their handlers work exclusively as a team and spend a huge amount of time together creating a lifelong bond. The general purpose dogs retire at around eight years old, normally into the care of their handler.

Tayside Police Dog Section

The Tayside Police Dog Section is based at Baluniefield Police Station in the Douglas area of Dundee, but has responsibility for providing police dogs throughout the whole force area.

The section comprises one dog instructor and eight dog handlers, one of whom is also an instructor. Each of the dog handlers has a general purpose police dog and a specialist search dog.

Dog handlers are operational police officers and as such they carry out intelligence-led high profile patrols in order to deter and catch criminals and to reassure the public. The dog handlers are a force resource and can be tasked to a specific area or police operation where their specialist knowledge can be of assistance.

Tayside Police's dog handlers and instructors need to be instinctively aware of a dog's potential for police work by gauging its intelligence levels and general temperament from an early stage. Officers involved in this process must show an affinity with and a dedication to the animals they work with, making the relationship between dog and handler one of mutual trust and absolute loyalty.

Officers must complete two years' probation as well as two years core policing work before being considered for a post in the dog section. They then have to submit an application and only those of a particular disposition and aptitude will be considered.

The Force's general purpose police dogs are all German shepherds. Members of the public have gifted most of these dogs to the police. General purpose police dogs start their training when they are between 12 and 24 months old and will work until they are between 7 and 8 years old.

Each new dog receives a minimum of 12 weeks intensive training and must pass a test to be licensed before becoming operational. Each dog receives a minimum of 16 days training per year after this and must be relicensed every year. Handlers also carry out further training on a day to day basis.

A dog handler will always issue a standard challenge to suspects who are running away. If the suspect stops running the dog will stop beside them and bark. However, if they carry on running, the dog will give chase and bring them down.

The force's specialist search dogs are labradors, springer and cocker spaniels and a German wire-haired pointer. The specialist search drugs dogs are trained to search for the main categories of unlawful drugs and in addition they are trained to search for cash and weapons. There are also some trained to scan and indicate people carrying unlawful drugs. A further two of the specialist dogs are trained to search for explosives.

The length of initial training they undergo can vary depending upon the specialist role they are being trained for. All of these dogs will also undergo regular training and along with their handlers must also be relicensed annually.

WALES

The South Wales Police (SWP) Dog Section opened its doors on 23 August 1960, after the arrival of four German shepherds and a team of fledging handlers. Since then the Dog Training School has gone on to become one of the most respected and influential institutions in the UK.

As part of the Operational Support Division, the Dog Section provides help and reinforcement for police officers across the South Wales region. With thanks to years of dedicated training, the SWP Dog School has helped to establish the dog as a vital member of the policing team. Working together with their handlers and divisional officers, the dogs ensure that South Wales remains safe.

A modern day police dog section needs to be able to tackle its current challenges and threats in a robust and dynamic manner. The present unit is experienced and equipped to track persons and property in a huge variety of emergency situations. Situations where they help include: vulnerable missing persons, locating criminals who've recently committed burglaries, car crime offences or violent crime such as armed offenders.

Canines have never been so utilised or in demand as they are today. With the ever-increasing crime rate rising, this trend looks set to continue and the future of police dogs in Wales looks likely to only increase.

Residing peacefully away from the hustle and bustle of Police Headquarters, the SWP Dog Section in Waterton is home to 74 operational dogs and their dedicated team of handlers. Listening to the cacophony of gruff barks reverberating around the training school, it's hard to believe that in 1960 just four dogs resided there. Bruce, Bess, Carl and Cora (the latter two hailing from Edinburgh City Police) were just four months old when they began their long and successful careers as the first South Wales Police dogs.

From this young age, the new recruits underwent numerous training courses with their fledging handlers before becoming fully operational. From the evidence of cases reported during 1960, it seems that the dogs took to their duties with ease. Despite being just six months old and only partially trained, Carl was responsible for the arrest of three men stealing Christmas trees in Tonyrefail during December 1960. Similarly, Bess gave an indication to her handler which resulted in the arrest of a man in Maesteg on a charge of breaking and entering, whilst she was still under a year old.

As the early police dogs moved from strength to strength in their roles, so the Dog Section looked to refine and expand the skills the animals could bring to the South Wales Police. The year 1969 saw the introduction of explosive search dogs to the force. Sergeant Ian Roderick explains how this proved to be a major step in the history of dog training: 'The explosive dogs were the first in the UK, and originated to tackle the rising number of attacks being carried out by the Free Wales Army. The Metropolitan Police were approached to train these dogs, but they claimed that it couldn't be done. We took it upon ourselves to train them instead, and the results were astounding. There are now around 380 explosive dogs in the UK which have all derived from the pioneering work done by the South Wales Police.'

Following the terrorist attacks in London and New York, major work was undertaken in the detection of liquid explosives. In 2007 the SWP rolled out the training for this threat at a national level, and in the process secured a reputation as one of the most respected and influential dog sections in the UK.

The hard work and dedication of the dog handlers and their animals continues to push the boundaries of crime detection. In 1991 they established narcotic detection dogs and in the same year introduced a firearms detection capability. Currency detection was then developed in 2002, and in 2008 a passport detection dog for the Immigration Service was introduced.

Dogs continue to be a vital asset to the policing team. Their most recent ground-breaking work is the training of dogs to detect mobile phones and SIM cards for Her Majesty's Prison Service.

Dog breeds used by SWP:

- German shepherds
- Belgian shepherds (Malinois)
- Springer/cocker spaniels
- Labradors
- Rottweilers

Dog roles at SWP:

- General duties dogs
- Firearms support dogs
- Pro-active drugs dogs
- Passive drugs dogs
- Explosive search dogs
- Cadaver dogs
- Conflict management dogs

The SWP Dog School has trained service dogs for forces all over the world, including police in Bermuda and Hong Kong. The school provides instruction not only for South Wales Police officers, but for handlers from the Welsh and South West of England regions. Police officers from Cheshire, Leicestershire. Members of the Police Service of Northern Ireland have also attended as students as have individuals from the Ministry of Defence, British Army, Prison Service and the Royal Air Force.

Taz to the Rescue

The following story is just a sample of what the dogs have achieved recently. Many of these crimes may not have been detected without the skill of the handlers and the instincts and training of the dogs themselves.

Sometime between 9 and 11pm on Wednesday 13 January 2010, a 75-year-old man suffering from Alzheimer's went missing from his home address. He was wearing only jeans, a jumper and two left boots. It was a very cold night with a recent fresh fall of snow and deep snow already lying from previous weeks. The man was a keen walker and was very fit for his age.

PC Galloway and his dog Taz were asked to attend some two hours after the man was thought to have set out, and located a track on a farm road 2 miles from his home. The track continued over numerous fields and hills, through very deep snow and over extremely rough and difficult terrain. The weather conditions were exceedingly poor with extremely cold, snowy and foggy conditions, but Taz continued to track for over two hours.

Taz finally tracked to where the man was kneeling in snow up to his middle and suffering from hypothermia due to his limited clothing. He would not have survived for much longer had he not been found by PC Galloway and Taz.

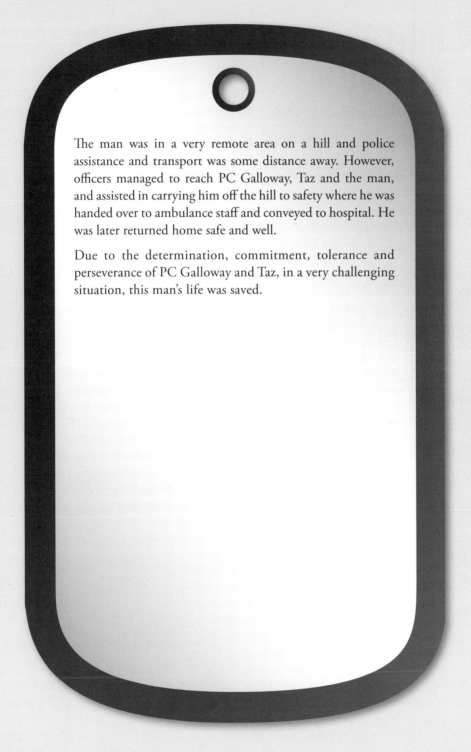

The man was in a very remote area on a hill and police assistance and transport was some distance away. However, officers managed to reach PC Galloway, Taz and the man, and assisted in carrying him off the hill to safety where he was handed over to ambulance staff and conveyed to hospital. He was later returned home safe and well.

Due to the determination, commitment, tolerance and perseverance of PC Galloway and Taz, in a very challenging situation, this man's life was saved.

BRITISH SPECIALIST POLICE K9 UNITS

Ministry of Defence Police

The Ministry of Defence Police (MDP) is a special police force that is part of the Ministry of Defence Police and Guarding Agency which was formed by an administrative merger of the MDP and Ministry of Defence Guard Service on 1 April 2004. The MDP is classed as a 'special police force' in UK law. It is primarily responsible for providing police, investigative and guarding services to Ministry of Defence property, personnel and installations throughout the United Kingdom. MDP officers are attested as constables.

The MDP has approximately 3500 police officers based at 110 police units at 86 locations across the United Kingdom. Within the force the dog sections consist of 400 dog handlers which use explosive, drug, tactical firearms support, and general purpose police dogs. The MDP has the most dogs of any UK police force.

General purpose (GP) police dogs and their handlers are deployed at 23 dog sections across the United Kingdom. The GP teams are trained and licensed in accordance with the National Police Dog Assessment Model. Selected teams will undertake further training to enable them to deploy in a tactical firearms support role alongside firearms officers. The force also operates several classifications of specialist search dogs which are deployed to search and indicate the presence of explosives and drugs, as well as firearms. All dog teams within the Force Dog Section undertake regular Refresher Course and Continuation Training, which is delivered by accredited instructors. MDP dogs are provided by the Defence Animal Centre at Melton Mowbray where both handlers and dogs are trained.

The majority of dogs used are general purpose police dogs, employed to contribute an additional policing and security dimension. The dogs are trained to search for property (evidence), to search and track persons, and to aid their handlers by restraining persons. Police dogs are used for high security patrols at some Minister of Defence locations. MDP dog teams are the only police dog teams in the UK to carry out high risk explosives searches.

Many dogs are trained in specialised areas:

- The tactical firearms support dog is deployed as a tactical 'less than lethal' option at any incident where there is the possibility that lethal force might be required

- The arms, explosive search dogs are a high profile, effective deterrent used as a pro-active response to the threat from terrorist activity

- Drug detection dogs carry out searches of buildings, vehicles and vessels for the detection of all types of controlled drugs

Canine welfare is a priority. The practices and procedures involved in the treatment, care, training and employment of MDP dogs are constantly appraised and reviewed. The Force Dog Officer represents the MDP on the Association of Chief Police Officers, Police Dog Working Group which includes representatives from all Home Office police forces across the UK.

The UK has several specialist police forces including the Ministry of Defence Police; a team used to patrol high threat government facilities.

The Civil Nuclear Constabulary

The Civil Nuclear Constabulary (CNC) has a very exclusive role; it provides protection for civil nuclear licensed sites and safeguards nuclear materials, nuclear site operators, policing and nuclear regulators as well as interlinking with Home Office forces. The CNC has a policing responsibility with a difference. With over 900 highly trained police officers and police staff, it protects 15 civil nuclear sites across England, Scotland and Wales, safeguarding nuclear material in transit and playing a key role in national security.

The CNC use dog teams extensively to patrol these sites. Becoming a CNC dog handler can involve being with your dog 24/7, as all handlers are required to home kennel. The role involves conducting offsite, fence and full site checks, patrolling the site and checking vast areas of land. This means it involves a lot of exercise and walking, and handlers require a high fitness level.

Dog handlers receive comprehensive training. The quality of their training means the CNC dog teams find themselves in demand from other forces to help them with incidents. CNC dogs are trained for a variety of roles, from general purpose police work to explosives detection. The CNC Constabulary Dog Training Facility provides full training for dogs and their handlers, as well as giving advice and guidance to all CNC units on the care, welfare and deployment of police dogs. The standard of training for all handlers, dogs and instructors is at Home Office levels and the CNC liaises closely with other Home Office forces.

One of the key challenges is maintaining the supply of replacement dogs, although in recent years CNC has started its own puppy breeding scheme. As some serving dogs are getting older, replacing them will still be a major challenge, as breeding and training a dog to the required CNC standards takes a long time.

British Transport Police

The first police dogs went on patrol at Hull Docks in 1908. Initially there were four dogs called Jim, Vic, Mick and Ben. Jim's handler was Sergeant Allinson, who was pictured in the local press and the nationally circulated *Pall-Mall* and *Penny Pictorial* magazines. The latter reported: 'In a novel experiment by the North Eastern Railway Police, dogs are used as detectives on the docks at Hull. They consist of a number of trained Airedale terriers which, in company with the railway police, patrol throughout the night and capture thieves, tramps and other persons who may be sleeping out. The dogs are trained to obey a police whistle and to chase and stop a man who is running away.'

On 26 November 1908 the scheme extended to Hartlepool Docks and shortly afterwards to the Tyne Dock and Middlesbrough Docks, all policed by the North Eastern Railway Police. The dogs were all trained at Hull where kennels had been erected and were issued with a coat to wear during bad weather.

These dogs were only used at night and were probably not specific to an individual handler. They were trained to protect the police uniform; indeed to attack anyone who was not wearing a uniform as anyone not in uniform in the docks at night could be considered a suspect. The dogs would even growl at their own handlers when they were not in uniform.

After World War I the dog section was subject to a review and in 1923 the Hull trainers decided to use Alsatians, the favoured dog of the German Army during the conflict. It took until the late 1920s for other 'non-railway' police forces to become interested in the use of police dogs and it was in 1934 that the Home Office set up a committee to evaluate their use. It was initially felt that dogs on the streets would harm the police's relationship with the public, but eventually the go-ahead was given in 1938.

After the war many different railway and dock police forces amalgamated to become the British Transport Commission Police. This new force, the second largest in the country, had a police dog strength of 24. A new police dog training centre was established at Inmans Farm, Hedon Hall near Hull, with the kennels located in converted stables. The Officer in Charge of this new school was Inspector John Morrell, who not only obtained gift dogs but begun to breed pedigree dogs for use by the force. It was under his stewardship, and with the support of Chief Constable Arthur West that the strength of the dog section was increased to 75.

In 1960 Inspector Morrell died at the age of 46 and his role was taken on by Inspector Herbert Shelton who was recruited from another force for the task. Inspector Shelton was responsible for the construction of a new police dog training centre at Elstree in Hertfordshire. This new facility allowed more dogs to be trained and dog handler posts were established at many stations and docks throughout the country including Southampton Docks which formed its dog section in 1962.

It was at Southampton in 1973 where Police Constable 'Spud' Murphy trained his general purpose dog to detect cannabis that was being imported into the country, often amongst goods and freight. The superintendent was so impressed he obtained a dog specifically for this purpose. Cap, named after a ship's captain who donated him, was multi-handled by four officers.

Between 1973 and 1974 arrests by dog handlers rose from 738 to 908 but this did not impress the new Chief Constable Eric Haslam, who had joined the force from the Kent County Constabulary. He reduced the dog section to 22 officers.

On 4 July 1974 Police Constable Don Gordon and his police dog, Jim, caught a man stealing cable at Grand Terminus Junction, Glasgow. The man slashed the officer around the face and stabbed Jim before escaping. Despite their injuries the team chased and again tackled the man but received further injuries. The officer required 38 stitches but the man is caught and officer and dog received the Whitbread Shield for their brave conduct. This is the first and only time a dog handler has won this award.

Police Constable Parkinson in Manchester became the first British Transportation Police (BTP) officer to undergo training for detecting explosives when in 1980 he and his dog attended a course with the Cheshire Police. In 1982 PC Margaret Lyall, stationed at Glasgow, became the first female dog handler in the force. In 1984 a new dog training school was opened on a site adjacent to the Force Training Centre at Tadworth, Surrey. In 1988 Sgt Ablard was awarded the BEM in the Queen's New Years Honours list for his services to dog handling within British Transport Police.

On 21 December 1989 a terrorist bomb exploded on Pan-Am 747 plane which crashed near the Scottish town of Lockerbie. Two dog handlers from the BTP in Scotland, Davy Connell and Alistair Campbell, arrived on scene within an hour and commenced a tour of duty that lasted 33 hours. The officers and dogs discovered 23 bodies. They were later joined by dog handlers Police Constable's Callum Weir and Neil Russell, who remained on site until the end of the searches four weeks later. The involvement of these four officers was such that they were called to attend court in Holland 11 years later to give evidence relating to the incident.

Passive alert detection (PAD) dogs were first used by Customs and Excise and the Prison Service, and in 1998 the use of such dogs was brought to the attention of Detective Chief Superintendent Peter Whent. As a result Police Constable Judy Bailey attended a Home Office training school with her dog Benji. British Transportation Police were used as a pilot force for this aspect of policing with dogs and the experiment was highly successful. In their first two years together, Judy and Benji made more than 4000 searches which resulted in 1546 arrests. Other forces have now followed the lead of the British Transport Police in training and using PAD dogs.

UNITED STATES OF AMERICA

The United States is one of the world's largest police K9 operators in regard to sheer numbers in the world. Unit sizes vary from over a hundred to just a single sheriff and his K9 in some instances. However, no one knows how many there is exactly and if anybody gives you a number it is a guess. In the US full-time officers, part-time officers, volunteers, search and rescue and fire services all use dogs, add to that the military, Customs, ATF, the Secret Service and many other agencies.

The United States Police Canine Association (USPCA) has about 3000 regular members but K9 police officers are not required to join and membership is strictly a handler's choice. The numbers are vast and to represent the canine police forces in the USA I have selected a limited number hoping to show some diversity in numbers, traditions and geographic locations. According to the United States Police Canine Association, the first K9 competition for police dogs took place in Jacksonville Beach, Florida, in 1964. Today, police dogs are typically considered officers of the law and issued badges and bulletproof vests and, if killed in the line of duty, afforded a funeral ceremony with full police honours.

Bakersfield Police Department K9 Unit

The Bakersfield Police Department K9 Unit in California was established in 1988 with the first teams being placed into service in January 1989. The original team consisted of four German shepherd police dogs which were imported from Europe. The unit has since expanded in size to its current complement of six cross-trained patrol dogs, one labrador retriever that is narcotics detection trained, and a bloodhound for tracking/trailing.

During the last 17 years, the unit has been responsible for thousands of arrests, from burglary to homicide suspects.

Dogs are selected in Europe (previously dogs have been obtained from Holland, Germany, Czechoslovakia, and Hungary), and most have a background in *Schutzhund* which is a dog training sport commonly practised in Europe. The dogs usually have a basic understanding of tracking, obedience, and handler protection. Once they are imported and arrive in Bakersfield, they are matched to a handler.

An eight-week training period follows during which the handler bonds with his dog and the teams are trained to effectively work together. During this training period, the teams are taught to perform open-area searches (industrial yards, orchards, cotton fields, etc.). They are also trained to effectively search the interior of buildings. The teams will also be trained to 'clear' felony vehicle stops. During this activity, the K9 will check the interior of a vehicle during a 'high risk' stop to make sure there are no potentially dangerous suspects attempting to conceal themselves inside the vehicle.

Tracking skills are reinforced, as is the emphasis on handler protection. The K9 teams are trained to locate and 'alert' or 'indicate' the presence of certain controlled substances. At the conclusion of this training, the dog teams are certified to their competence. However, they must still complete a two-week field training period with another experienced K9 team.

All the teams train together twice a month and the handlers often individually train daily to reinforce the skills that have been previously taught.

There are numerous police dogs throughout the USA, most Police or Sheriff's Departments have them. There are so many in fact that exact numbers cannot be calculated.

Anchorage Police Department's K9 Unit

The mission of the Anchorage Police Department (APD) Canine Unit is to train, develop and deploy police service dog teams to support the various operational sections of the department in achieving the police mission in the safest and most efficient manner possible.

The canine unit has been able to achieve a high level of performance due to the financial support of Dollars for Dogs, Inc., the leadership provided by the Anchorage Police Department commanders, and the commitment of all the handlers.

APD Canine provides assistance to both law enforcement and non-law enforcement agencies, for example FBI, Ft Rich, EAFB, Kulis Air National Guard, State of Alaska Dept of Corrections Probation Officers. Anchorage School District regularly asks for a police canine to check schools for any guns or ammunition hidden in lockers or around the school.

It's not unusual for a newly purchased canine to have already been given a name by the breeder or kennel. However, when the dog is selected for the canine unit, it is renamed. The group or organisation providing the funds to purchase a dog are given the opportunity to choose a new name for the canine.

APD uses the Bark and Detain method as opposed to the Find and Bite used by other law enforcement agencies. Bark and Detain is an apprehension technique where the canine provides a clear indication (bark) while guarding (detain) a passive (still) person. This technique requires more training for the handler and canine, and performance at a higher skill level.

Additionally, 40 hours are spent in quarterly training, and once a year the unit will train as a group. This is all in addition to the daily maintenance training done to reinforce learned behaviours.

Belgian shepherds (Malinois), German shepherds and Dutch shepherds are the preferred breeds used. Most of them were bred in Europe, Holland, Czech Republic, or Germany. Then they were brought to the United States by the kennels who purchased them. Before APD chooses one for the canine unit, the canine has to pass rigorous selection tests for law enforcement work.

Training begins in a Canine Academy that can last for eight weeks or more. After that, every day the handler does some obedience work with the canine. For every three months of patrol work, they spend one week working on specific drills. And once a year they are tested and if they pass, they're certified to continue to work for another year. All of the dogs live with their handlers at home with their families. When they're off duty they get all the same perks as a regular house dog.

Dollars for Dogs is a non-profit organization that fully supports the Anchorage Police Department's K9 Unit. Dollars for Dogs raises funding for the local K9 Unit, purchases and trains the dogs, acquires all equipment for the K9s and their handlers, and pays for travel to events such as the Police Olympics. K9s are the invisible eyes and ears of the police in crime detection, prevention and investigation, and are an integral part of a well-equipped police force. All patrol dogs are selected by trained APD dog handlers, and subjected to a series of rigorous tests to evaluate their potential to work as police service dogs. After selection by APD, the dogs are purchased by Dollars for Dogs, and donated to the Anchorage Police Department. Without the financial support received from Dollars for Dogs, Inc. the Municipality of Anchorage could not achieve and maintain the APD K9 Unit as it is today.

Los Angeles Police Department (LAPD)

The K9 Platoon is the unit within the LAPD in charge of the training and use of K9 dogs throughout Los Angeles. It deploys highly trained handlers and their canine partners to conduct searches and apprehend felony suspects. K9 personnel are deployed around-the-clock, seven days a week. They are available to assist any department entity with searches for felony suspects. Two K9 officers have also been trained in search and rescue operations using dogs.

The Liberty Award, an award for bravery, was created in 1990 and has only been awarded once in the department's history. It is a medal for police dogs who are killed or seriously injured in the line of duty. The award is named after Liberty, a Metropolitan Division K9 who was shot and killed in the line of duty. Liberty's handler received the Medal of Valour for the same incident.

The mission is to support department field and detective operations in the search of outstanding felony suspects, misdemeanour suspects armed with a firearm, lost and missing persons, and evidence. K9 teams respond to assist field and detective operations on a city-wide basis, seven days a week, 24 hours a day. K9 teams also assist with emergency calls for service including 'officer needs help', 'assistance' or 'back-up' calls.

The K9 Platoon is one of the field platoons of Metropolitan Division, and as such is deployed at the direction of the Commanding Officer, Metropolitan Division. The K9 Platoon is supervised by a Lieutenant Officer-In-Charge, five K9 Sergeants, a K9 Chief Trainer, and 16 Police Officers as K9 handlers.

The Bomb Detection K9 Section is a specialised group of bomb detection canine handlers whose mission is to deter and detect the introduction of explosive devices in transportation systems and the City of Los Angeles. All of the officers assigned to the section attend a ten-week bomb detection canine course put on by the Transportation Security Administration's (TSA) National Explosives Detection Canine Team Program in San Antonio, Texas, Lackland Air Force Base.

The Los Angeles Police Department (LAPD) began participating in the National Explosives Detection Canine Team Program in 1997. The section works in cooperation with TSA and the Los Angeles World Airport Police. The section also works with LAPD Bomb Squad and provides an invaluable service to the airport community as well as the City of Los Angeles. The use of highly trained explosive detection canine teams is a proven deterrent to terrorism directed towards transportation systems. The explosive detection canine teams are used provide security and a visible deterrent at airports, rail stations, passenger terminals, seaports and surface carriers.

New York Police Department (NYPD)

The Emergency Service Unit of the New York Police Department is manned by over 300 staff. Its canine unit structure supports all major NYPD operations. The Canine Services Detail is primarily responsible for assisting patrol stations by conducting searches for felony and/or armed suspects with the use of specially trained dogs and their handlers. The police service dogs assigned to the Canine Services Detail are also tasked with locating evidence discarded by outstanding suspects.

The Canine Services Detail also supports the Special Weapons Teams on all activations, as well as during the service of high-risk search/arrest warrants. Canine handlers regularly train and work in conjunction with the Special Weapons Teams and have attended the same SWAT Schools. They are generally the first responders to situations that will eventually necessitate the activation of a Special Weapons Teams and it is often a Canine Deputy at the scene who will assist in making the determination that an incident will require more than a tactical area search, particularly in barricaded suspect situations. The Canine Services Detail is a valued resource at the Special Enforcement Bureau, and provides tactical support to the entire department 24 hours a day. In addition to supporting the department, the Canine Services Detail also provides assistance to local law enforcement agencies that do not possess a canine program.

The Emergency Service Unit also receives assistance from another Special Operations Division unit, the Canine Unit, consisting of 17 specially trained officers. The unit currently includes 16 dogs: seven patrol dogs, six narcotics dogs, and six bloodhounds each trained from about one year to assist on tactical search operations, searches for contraband materials, and to aid in high-risk crisis situations that might arise.

St Paul Minnesota

The St Paul, Minnesota K9 Unit was formed in 1958 with three K9 teams. It has expanded throughout the past 52 years and currently has an authorised strength of 22 K9 teams. There is one single purpose explosives detection K9 team and 21 Patrol K9 teams. Of the 21 Patrol K9 teams 16 are cross trained for narcotics detection and 5 are cross trained for explosives detection. The St Paul Police K9 Unit has K9 teams working 24 hours a day 365 days per year. The primary function of the K9 team is to be used as a locating tool, utilising the enhanced scenting capabilities of the dog.

K9 teams search buildings for hidden suspects, track suspects that have fled on foot and are used to locate evidence as well as detect narcotics, explosives and firearms. The secondary function of the K9 team is to enhance officer safety. All patrol K9s are trained to apprehend criminal suspects on the command of their handler. Over the past several years about 95 per cent of criminal suspects have decided to give up peaceably when confronted with a K9. The remaining 5 per cent were apprehended by the K9 allowing the human officers to remain behind cover and concealment. Whenever tactically possible criminal suspects are issued a warning to surrender themselves or the K9 will be deployed.

The St Paul Police Department, in addition to using K9 teams, also trains all officers and officers from police jurisdictions throughout the upper Midwest of the United States. Officers from all over the states of Minnesota, Wisconsin, Iowa, North Dakota, South Dakota and Illinois have trained at the St Paul Police K9 Unit 12 week Basic Canine Handler's School held each year. The 12-week Basic Canine Handlers Course begins with a new K9 handler and an untrained K9. The dog and the handler are trained at the same time. Each handler is responsible for the training of his/her own K9 under the supervision of the St Paul Police K9 Training Staff. K9 teams are instructed in obedience/ agility/ open area searches/ building searches/ evidence searches/tracking and criminal apprehension. Each year 10 to 15 K9 teams graduate from the Basic Canine Handlers Course.

The St Paul Police K9 Officers are all members of the United States Police Canine Association (USPCA). Each year every K9 team must certify, at regional certification trials, to the standards of the USPCA in order to continue working on the streets. In addition each year St Paul Police K9 Unit sends a Department

Team consisting of 5 K9 teams to the USPCA National Field Trials to certify under more rigorous judging and to compete for national awards. The St Paul Police K9 Unit has been named the Top Department Team, by the USPCA, 9 times in the past 20 years as well as receiving individual awards too numerous to list. Each year every K9 team must also certify to the proficiency standards of the USPCA in narcotics detection or explosives detection.

The St Paul Police K9 Unit is supported by the St Paul Police K9 Foundation, a group of volunteers from the community. The K9 Foundation raises moneys through fund raising events and donations to support the St Paul Police K9 Unit. The K9 Foundation purchases dogs, provides training equipment, training facilities and provides funds for the training of officers.

During the first 40 years the St Paul Police K9 Unit depended on dogs that were donated by the public. For the past 10 to 12 years all St Paul Police K9s have been purchased from Europe. The unit purchases 'green' dogs approximately one year old and begins training them on their arrival in St Paul. The St Paul Police K9 Unit primarily uses male German shepherd dogs. The GSDs have proven very reliable and easily acclimate to the harsh winter conditions in Minnesota.

The St Paul Police K9 Unit was featured in 2008/2009 in a television series called *K9 COPS* which has aired worldwide on the Animal Planet Network. The series was based on live film footage shot during actual street deployments of St Paul Police K9s. The television series was designed to educate the public of the value of Police K9s, and to show the public the multiple ways that K9s can be utilised by law enforcement.

Although they are very proud of the accomplishments of their K9s on the competition fields and the recognition they received from the television series, their true pride rests on their ability to perform on the streets of St Paul. Each year they deploy K9 teams on over 3000 cases. K9s are responsible for the capture of nearly 1000 criminals in St Paul each year, in addition to the recovery of hundreds of pounds of illegal narcotics and the recovery of valuable evidence that would otherwise have gone undetected. St Paul K9 teams undergo rigorous training in high risk searches for armed suspects and deploy regularly with the St Paul Police SWAT Team to support their operations. There have been three St Paul Police K9s killed in the line of duty; two by gunfire, the other in a fall. There has also been several K9s injured by gunfire, stabbing and blunt trauma. One St Paul Police K9 Handler has been killed in the line of duty from gunfire.

The St Paul Police K9 Unit has a long and proud history. Each year it invites all present and retired K9 handlers to unite at a picnic where they share some food and the stories of the courageous acts of the more than 100 K9s that have gallantly served for the past 50 years.

Orange County

In Orange County there are many police departments. Most have their own K9 programs that range in size and tasks. It is a heavily populated area with major tourist attractions such as Disneyland within its area. Some of the K9 programs have as few as a single team and others have dozens. Listed below are three examples.

Anaheim Police Department Canine Detail

The Anaheim Police Department Canine Detail was established in 1981 with three police service dogs. Over the years, the police department has expanded the canine detail to its current strength of six patrol dogs. Most of the patrol dogs are cross-trained to detect narcotics. Since its development, the canine program has become one of the most respected in Southern California.

The current canine detail comprises one lieutenant, two sergeants and six handlers partnered with their police service dogs. The Canine Teams are on duty or on call 24 hours a day, seven days a week and operate throughout the City of Anaheim. The teams also assist other police departments throughout Orange County.

The teams currently use German shepherds imported from Europe for patrol dogs. A police service dog's primary purpose is to locate, whether it's a dangerous criminal hiding in a neighbourhood or illegal narcotics being concealed in a vehicle or building. Without their heightened senses, the job would be much more difficult.

Some of the duties of a police service dog team are:

- Searching for dangerous criminals hiding in urban and rural areas
- Searching for concealed narcotics and contraband
- Patrolling high crime areas to deter criminal activity
- Assisting other law enforcement agencies throughout the county
- Supporting other specialised units of the Anaheim Police Department
- Deploying with the Special Weapons and Tactics (SWAT) Team
- Serving the community by participating in public relations demonstrations

The Kindness of Strangers

The history of the Anchorage Police Department (APD) K9 Unit started in 1975, which was the year Officer John Flora was shot and killed while investigating a burglary. His widow established a memorial fund in his name, with the express purpose of raising money to start a canine unit for APD. The citizens of Anchorage liked that idea: local clubs, a radio station and even the Alaska Army National Guard joined together for a fundraiser in the Sears parking lot.

A surprising multitude of Anchorage residents showed up that sub-zero November Saturday to see dog obedience training demonstrations, a National Guard helicopter, vehicle displays and watch local radio and television personalities take cream pies in their faces in return for financial pledges. By the time the event was over, late in the evening, enough money had been raised to purchase and equip two canines. In the following weeks donations kept coming in, and the APD K9 Unit was formed with four dogs and handlers.

Ten years later, Officer HB Hanson, a K9 handler, was fatally wounded while helping another K9 team apprehend an armed suspect. A memorial fund in his name was also established to benefit APD's K9 Unit. Both memorial funds were combined, and Dollars for Dogs, a volunteer organisation, was entrusted with the management of the funds.

Fullerton K9 Program

The Police K9 Program began in 1983 with three K9 Teams. The K9 Program is an essential tool in the fight against crime, and provides protection for the officers and the community. When K9 officers are not responding to calls, they patrol the business and residential areas of the city in an effort to deter and detect crime.

The canine team's primary functions are to:

- Respond to alarm and prowler calls

- Conduct building and article searches

- Sniff out drugs

- track suspects

Before an officer is chosen to be a canine handler, the officer goes through a testing process. The officer must show a unique dedication toward the canine unit, and must have accommodations at home for their new partner. The dogs are imported from Germany.

The police officer handler will go through a 16-week initial training session. The bonding between the officer and the canine is very important during this time. In order to solidify this bonding, training is ongoing throughout the partnership of the canine team. When the officer is not working, the canine stays at home with the officer and his or her family. Retired dogs normally live with handlers for the rest of their lives.

Orange County Sheriff's Department

The combined efforts of the Orange County Sheriff's Department Canine Team provides the department with almost 24–7 coverage, which is greatly needed considering the team is already up to 800 deployments for the year. The Sheriff's canines are tasked with three missions in the field: suspect apprehension, narcotics detection and the recovery of evidence. The Sheriff's Department is unique within the County of Orange. it is one of the few agencies assigned a particular patrol area. Most canines throughout the county are able to roam and go where they are needed. In addition to the normal patrol responsibilities, canine teams are often called upon to assist on alarm calls, burglary calls, building searches, article searches, suspect tracking, area and building searches for suspects, along with narcotics and officer safety assists.

The Orange County Sheriff's Department also have reserve teams; they conduct K9 narcotics detection and evidence searches for Dana Point, Mission Viejo, Laguna Hills, Laguna Niguel, Lake Forest, Rancho Santa Margarita, San Clemente, San Juan Capistrano, Stanton, North & South Investigations, GET, Narcotics Interdiction Unit, Garden Grove, Laguna Beach, DEA and California Highway Patrol.

The two reserve teams, Reserve Deputy Scott Klappenback & K9 Roan and Reserve Deputy Jim Wharrie & K9 Mona have been assigned to the City of Lake Forest for the past five years. The two reserve K9 teams provided patrol and narcotics K9 coverage on every Friday and Saturday night throughout 2008.

The statistics outlined below summarise the Reserve K9 Teams' collective accomplishments in 2008:

- 109 patrol shifts completed (1153 total patrol hours)

- Participated in over 832 hours of formal K9 Section training, including monthly evaluations and annual narcotics certification

- Responded to 13 off-duty call-outs for K9 narcotics searches

- Conducted 6 K9 demonstrations for the community

- During routine patrol responded to a total of 582 calls for service

Of the 582 total calls, 232 (40 per cent) were K9 narcotic detection or evidence search deployments with the following results:

- 70 (30 per cent) resulted in a narcotic related arrest (cocaine, heroin, marijuana, methamphetamine, opium)

- 121 (52 per cent) resulted in a narcotic 'alert' without an 'arrestable' quantity of narcotic present (confirmed residue, debris, paraphernalia or odour present)

- 35 (15 per cent) resulted in no 'alert' but significantly increased thoroughness of search while reducing the consumed search time for the patrol deputy

- 6 (3 per cent) resulted in an unconfirmed alert (unable to substantiate presence of narcotics)

In Orange County there are many police departments. Most have their own K9 programs that range in size and tasks. It is a heavily populated area with major tourist attractions such as Disneyland within its area. Some of the K9 programs have as few as a single team and others have dozens.

Honolulu Police Canine Unit

The Honolulu Police Department (HPD) is the 21st largest police department in the United States. Unlike the other 49 states, Hawaii does not have state police or separate city departments. Instead each county has its own law enforcement agency.

The Specialized Services Division performs a number of diverse functions that require unique skills. The roots of HPD's Specialized Services Division go back to 1946 when a seven-member quick response unit known as the Metro Squad was created to battle gang violence. Over the years the unit grew and expanded its duties and responsibilities. In 1972 it was known as the Tactical Operation

Division. In 1988, the Specialized Services Division as it is known today was created. Within division are officers in the Canine Unit who are called upon to search for prison escapees, missing persons, and felony suspects. They are also used in narcotics and explosives detection.

The Honolulu Police Department's Canine Unit began as a pilot program in 1957, under Chief Dan Liu. The first canine unit consisted of 12 officers. The dogs, mainly German shepherds, were donated by the residents of Honolulu. The officers constructed their own training facility including an eight-stall kennel using their personal donations of money and labour. The officers also trained during off-duty hours. By 1961 the canine unit had become a fully fledged part of the Honolulu Police Department, when the Metro Squad, the forerunner of today's Specialized Services Division, employed police dogs as a part of their patrols of Waikiki.

In 1989, dogs trained in the detection of narcotics were first used by the Narcotics/Vice Division and since that time they have helped police seize millions of dollars in drugs and cash. The canine unit's tasks also include explosive detection, tracking, suspect apprehension and the location of articles or evidence at a crime scene.

As times and task requirement changed, the German shepherds were replaced by a more durable breed of dogs, the Dutch shepherd and the Belgium shepherd (Malinois). There are three dogs used by Narcotics/Vice airport division: a golden retriever, short-haired pointer and a labrador. Each dog has a badge designation and they are considered officers assigned to the Honolulu Police Department's Specialized Services Division.

New England State Police K9 unit

The State Police K9 unit deploys approximately 75 highly trained canines to agencies throughout New England for search and rescue, criminal apprehension, narcotics detection, crowd control, missing persons searches, cadaver recovery searches, site security, arson detection, explosive detection, and other missions. Depending on specific mission requirements, members of the canine unit would work in support of, or in conjunction with, other specialised units including the Air Wing, Special Tactical Operations team, Marine Unit, Dive Team, and the Special Emergency Response Team. Their services are available upon request, without cost to the requesting agency. The State Police uses dogs such as the labrador retriever, the German shepherd, the Dutch shepherd, and the Belgian shepherd (Malinois). In order to become a K9 officer candidates must be on the force for at least five years.

State Police K9 Unit handlers are trained as Tactical Team Leaders, certified in Search Management as well as Incident Command, and other search tactics such as 'Hasty Team' Searches. All State Police K9 Teams are trained to locate human scent by tracking, air scenting, or locating last known places. They have specialised equipment and are capable in protracted wilderness search operations. State Police K9 supervisors have been working closely toward certifying those qualified Civilian Volunteer K9 Unit handlers.

The Fire & Explosion Investigation Section has a number of specialised resources available to assist municipal fire and police to conduct fire or explosion investigations 24 hours a day, 365 days a year. These include five nationally certified Accelerant Detection Canine Teams (AK9) which are regionally deployed. Each AK9 team was trained in the Connecticut State Police/AT AK9 (food reward) method. Each AK9 team is able to respond around the clock to assist investigators anywhere in the state at any fire or explosion where there is a possibility of arson. Each AK9 team is also available for fire prevention programs in schools and related civic events.

Sacramento Sheriff's Department

The Sacramento Sheriff's Department uses several canines on call-outs handled by the Special Enforcement Detail. All of the canines are regularly trained in searching and working with SWAT teams and all handlers are SWAT trained.

The Special Enforcement Detail uses canines on search teams, on perimeters in case the suspect tries to flee from an area of concern, and with the primary arrest team in case a suspect tries to fight or run from the arresting officers. In all cases, the use of the canine provides an extra tool for SWAT teams to assist them in conducting their jobs in a safer, more efficient, and reliable manner

Most of the areas of Sacramento County are highly populated urban settings with homes, businesses, parks and schools. In the past the canines would be deployed on an area search to look for fleeing suspects or missing people, but today canine handlers also track suspects and missing people.

Handlers will attempt to track from scenes of robberies that have just occurred. The track will assist officers in establishing a direction of travel and if the track stops abruptly in a parking lot that information would assist investigating officers in determining where the suspect(s) may have had a vehicle parked.

Tracking becomes an essential tool on deployments in the rural parts of Sacramento County. Tracking can assist in narrowing the scope of a search in a vast search area. Handlers have had numerous successes with the deployment of the canine on a track.

The area search is by far the most common usage of the canines. An area search may be conducted on a long line or offline where the K9 can roam unrestricted. Using the canines on an area search is not always done to locate criminals. At times dogs are used to look for missing people. However, the majority of the time when you see a canine team working in your neighbourhood conducting a yard-to-yard area search they are looking for a suspect.

The Sheriff's Department has two canines assigned to the Narcotic Detail and one assigned to the Elk Grove Police Department (a contract city patrolled by the Sheriff's Department). The canines assist narcotic officers in locating narcotics hidden by criminals. Paranoid drug abusers hide their illegal drugs in some remarkable places. It is certain that without the use of a well-trained canine and the canines keen since of smell many narcotic stashes would go undiscovered.

The canines are commonly used on probation searches of known 'drug houses' and for warrant sweeps. The canines can also be used on traffic stops to search vehicles. The canines are there to assist officers in many ways. Four of the patrol canines are crossed trained in narcotic detection. The canines are trained in locating the four most common illegal drugs, methamphetamine, cocaine, heroin, and marijuana.

The Sheriff's Department has canines assigned to the Sacramento International Airport as well as canines assigned to the Explosive Ordinance Detail (EOD). The canines working the airport all have attended a 10-week National Explosive Detection Canine Team Program training course at Lackland Air Force base put on by the Department of Homeland Security Transportation Security Administration (TSA) Support Branch. Five out of the six canines are TSA canines, which are assigned to the airport. TSA requires the handlers to continually train and they monitor the training and utilisations. TSA sets the standards and the department makes sure the training is done correctly. The canine teams are evaluated once a year.

The canines assigned to EOD follow similar training guidelines; however, they train within the department. The canines are certified on the odour recognition of several types of explosives and common components. TSA and the Sheriff's Department mandates that the information is classified.

A Night with Deputy Brown and Lycos

Deputy Brown has a special attachment to K9 duty. 'It's a privilege to work with these dogs,' he said. 'During the first year or two, it's a learning curve with the dog, but now we work better as a team.'

Deputy Brown is teamed with Lycos, from Holland, an eight-year-old certified Royal Dutch police dog. He and Deputy Stephen Brown have worked together for seven years.

'Lycos will find evidence such as guns and knives contaminated with a suspect's odour,' Deputy Brown said. 'His nose is sensitive enough to find a key inside of a good sized park.' Along with human odour Lycos can find the four major drug odours: marijuana, heroin, methamphetamine, cocaine and their derivatives. 'No other tool is as versatile to law enforcement as canines are.' Not only are the canines capable of apprehending criminals hiding on the street, they are social enough to regularly participate in public demonstrations at schools and Boy Scout meetings. 'Not every agency has canines as well rounded as the Sheriff's Department.'

Here is a window on one patrol night. At 22.30 there is a car stop off of Katella in the unincorporated area of Anaheim. The suspect smells of marijuana and admits he has been smoking in his car for a while. The suspect is in the Black and White and the patrol deputy rolls up the windows of the suspect's car to seal in the odour for Lycos.

Deputy Brown takes Lycos to the suspect's car and walks him around the outside. It appears to be play, but the deputy is working with the dog's play drive. Inside the car, Lycos alerts to several places, in the centre console, under the front passenger side floor mat and in the rear seat. Deputy Brown has Lycos check the trunk. He opens the hood of the car but checks the engine to insure it's not too hot before allowing Lycos to check it out.

Nothing is found beyond a small package of marijuana that the suspect had admitted having. The dog's activity is likely the result of marijuana or other drugs being kept in the car earlier and leaving a residual odour. The car appears to have a lot of residual odour.

At 23.30, Deputy Brown stops to assist two Los Alamitos Police Department units. They have stopped a parolee who is being given a field sobriety check. They ask Deputy Brown to have Lycos check the car for drugs.

The parolee said he has never had drugs in the car and hasn't used methamphetamine since August 2005, the day he was last arrested.

Brown walks Lycos around the outside of the car and through the interior. Lycos only alerts on a bag, which is then removed from the car. He leaves the bag for the Los Alamitos police to check thoroughly. When Los Alamitos Police handcuff the

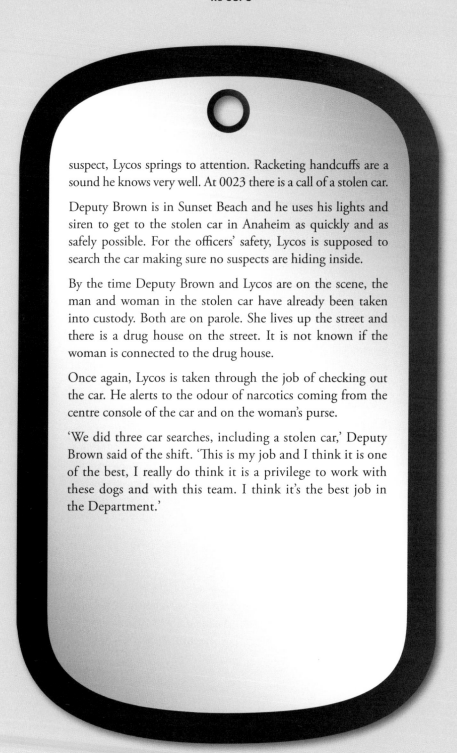

suspect, Lycos springs to attention. Racketing handcuffs are a sound he knows very well. At 0023 there is a call of a stolen car.

Deputy Brown is in Sunset Beach and he uses his lights and siren to get to the stolen car in Anaheim as quickly and as safely possible. For the officers' safety, Lycos is supposed to search the car making sure no suspects are hiding inside.

By the time Deputy Brown and Lycos are on the scene, the man and woman in the stolen car have already been taken into custody. Both are on parole. She lives up the street and there is a drug house on the street. It is not known if the woman is connected to the drug house.

Once again, Lycos is taken through the job of checking out the car. He alerts to the odour of narcotics coming from the centre console of the car and on the woman's purse.

'We did three car searches, including a stolen car,' Deputy Brown said of the shift. 'This is my job and I think it is one of the best, I really do think it is a privilege to work with these dogs and with this team. I think it's the best job in the Department.'

United States Specialist Canine Units

United States Park Police Canine Unit

The United States Park Police Canine Unit was established in 1959, the first in the Washington, DC, area. Two years earlier, Chief Stewart sent Sergeant Alfred Beye to the Royal Canadian Mounted Police Training Kennel in Nova Scotia, Canada. Sgt. Beye then trained with the Baltimore City Police Canine Unit and returned to train the first canines employed by the US Park Police.

The first handlers were members of the Horse Mounted Unit. They trained each dog in different language commands, so that others could not control them. These included Spanish-Indian, German and Japanese. Once they trained the dogs, they would trot along next to the Horse Mounted handler while he patrolled the horse trails. Eventually, the force only assigned the canine handler the duties of working with a trained dog. By the early 1970s, only one canine team remained.

This canine unit is specifically trained for drug and explosives detection. It also provides search and rescue services and assists in securing areas prior to the arrival of the President, Vice President, and visiting Heads of State. In 1974 the force added the first explosives detector dogs.

Over the years the canine unit has moved between the Patrol Branch and the Special Forces Branch, to which it is currently assigned. The force currently has a number of canines which are assigned in WDC as patrol dogs. Several of these dogs are also cross-trained in narcotics detection. The force also has officers and canines assigned as explosives detector teams in WDC. The force has a number of dog teams assigned in the New York Field Office and the San Francisco Field Office.

The Bureau of Alcohol, Tobacco, Firearms and Explosives (ATF)

From the nation's capital to the crossroads of rural America, the increased threats of violence is unsettling. Often these threats are carefully hidden from human detection, but thanks to ATF's explosives detection canines, they can still be found.

After an initial course of ten weeks duration the newly certified explosive detection dog has the capability to detect many types of explosives, explosive residue, smokeless powders and search for post blast evidence. ATF canines are capable of conducting these searches under all operational conditions including locating substances in hidden objects or on persons.

While there is a great need for explosives-detecting instruments, there is also a great need for law enforcement agencies to have an explosives–detecting canine capable of detecting explosives and firearms threats. To support ATF's mission and that of other law enforcement agencies, ATF applied knowledge gained from its long established accelerant detection canine program and developed a scientifically based explosives detection canine program that trains dogs capable of detecting a myriad of different explosives compound.

ATF trained and certified canines learn explosives odour recognition through food and praise reward conditioning. This training methodology allows for a canine to be repeatedly exposed to various explosives odours daily, thus reinforcing these odours to the canine continually.

As a public service, ATF sponsors educational programs and training for schools, civic groups, and other law enforcement agencies about explosives and firearms, explosives and firearms detection, and other safety issues. During many of these programs, a canine team will promote community safety issues through prevention and detection demonstrations.

As the Federal Government explosives and post blast experts, ATF offers certified explosives detection canine to other federal, state, local and foreign law enforcement agencies. ATF uses a food and praise reward training methodology that exposes canines to five basic explosives groups, including chemical compounds used in an estimated 19,000 explosives formulas. It is believed by ATF that exposing canines to various explosives from the basic explosive families will give the dog the ability to detect the widest range of commercial or improvised explosives possible when working in field. Successful detection of an explosive or firearm earn the canine a food and praise reward, which encourages repetition.

To earn ATF certification, all dogs must pass a blind test wherein they must successfully detect 20 different explosives odours, two of which they were never exposed to during training. The scientific methodology, and the training and testing protocols are certified by the ATF National Laboratory, and produce an extremely versatile, mobile, and accurate explosives detection tool.

ATF began training Accelerant Detection Canines in 1986. These specialty canines are trained to detect a variety of ignitable liquids that could be used to initiate a fire. The Accelerant Detection Canine Program is available to state and local law enforcement/fire service agencies that meet various criteria and are willing to commit to a five-year memorandum of agreement. Handlers attend a five-week training course at the ATF Canine Training Center in Front

Royal, Virginia, then return to their respective departments to begin working operationally. These teams are utilised by the ATF National Response Team on fire-related callouts. All ATF ADC teams are recertified on a yearly basis.

Currently, there are approximately 50 canine teams across the country participating in the ADCP. Since 1991, ATF has trained 676 explosives detection canines and 149 accelerant detection canines. The dogs and their ATF-trained handlers are located throughout the United States in local police and fire departments, fire marshal offices and federal and state law enforcement agencies. Teams are also located in 21 foreign countries.

Central Intelligence Agency K9 Corps

The Central Intelligence Agency (CIA) is an independent US Government agency responsible for providing national security intelligence to senior US policymakers.

The CIA has a diverse work force — from engineers and linguists to doctors and analysts. But it has a special breed of employees — CIA K9 Corps. The CIA established the K9 Corps in 1991. Since then, the number of K9s and their human partners has increased, and the corps has plans for more growth. The CIA K9 Corps' main responsibility is to protect the CIA and its employees. All of the canines are federal police officers and are assigned their own police badge. What makes the K9 Corps so special is the dogs' ability to sniff out 19,000 explosive scents, which makes them ideal explosive detection officers.

The CIA K9s learn all of these scents in a 10-week training program. At the end of the training, the dogs and their human partners take 10 indoor and outdoor tests. Some of the canines receive street training, which sharpens the dogs' skills in obedience, agility, article search, suspect search, and criminal apprehension. When that training ends, the dogs have to pass a final exam. The top dogs then report for duty as members of the CIA K9 Corps.

To keep the dogs at the top of their game, the K9s and their handlers also participate in competitions throughout the year. Each year, members of the corps look forward to the regional and national competitions sponsored by the United States Police Canine Association (USPCA). When the dogs score enough points in the regional events, they go on to the national competitions. At the national level, teams compete against other teams from all over the United States and Canada.

Due to their extensive training and unique skills, the CIA K9 Corps often at times work with other law enforcement teams. There K9s assist the US Park Police, the Fairfax County (Virginia) Police Department, and the Drug Enforcement Administration. The K9s and their handlers also travel regularly to locations within the United States and abroad.

Most people work 40 hours a week, but the members of the K9 Corps work 60 hours a week. They also are on call around the clock. Fortunately, the dogs love their work and they are rewarded for being the best in their business. CIA dogs live with their caring human partners and get top care. The 'top dogs' in the CIA K9 Corps are just like all of the CIA's best employees: enthusiastic, hard working, loyal and dedicated. And their handlers will tell you that the dogs love their jobs.

The Pentagon

The Pentagon Police Department pursue excellences in the delivery of professional law enforcement services to the Department of Defense community in the National Capital Region. It also stands ready to support the overarching Pentagon Force Protection Agency's mission using highly trained, dedicated police officers, state-of-the-art technology and with effective partnerships with other federal, state and local public safety agencies.

The Pentagon Force Protection Agency traces its roots directly to the General Services Administration's (GSA) United States Special Policemen (USSP) and a variety of security and security related functions originally located throughout the Office of the Secretary of Defense.

Prior to 1971 the GSA's USSP provided law enforcement, safety and security functions at the Pentagon. The protection programs were a 'guard-watchman' operation, where USSP focused primarily on the protection of property. However, as a result of a growing number of disruptive incidents throughout the country, GSA re-examined its security program. In response to the mass demonstrations, bombings and bomb threats of the era, the Federal Protective Service was established to provide comprehensive protection of the Pentagon and its personnel rather than the previous policy of concentration on property.

The Pentagon Police K9 Unit was formed in July of 1998 with four handlers. The unit currently has 21 handlers. The unit was formed in order to take a more proactive approach to the growing threat of terrorism. The K9 teams assigned to the Pentagon provide protection for the Secretary of Defense, visiting dignitaries and all Department of Defense personnel at the Pentagon and throughout the National Capital Region. In addition to numerous proactive assignments for explosive detection, the K9 teams respond to bomb threats, suspicious packages and suspicious vehicles. The K9 unit also provides support to other law enforcement agencies in the area.

Transit Police

The Transit Police Canine in New York City (NYC) consists of four units: the Transit Bureau Canine, Emergency Service Canine (vehicle-based street response), Bomb Squad Canine and Narcotics Canine. Collectively it is the largest canine unit of any municipal police department in the United States with around 100 canines (exact numbers are not divulged for security reasons) among the four units.

Prior to 1995 there were three police departments in NYC: the NYPD, NYC Transit Police (subways and buses) and the NYC Housing Police (public housing). Then, in 1995, Mayor Giuliani merged the three departments into one.

Prior to the merger, the NYC Transit Police had the largest and perhaps best trained canine unit in the city. It was a centralised unit that policed the NYC subway system. The NYPD had decentralised precinct-based units. The merger happened in 1995 and this was effectively the end of the Transit Canine Unit. The canine teams were absorbed into street patrols. Upon merging with the NYPD the NYC Transit Police K9 Unit and the NYPD Precinct based K9s were absorbed into a new centralised sub-unit of the NYPD Emergency Service Unit, becoming ESU K9.

In 2005 Police Commissioner Kelly saw the need to recreate a canine unit that would be deployed exclusively to mass transit. Starting on 1 January 2006 it still is a work in progress.

What is unique about Transit Canine is that they are unlike any traditional canine unit. Traditional canine units typically are vehicle-based reactive units. They are usually requested to the scene of an incident. The canine teams assigned to Transit Canine are pedestrian-based, proactive patrol units that utilise mass transit. Their primary focus is the NYC Subway, one of the busiest in the world, but they also police the buses, ferries, trams and anything that can move people. NYC Subway moves about five million people per day in the system.

This is one of the most difficult environments to do canine policing in. The unit face daily challenges that would frighten most police canines. Transit Canine Policing is a specialty within a specialty; it is very difficult to do train patrol on a crowded train at rush hour with a canine that is trained in criminal apprehension (un-muzzled). Fortunately Transit Police have a highly trained group of officers and canines that are talented enough to meet the challenge.

The unit's purpose is counterterrorism as well as traditional crime fighting. The teams have been effective at both. In regards to counterterrorism, they have the ability to prevent an attack through deterrence and to respond to the aftermath of an attack, but what is unique is that they also have the unique ability to respond to an ongoing attack.

Some specialised transit canine capabilities:

- Criminal apprehension
- Building searches
- Field searches
- Tracking/trailing
- Evidence recovery
- Firearms recovery
- Search and rescue
- Cadaver
- Traditional explosives detection (static packages)
- Vapour wake explosive detection
- Narcotics

It takes a lot of work, dedication and training to have all these skills and most of the canines are dual purpose.

The Amtrak Police Department K9 teams are strategically deployed at stations throughout the system and involved in up to 1000 train trips a month. The Amtrak Police Department K9 teams provide a psychological and physical deterrent to potential threats from explosives. These teams are part of a collaborative interagency initiative that includes the Transportation Security Administration, federal and state Departments of Homeland Security, and state and local law enforcement agencies.

For explosives detection, the teams undergo an 11-week training program at either the Auburn University Canine Detection Training Center in Alabama or the Transportation Security Administration facility at Lackland Air Force Base in Texas, where dogs are trained in odour recognition. During that time, handlers are taught to recognise changes in their dog's behaviour as a response to 'alerting' on a potential threat.

Part of the standard explosives detection training includes vapour wake training, where the dogs are trained to alert on scents left in the wake of a passing individual. Amtrak currently has the most K9 units in the railroad industry with vapour wake capabilities.

Airport Police

The Los Angeles Airport Police (sometimes referred to as LAXPD) Los Angeles Airport Police Division is the fourth largest law enforcement agency in Los Angeles County, with more than 1100 law enforcement, security and staff personnel. The Airport Police is a division of Los Angeles Department of Airports, Los Angeles World Airports (LAWA). Although currently working very closely with the Los Angeles Police Department, the Los Angeles Airport Police is a separate entity, primarily due to the Airport Police having specialised training and funding resources.

The Airport Police fields over 20 explosive detection (EDK9) and patrol (K9) dogs Los Angeles Airport Police, combined with the Los Angeles Police Department, maintains the largest Transportation Security Administration (TSA) canine explosive detection program in the country in an aviation environment. This unit is specially trained to search for and apprehend fleeing suspects, explosive materials, and other evidence. Canine teams provide high-visibility patrols of the terminal areas, respond to unattended-article calls, and provide assistance to nearby law enforcement agencies. Black NOMEX uniforms are worn by officers assigned to K9 duties.

Deputy Lynn Ridenour and K9 Rico, a two-year old Belgium shepherd (Malinois) have recently joined the Explosives Detection K9 Program at John Wayne Airport. Rico has undergone more than a year of training and for 10 weeks the new team trained together at the Transportation Security Administration's Explosives Devices Canine Team Program at Lackland Air Force Base in Texas.

Deputy Ridenour and Rico join several other teams at the airport. All of the deputies working on the team are skilled both as dog handlers and as bomb technicians. The Explosives Devices Canine Team Program was established on 9 March 1972. It was created by order of President Richard Nixon following an incident in which a Los Angeles bound plane had to return to JFK Airport in New York following a report of a bomb on board. Upon landing, a search of the plane was made by a bomb sniffing dog named Brandy. Brandy found the bomb just 12 minutes before it was set to explode. President Nixon ordered the new program later that day.

John Wayne Airport became part of the program after 9/11. Three teams of deputies with K9s trained in explosives detection have worked at John Wayne Airport since 2003.

The purpose of the program is to protect the public at the airport from explosive devices and, at the same time, create the least possible disturbance to the airport's routine. To best fulfil that task the K9 teams work the area methodically without following a regular pattern that can be predicted.

Captain Dennis DeMaio, commander of the Airport Operations Division, said the K9 teams have served John Wayne Airport well. He said that while K9 teams at airports are fairly common, his teams are a rarity in that the K9 deputies are trained as bomb technicians.

'When we have a suspicious package we can have the skilled bomb technician and the explosives dog check it out quickly without having to cordon off a 500 square yard area or evacuating the terminal,' Captain DeMaio said. 'It's the best combination for ensuring the safety of the public and keeping the flights on schedule.'

Deputies check the bags that are unattended and walk through the crowds at the airport; the K9s sniffing at each bag they pass. The K9s are almost always working when at the airport, seeking one of the scents they have been trained to find. For the K9s it is a game, a a chance to impress their handler and win a reward: a toy that they get to play with whenever they discover a scent they have been trained to find. The dogs are trained so that they can walk through crowds and find explosives in luggage or on a person. They have been loaned for use at the World Series and the Stanley Cup when those events have been in Orange County.

The K9s can help determine whether an unattended bag is a suspicious bag. If the bag is too suspicious it can cause the airport terminal to be evacuated. The K9s can help keep evacuations, with their attendant flight delays, to a minimum. Their presence creates a deterrent to those who would plan to bring a bomb to the airport. They are constantly patrolling the airport, along the curb where luggage is unloaded, in the terminal and in the cargo warehouse. The K9s are also used to check out planes between flights.

When the K9s patrol in the terminal, the faces of the passengers often light up with big smiles. One of the biggest challenges to the teams is keeping the public from distracting the dogs with petting and fawning.

Homeland security in the USA has seen the increased use of explosive detection dog teams, which are the most efficient and cost effective tool in the war against terrorism yet devised.

Barking Mad

One weapon a police dog has to quell violent offenders is its bark. The sound of a police dog barking is usually enough to stop any would-be offender; however, a university student was once charged for allegedly hissing and 'making barking noises' at a police dog. The 23-year-old was accused of teasing the police dog in the university grounds.

According to a police report, Officer Bradley Walker was outside his squad car investigating a car crash early one morning when he heard Timber, his K9 partner, 'barking uncontrollably' in response to the offender's taunting.

The offender was barking while in a 'highly intoxicated' state, and refused to stop teasing the animal. The officer says he asked the offender why he was harassing the dog, and he replied, 'The dog started it.'

San Diego Harbour Police

The Harbor Police K9 team was initially formed in 1997 and is currently composed of three officers, two corporals, a sergeant and their K9 partners with two officers in the narcotics K9 team. The K9 team is the only Transportation Security Administration (TSA), certified explosive detection team south of Los Angeles International Airport.

The team is assigned primarily at Lindbergh Field, but they are available to respond to all parts of San Diego County through a mutual aid agreement.

The Harbor Police K9 team is required to attend a three-month school at Lackland Air Force Base in San Antonio, Texas, where they learn how to work with their canine partner in detecting explosives. The canine team works around the clock and is on-call 24 hours a day. Although they operate with very little attention, the team is one of the most in-demand in the Harbor Police Department. The team spends the majority of its time in training and conducting training drills. They are evaluated annually by TSA personnel, and are subject to surprise checks and tests at any time. During the annual re-certification, each officer and his K9 partner must have an extremely high success/find rate or they do not certify. This is an important aspect of the program because if an officer and his K9 partner do not certify, they may be removed from the detection program.

These finely tuned canines are working animals and the public needs to keep in mind that these animals are not pets and need to stay focused on their important task. These dogs are for the protection of the travelling public and the area they serve.

The San Diego Harbor Police Department is the premier police presence in San Diego Bay, the San Diego International Airport (also known as Lindbergh Field), and on all Tidelands around the bay. Its jurisdiction extends through the five member cities of the Port District, which include San Diego, Chula Vista, Coronado, Imperial Beach, and National City.

Los Angeles School Police Department (LASPD)

From some of the largest K9 units in the world the USA also deploys K9 teams of single officers in some sheriff departments. One small K9 unit performing an immensely important role to protect kids is the Los Angeles School Police Department. It was established in August of 1948 to create a safe and tranquil environment for the students, teachers and staff of the Los Angeles Unified

School District. The men and women of the LASPD have accepted this duty with an unyielding commitment that has not wavered for over six decades. This dedication to public safety is the standard for the fifth largest law enforcement agency in Los Angeles County and the largest school district police department in the nation.

The Los Angeles School Police Department Canine (K9) Unit consists of one sergeant and six officers, each assigned their respective canine partner. K9 handlers are required to complete many hours of extensive training to achieve trust and cohesion with their canine partner. Canines are police officers, each with their own serial number, police officer badge and photo ID.

Two of the department's six canines are deployed directly into the Day School Program, where they have been specially trained to serve as narcotics detection dogs. Working directly with school staff, the K9 unit has a positive impact on reducing the ingress and egress of unlawful drugs at Los Angeles schools. The department's additional four canines have been specially trained as police service dogs and are deployed to assist the Patrol Division with the apprehension of outstanding suspects, and two are cross-trained to locate explosives as well as firearms.

US Forest Service

The first known use of canines in the Forest Service (FS) is found in an article titled 'Using Bloodhounds to Prevent Forest Fires'. This article was written by Eastern Regional Forester D.W. Beck and was published in the October 1946 issue of *Fire Control Notes, A Periodical Devoted to the Technique of Forest Fire Control*. It discusses the use of bloodhounds to trail and find the guilty persons or scare them so thoroughly that they will start no more fires. The dogs were used in Arkansas, West Virginia. Virginia, and Kentucky and were credited with markedly reducing man-caused fires in areas where they had been numerous.

The next known use of canines in Forest Service law enforcement began in 1983 when two law enforcement officers (LEO) from the Angeles National Forest were approved to train and use patrol/officer protection dogs. Dogs are located within Forest Service Regions, which are numbered. Dogs employed in Region 5 were soon followed by Region 8 in 1985. Since beginning in 1983, 29 Forest Service LEOs have handled 33 different dogs. To date, Forest Service K9 teams have been located in every region except R9 and RIO.

Most dogs were trained for patrol/officer protection, although three were trained for narcotics or narcotics/tracking only. Only a few were dual purpose or trained for patrol and narcotics detection both. Past dogs were both personally owned and government owned and most were male German shepherds. Many were purchased from vendors, although the source of several previous dogs is unknown. Training was done with local departments, vendors, by private trainer, and by the handler. Canine programs started at a grassroots level, with handlers indicating an interest and essentially starting their own programs with district support.

Trends can be seen over the years the FS has been using canine teams. Originally, all the handlers were male, but as women entered FS law enforcement, they have been consistently represented. The breed of dogs used has shifted from almost all German shepherds to a mix of German shepherds and Belgian shepherds. The gender of dogs has shifted from all male to a male and female mix.

Early on, Forest Service dogs started out 'green'. Currently, most dogs are already 'started' prior to their purchase. Training time has shortened considerably, reflecting the shift to started dogs. Early on, almost all dogs were single purpose. Now, most are dual purpose. All of these changes are in concert with what has happened in the greater police K9 community. The only obvious difference between FS K9 and the rest of the police K9 world is a lack of dogs who only perform detection duties. Detection-only dogs are common outside the FS.

Today the most important, and most easily overlooked, purpose of K9 teams in the Forest Service is crime prevention. When the public sees that the Forest Service has spent the time and money to establish and maintain this specialised skill, it's a subtle reminder that the agency takes its law enforcement mission seriously. The mere presence of a K9 team reduces crime.

The best known uses of canine teams in the Forest Service are protection of the officer and narcotics detection. Assaults on employees are infrequent, hut they do occur. Assaults on K9 handlers are extremely rare as are assaults on any employee at an incident where a K9 is known to be present. As for narcotics detection, hundreds of drug cases are made each year based on Forest Service K9 alerts.

Forest Service canines have been used to locate felony suspects in buildings and outdoors, to apprehend suspects fleeing from marijuana gardens, and to find escaped prisoners. This is particularly important in that most of these subjects would have escaped arrest entirely had the dog not been present.

Use of Forest Service K9 teams has not only prevented injury to several employees, but also to suspects themselves. One LEO was being approached by a suspect with a knife. The assault stopped suddenly, without injury to the suspect or LEO, when the LEO's canine partner deployed from the vehicle. Without the dog, it is possible the suspect would have been shot and killed. The use of a K9 team as a 'wedge' allowed assistance to reach two LEOs who had been intentionally surrounded and isolated by hundreds of people at a Rainbow Gathering. The arrival of one dog put a stop to a wrestling match involving a Forest Service LEO and a felony suspect.

The above examples are just a few that have been reported. What can never be reported is the number of times the mere presence of a K9 has prevented an assault on an LEO or other employee. Additionally, the mere presence of a K9 frequently allows the LEO to deal with situations that would otherwise be left unhandled due to lack of backup.

Forest Service canines have been used to locate numerous lost people. One team was able to locate a suicide victim by simply tracking from the victim's vehicle. Without this tool, the search might have taken days or been unsuccessful. One team located a subject just as she was starting to become hypothermic, possibly saving her life. An often overlooked fact is that when a canine team is able to locate a lost person, this can literally save thousands of man hours of searchers time. Even when location fails, tracking can indicate the lost person's direction of travel, significantly reducing the area to be searched.

Forest Service canine teams have been used successfully to detect the presence of timber sale protesters and, alternatively, to declare a timber sale area clear of protestors. They have been used to locate stashes of supplies that protestors have hidden in closed areas, narcotics buried near FS roads, evidence, weapons and sites of big game poaching. Canine teams have also been used to locate subjects illegally harvesting forest products, evidence in cedar thefts, and other cedar theft sites that were previously unknown.

A last use of K9s in the Forest Service is public relations. Forest Service K9 teams have given numerous demonstrations at schools and civic functions. Much of the public likes dogs, especially children. While not all police dogs are suitable for this activity, those used for demonstrations have been well received around the country.

As for the future, several new uses come to mind. Two current K9 handlers have indicated a desire to train their dogs to locate marijuana gardens. Historically, that is thought to be impossible, but current information indicates otherwise. Considering how much marijuana is grown on Forest Service land, this would be a very useful skill. Other untapped skills include game detection in areas that have a significant poaching problem and accelerant detection for arson fires.

The use of personally owned dogs has been in effect since 1985. No problems have been identified with this practice. Using a personally owned dog can reduce initial start-up costs by several thousand dollars. Also, it may result in a more effective team since these dogs are usually trained by their own handlers and the training time is usually significantly longer than received at a vendor.

Zimbabwean Republic Police

Royal Swaziland Police and the Zimbabwean Republic Police dog handlers held a graduation ceremony in 2010, at the Zimbabwean Republic Police Canine Training School. Eight Royal Swaziland Police Dog Unit officers were passing out alongside their Zimbabwean colleagues after taking part in a three-month training program which commenced in early 2010. Five of the officers were undergoing training in the handling of drug sniffer dogs and tracker dogs.

This may sound routine but for many African nations, having police dogs has broken several barriers. Firstly and perhaps traditionally, colonial powers who governed these countries for many years used dogs to suppress riots and track down terrorists (now known as liberators). Secondly, even though dogs are present in all villages and part of life they tended to be regarded as a food source with occasional guarding and herding abilities. Thus it has taken a few generations and forward police thinking to change opinions here to use and care for them as law enforcement tools.

Tracker dogs are used in tracking and following the scent of fleeing criminals. Three were trained to be dog unit instructors. Also the program encompassed the training of the dogs themselves to be specialised police dogs. The Dog Section should make a meaningful contribution in the policing of Zimbabwe, particularly in reducing drugs and firearms.

The participants have been moulded into vigilant and professional dog handlers determined to keep criminals at bay. It is without doubt that the 2010 FIFA World Cup required the southern African region to have effective and sophisticated crime management instruments, such as dogs which possess acumen in crime detection.

Final Tour of Duty

On Thursday 28 September at 11.45 am, Deputy Sheriff Matt Williams and his K9 partner DiOGi, responded to a call to assist Deputy Douglas Speirs after a suspect fled on foot into a wooded area from a traffic stop. Deputy Williams deployed DiOGi into the dense brush from the scene and began trailing the suspect deeper into the woods near a creek. Matt was alone with DiOGi at this time when the suspect was located. Although details are still hazy, the suspect is believed to have been hiding in the hole created by a downed tree and produced his own handgun, firing on and killing DiOGi as the K9 engaged the suspect. The suspect immediately continued the attack firing on and striking Matt eight times. Deputy Speirs was also shot and wounded in the leg.

The suspect took Deputy Williams' pistol and magazines and fled deeper into the woods, emerging a short time later behind a house. The suspect engaged in a shootout with Lakeland police officers and once again fled into the same dense brush. Polk County K9 handlers responded after Deputy Williams did not respond on the radio and initiated a search into the woods for Matt. He was located by the K9 teams, who entered with full knowledge of the armed suspect hidden within. They located their fallen brother and his partner and brought them back out.

Tactical, SWAT and K9 teams from all agencies surrounding Polk County responded immediately. A seamless perimeter around the area was put into place with hundreds of law enforcement officers. As dark fell, the perimeter remained and helicopter searches tracked small movements of the suspect throughout the night as he remained pinned within the woods. At daybreak, on Friday 29 September, nearly 500 officers responded from around the State of Florida to assist in the manhunt to bring the killer to justice. At approximately 9.50am, as SWAT teams moved in a line combing through the area, the killer was spotted burrowed underneath a fallen tree. He refused to surrender and, concealed under a cloth, he held Deputy Williams' service pistol, bringing it to bear on the officers. The killer was pronounced dead at the scene.

Deputy Vernon Matthew Williams, better known as Matt, was a Deputy Sheriff for Polk County since 1994, serving in the capacity of K9 handler for the past eight years. Deputy Williams was revered as the head trainer of the Polk County K9 Unit. He will be remembered as a light-hearted prankster who always saw the good in people. His enthusiasm was contagious and motivational to all around him. He always said, 'As long as I get up in the morning and I see my patrol car still says "CAUTION K9", I know it's going to be a good day.'

Deputy Williams and DiOGi (pronounced Dee-oh-gee) or 'DOG with two lil Is' as Matt always said, made the ultimate

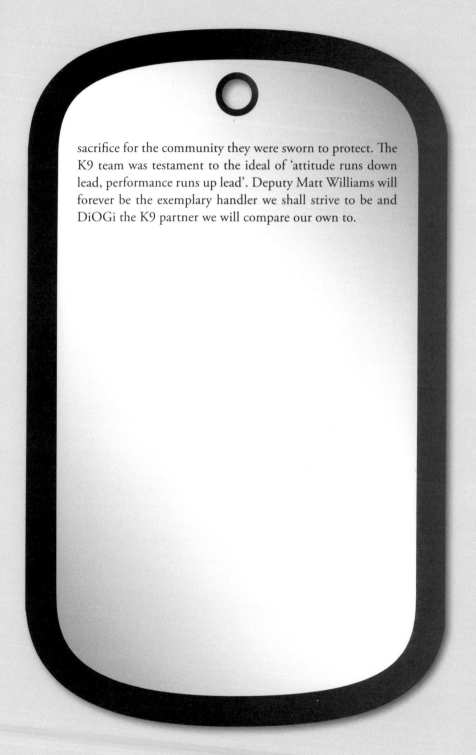

sacrifice for the community they were sworn to protect. The K9 team was testament to the ideal of 'attitude runs down lead, performance runs up lead'. Deputy Matt Williams will forever be the exemplary handler we shall strive to be and DiOGi the K9 partner we will compare our own to.

POLICE K9 ACRONYMS

ACPO   Association of Chief Police Officers or Administration Officer
                or non sworn officers

ACT   Australian Capital Territory

ADC   Accelerant Detection Canines

AES   Arms Explosive Search dogs

AFB   Air Force Base

AFP   Australian Federal Police

AK9   Accelerant Detection Canine Teams

APD   Anchorage Police Department

ATF   Alcohol Firearms and Tobacco Agency

BDTC   Neeme Border Guard Dogs Training Centre

BORSTAR   Border Patrol canine search, trauma, and rescue

BTP   British Transportation Police

C-17   Military Cargo Plane

Carabinieri   Military Police

CBP   US Customs and Boarder Protection

CBSA   Canada Border Services Agency

CCFR   Canine Training Centre Front Royal

CDD   Cadaver Detector Dogs

CENTREX   UK Quality Assured

CEP   Canine Enforcement Program

CETC   Canine Enforcement Training Center

CGSU   Coast Guard Support Unit

CIA	Central Intelligence Agency
CID	Criminal Investigation Department
CIS	Criminal Investigation Service
CNC	Civil Nuclear Constabulary
CNICG	Canine Section of the Gendarmerie
CR	Czech Republic
CSI	Central School of Instruction
CTT	Combat Tracker Team
DDR	German Democratic Republic
DEA	Drug Enforcement Administration
DGP	Director General of Police
DLHP	Dutch Mounted Police and Police Dog Service
DOG	Deployable Operations Group
DSU	Dog Support Unit
EDD	Explosive Detection Dog
EOD	Explosive Ordnance Disposal
EORT	Explosive Ordnance Response Team
EPS	Edmonton Police Service
EPSA	The Estonian Public Service Academy
ESU	Emergency Service Unit
FARC	The Revolutionary Armed Forces of Colombia
FBI	Federal Bureau of Investigation
FBS	Federal Border Service
FEDD	Firearms & Explosive Detection Dog
FS	Forest Service

FSCCP	Federation of Swiss police dog handlers
GARD	Republic of Ireland Police Constable
GIGN	National Gendarmerie Intervention Group
GP	General Purpose Police Dog
GSA	General Services Administration´s
GSD	German Shepherd
HPD	Honolulu Police Department
HQ	Headquarters
HRD	Human Remains Detection
HRDSN	Himalaya Rescue Dog Squad Nepal
HRT	Hostage Rescue Team
IDF	Israeli Defence Force
Inspector	A Police Commissioned Officer
K9	a police dog
K9 Officer	Police dog handler
KEM	Turkish National Police Dog Training Centre
KLPD	Dutch National Police Services Agency
KOM	Department of Anti-Smuggling and Organized Crime
LAPD	Los Angeles Police Department
LASPD	Los Angeles School Police Department
LAX	Los Angeles Airport Police
LEO	Law enforcement Officer
MDP	Ministry of Defence Police
MGS	Ministry of Defence Guard Service
MOD	Ministry of Defence

MPS	Metropolitan Police Service
MSRT	Maritime Security Response Team
MSST	Maritime Safety and Security Team
NAS	Narcotics Affairs Section
NDD	Narcotic Detection Dog
NEDCTP	National Explosives Detection Canine Team Program
NGO	None Government Organization
NPC	National Police Dog Centre
NSW	New South Wales
NT	Northern Territory
NYC	New York City
NYPD	New York Police Department
NZ	New Zealand
OFO	Office of Field Operations
PAD	Passive alert detection
PAP	People's Armed Police
PC	Police Constable
PD	Police Dogs
PDI	Policía de Investigaciones de Chile
PDU	Police Dog Unit
PFPA	Pentagon Force Protection Agency
PNH	National Police of Haiti
Polizia di Stato	Italian State Police
POLRI	Indonesian National Police
POVIAT	Polish police agencies

POW	Prisoner of War
QPS	Queensland Police Service
RAAF	Royal Australian Air Force
RAF	Royal Air Force
RAVC	Royal Army Veterinary Corps
RCMP	Royal Canadian Mounted Police
RSPCA	Royal Society for the Protection of Animals
SA	South Australia
SAG	Canine Brigade of Servicio Agricola y Ganadero
SAPS	South African Police Service
SAR	Search & Rescue Dog
SD	Security Dogs
SDTC	Estonian Service Dogs Training Centre
SDU	Nepal's Ministry of Home Affairs
SED	Special Enforcement Detail
SERT	Special Emergency Response Team
SGT	Sergeant a Police rank
SNCO	Senior non-commissioned officers
SOG	Special Operations Group
SPF	Singapore Police Force
SRT	Special Response Team
SSD	Specialized Services Division
STOP	Special Tactical Operations Team
SWAT	Special Weapons and Tactics
SWP	South Wales Police

SWRU	Snow Wolf Commando Unit
TOD	Tactical Operation Division
TSA	Transportation Security Administration's
UK	United Kingdom
UNDCP	United Nations Office of Drugs and Crime
USA	United States of America
USAR	Urban Search and Rescue
USPCA	United States Police Canine Association
USSP	United States Special Policemen
USSR KGB	Union of Soviet Socialist Republics Russian Security
VCP	Vehicle Check Point
VIC	Victoria
VIP	Very Important Person
VS	Verein für Deutsche Schäferhunde
WA	Western Australia
WDC	Washington, DC

BIBLIOGRAPHY

Books

Law Enforcement Dogs In Australia & NZ Queensland Police Service, Adkins, G & Whittaker, A, 2009, Queensland Police Service, Queensland.

Police Dogs Training and Care Home Office Books, 1986, HMSO Books, UK.

RNZAF Police Dogs Manual, 1980, RNZAF, New Zealand Air Publication, New Zealand.

Journals

Forensic Science Centre Scent Identification, Aleksandravičius, A, 2011, Lithuanian Police and Dog Training Board.

Canine Courier magazine, Griffeth, B, 2009, United States Police Canine Association Vol 20, pp 40.

The Detonator Magazine, 2010, Vol 5, pp 39.

K9 Cop Magazine, 2009, Feb/March edition, USA.

North American Police Work Dog Association.

Department Ministry of Defence, 2010, Public Relations and Information unit, Croatia.

Chiron Calling, Green, D, 2009, Magazine of the Royal Army Veterinary Corps Vol 2.

Websites

United States Police Canine Association, USA, viewed 2010, http://www.uspcak9.com/

Police K9 magazine, USA, viewed 2011, http://policek9magazine.com/

Ray Allen, Professional K9 equipment, USA, viewed 2011, http://www.rayallen.com/

Police Dogs, viewed 2011, http://en.wikipedia.org/wiki/Police_dog

North American Police Work Dog Association USA, viewed 2009, http://www.napwda.com/